GHOST TAVERNS

An Illustrated Gazetteer of Haunted Pubs
in the North East of England

GHOST TAVERNS

An Illustrated Gazetteer of Haunted Pubs
in the North East of England

Darren W. Ritson & Michael J. Hallowell

AMBERLEY PUBLISHING

First published 2009

Amberley Publishing Plc
Cirencester Road, Chalford,
Stroud, Gloucestershire, GL6 8PE

www.amberley-books.com

British Library Cataloguing in Publication Data.
A catalogue record for this book is available from the British Library.

ISBN 978 1 84868 140 8
Typesetting and Origination by diagrafmedia
Printed in Great Britain

From Darren:
To my partner Jayne Watson, and our daughter Abbey May Ritson.
To my mother, father and my brother, Gary, who have supported me
throughout my 'spooky' adventures.

From Mike:
To the haunted pubs that are no longer with us, and the invisible
patrons who, in another world, may still gather inside their
welcoming walls.

OTHER BOOKS BY DARREN W. RITSON:

Ghost Hunter – True Life Encounters from the North East (GHP, 2006)
In Search of Ghosts – Real Hauntings From Around Britain (GHP 2007)
In Search of Ghosts – Real Hauntings From Around Britain (Amberley Publishing, 2008)
Haunted Newcastle (The History Press, 2009)

OTHER BOOKS BY MICHAEL J. HALLOWELL:

Herbal Healing – A Practical Introduction to Medicinal Herbs (Ashgrove Press, 1985)
Ales & Spirits (People's Press, 2001)
Invizikids (Heart of Albion Press, 2007)
Mystery Animals of Northumberland & Tyneside (CFZ Press, 2008)
The House That Jack Built (Amberley Publishing, 2008)
Christmas Ghost Stories (Amberley Publishing, 2008)
South Shields Through Time (Amberley Publishing, 2008)

Co-authored by Michael J. Hallowell & Darren W. Ritson:
The South Shields Poltergeist – One Family's Fight Against an Invisible Intruder (The History Press, 2008)

Contents

Acknowledgements

We wish to acknowledge the following individuals and organisations for their invaluable help:

Ivor Muncey, for supplying some of the rare photographs included in this volume.

Alan Tedder, author and researcher, for supplying details of numerous haunted public houses in the north-east, and for his kind permission to reproduce photographs in this volume.

The Durham Constabulary, for help in researching the story behind the spectre that allegedly haunts the Clock Hotel.

The North East Ghost Research Team, including Suzanne Hitchinson (nee McKay), Glenn Hall, Claire Smith, Darren Olley, Julie Olley, Mark Winter and other past members.

The *Northumbrian Gazette* and the *Hexham Courant*, for kindly publicising our request for stories regarding haunted public houses.

The Ghosts and Hauntings Overnight Surveillance Team (G.H.O.S.T)

Psychic medium Ralph Keeton and investigator Nikki Austwicke.

Cindy and Colin Nunn.

South Tyneside Libraries, for permission to quote from The Borough of South Shields, by George B. Hodgson.

And finally, sincere thanks to all the publicans, brewers, librarians and others who have gone beyond the call of duty in assisting our research.

Foreword

For over a quarter of a century I have ran and lived in some of Tyneside's most characterful public houses. My company currently owns three inns – The Albion Inn in Bill Quay, The Robin Hood in Jarrow and The Maltings in South Shields. I am also the proprietor of the only brewery in South Tyneside – the Jarrow Brewery – after the closure of the previous Westoe Brewery in the 1950s.

During this period I have never ceased to be amazed by the strange happenings within these premises.

The Robin Hood itself was subject to a series of strange incidents just recently, when a large (and extremely heavy) brewery clock kept jumping off the wall and landing in the middle of the bar when no one was there. It is occurrences like these that Darren and Mike have investigated with gusto.

Darren and Mike's book, *Ghost Taverns: An Illustrated Gazetteer of Haunted Pubs in the North East of England*, recounts fascinating stories of weird encounters that are guaranteed to make the hairs on the back of your neck stand on end.

I can thoroughly recommend this book to anyone who thinks that nothing compliments a pint of ale better than a genuine ghost story.

Jess McConnell,
Proprietor,
The Jarrow Brewery.

Introduction

When Mike first began writing his WraithScape column for the *Shields Gazette*, he quickly accumulated a hard core of dedicated readers who would frequently supply him with what would once have been called – to use 1940s comic book terminology – 'ripping yarns'. Rejecting a story is a decision which he does not take lightly, and often with great sadness. He will not publish anything that is patently false, or where it has became obvious to him that his informant is 'telling porkies', as they say.

However, Mike occasionally comes across a story that may not necessarily be true, though it is obvious that the teller of the tale really believes it to be true. He has always been candid in admitting that some tales – particularly those of great age – are essentially unverifiable. The witnesses may be long dead, and the premises in which the haunting was said to have taken place long demolished. What we are left with, in the final analysis, is hearsay. This should not stop the story getting in to print. It is sufficient that the reader be directed to make up his or her own mind regarding its veracity.

Darren, on the other hand, is a much more 'hands-on' investigator. Like Mike, he frequently receives correspondence from people about allegedly haunted buildings and ghostly experiences, which he follows up with great relish. Hence, since 2003 he has travelled across the United Kingdom investigating scores of haunted properties, although his interest and research in this subject actually spans over two and a half decades.

Essentially, this book is about dozens of haunted pubs throughout the north-east of England. Some entries are relatively brief, whilst others are presented to the reader under the heading In-Depth Case Study. These also detail thorough investigations into some of the reputedly haunted pubs and alehouses in the north-east region, but go into far greater detail.

Darren's goal is simply to obtain objective, scientific evidence for the existence of ghosts. Having said that, with the rapid progression of modern technology and advanced photographic enhancement software, the ability to fake or at least duplicate good ghost pictures is becoming far easier and, unfortunately, a lot more common. This, combined with the relentless broadcasting of irritating 'ghost-hunting' programmes that are quite clearly hamming things up for the sake of good ratings (and to make lots of money) does not do the dedicated psychical researcher and the respected research society any good whatsoever. When a good piece of evidence comes to light, no one will believe it. It is the classic case of 'crying wolf'. However, the authors keep persevering and the selection of In-Depth Case Studies presented herein comprises a mere fraction of the haunted pubs and inns Darren has had the privilege of investigating; we think the reader will find them most intriguing.

The rest of the inserts contained within this volume are shorter, and, like our 'overnight investigations', contain fascinating narratives elaborating on the establishment's history, folklore and – of course – ghosts. The authors have to admit that during their painstaking research and the compilation of the Gazetteer itself, the on-site field research and interviews they carried out in their quest to compile this ultimately resulted in them hearing some of the most remarkable first-hand accounts of ghost stories. The authors also found themselves sampling some of the finest ales and pub grub in the region – it's a difficult job, but someone has to do it.

So where did it all begin? Well, for Darren it could have begun at The Albion Inn at Bill Quay which, ironically, is the first pub mentioned in this volume. Darren's father had told him about 'the ghost' at the Albion Inn many years ago when out on one of their many bike rides 'owa the watta'. Every time they passed the inn they would pop in for a refreshing drink. On one occasion, whilst it was raining heavily outside, Darren's father pretended to show him how his Nikon SLR camera worked whilst simultaneously – and on the sly – taking random shots inside the pub in the hope they might catch the ghost on film. They did not. This was the beginning of something special for Darren: an interest, in photography, ghosts (and, of course, the traditional local pub). The Albion Inn holds fond memories for Darren, and something stirred within him all those years ago; it is something he has not been able to leave behind.

Public houses have a very special allure, and the authors would be lying through their teeth if they said that some of that allure wasn't alcohol based. However, successful drinking houses can no more rely purely on the quality of their beverages for their reputation than a good motor car can rely solely on the quality of its tyres. Pubs are not just about drinking; the public house is an experience composed of many different aspects: the clientele, the décor, the food ... and, of course, the ghosts.

What about Mike? Well, truth be told he can't remember exactly when the connection between pubs and ghosts was first made in his mind. Perhaps there never was a defining moment; maybe the relationship between drinking establishments and denizens of the netherworld just grew naturally within the confines of his cerebellum without him ever noticing it.

But there did come a time when he came to appreciate that relationship. A pub without a ghost is like a pub without beer; superficially everything may look okay on the outside, but it isn't long before patrons find out that something is horribly, terribly wrong. A good ghost, like a highly polished bar and a wide selection of spirits, just adds that extra-special something that simply can't be substituted.

In 2001, Mike's book *Ales & Spirits* was published – a history of over twenty haunted public houses. He toyed with the idea of writing a second volume, but wasn't sure whether his liver would stand it. Spending one's days in pubs, drinking ale and listening to eerie narratives about the shades of long-dead bartenders, may be good fun but carries inherent dangers. He used to operate on the ratio of one pint to one ghost story, but as many pubs lay claim to having seven or eight resident spectres ... well, you get the idea.

And then Darren came onto the scene and resurrected Mike's desire to once again enter the fray and explore the world of haunted hostelries. Unsure at first, Darren rapidly charmed away his reluctance and Mike is glad he did.

The bulk of the stories in this book concern public houses that are still standing. However, there are several excellent ghost tales which relate to premises that were either pulled down long ago or are still standing but boarded up and awaiting demolition. The following chapters will focus both on drinking houses of yesteryear – those that no longer exist – and currently standing inns and taverns which are also reputed to be haunted.

A small number of pubs mentioned within these pages have featured previously in other publications, including Mike's book *Ales & Spirits* and Darren's *Ghost Hunter* and *In Search of Ghosts*. Those sections have been fully updated and now contain new material which we are confident will prove to be of interest to the reader.

Whichever pub you frequent, from here on you should look at it with fresh eyes. Not all the patrons standing at the bar may be visible, and if the barmaid looks to be dead upon her feet ... who knows? Maybe she really is ...

Darren W. Ritson & Michael J. Hallowell

2009

The 'Good Ghost' Rating System

Rating the selection of inns and taverns in this book for their 'ghost factor' was an extremely difficult task. The authors spent over three weeks carefully assessing and analysing both the historical and psychical evidence before arriving at their decisions.

We need to point out at the outset that a 'low' rating is no reflection whatsoever on the quality of the establishment itself; a back-street 'spit and sawdust' boozer is as likely to get a high rating as any other establishment, and an upper-class, expensive hotel may just as easily get a low rating.

All the pubs and inns mentioned in this book are 'good', as they all have genuine ghost stories attached to them (and they all sell beer). Even a low rating of '1' indicates that the premises is still reputed to be haunted and well worth a visit. So, what gets a haunted pub a high rating – say, 10 – and what merits a low one? The authors looked at several factors, including the variety of phenomena that present themselves, the frequency of sightings and, of course, the 'scare factor'. Some inns may only have one ghost, that has merely been sighted twice or thrice over the course of a century, thus only meriting a relatively low mark. Others, such as the Alum Ale House in South Shields, are reputed to have a veritable clan of spirits vying for space and probably haunting the premises on a shift system. One spectacular sighting may bump up a pub's rating, whilst a frequently seen (but relatively boring) ghost may demand only an average mark.

In the final analysis, the ratings given are purely the opinions of the authors and are largely subjective. No one should be offended if their local watering hole has a low mark, because it isn't the landlord's fault (or indeed ours) if the place is only visited by shades of the netherworld infrequently. Every pub in this book should feel honoured at its inclusion, regardless of its rating, for we believe that they all represent the very best of the haunted hostelries in the region.

But the authors aren't perfect, and we accept that of the thousands of pubs in the region a good number of landlords and patrons may be disappointed that their pub is absent from the pages of this volume. If you own, manage or drink in a haunted pub and you feel that it should be included in future editions of Ghost Taverns, then write to us. The reason you haven't been included is simple: we didn't know your local inn was haunted and now wish we had.

PART ONE

A History Of Drinking

CHAPTER ONE

Ancient Echoes

Man has always had a fascination for – and an intense relationship with – alcohol. Alcohol is, for those who enjoy a tipple in the company of others, complementary to social bonding. To be honest, we have to say that the demon drink has a lot going for it in this respect. Public houses are great levellers. When we pop into the Red Lion in West Boldon or the Old George in Newcastle upon Tyne's Cloth Market, we are equal to all those gathered therein, whether they be doctors, lawyers, farmers or rocket scientists. And, just as importantly, they are equal to us. Like King Arthur and the knights of the round table, those who sit with pint in hand share a democratic status which is only influenced by the question of whose turn it is to pay for the next round.

Another powerful predominance in public houses used to be tobacco, although by the twenty-first century its influence was nowhere near as great as it used to be and, by the time you read this book, the use of tobacco in taverns and hostelries across the land will have been banned completely.

Say what you will about the evils of tobacco, the fact remains that its use has always been a bonding ritual of great significance within alehouse and tavern alike. An echo of this ritual used to be seen until very recently, although in a somewhat disguised format. Until 2007, if you watched any large group of drinkers in a public house, at least several would almost certainly have been tobacco users. Some would occasionally pull out a packet of twenty, purchased that morning from the local corner shop. However, some brave souls would partake of this popular narcotic by an altogether more complex route. Back then, it was a fascinating pastime to look carefully for the person who rolled his (or even her) own.

Smokers who roll their own cigarettes are engaging in a fascinating custom which is carried out with great seriousness. In fact, it can be almost sacramental in its intensity. One friend of Mike's who has 'rolled his own' for a good many years said, 'You know, I enjoy the ritual nearly as much as the smoke'. Of course, he was referring to the ritual of creating an object of desire from nothing more than a few dried leaves and a piece of paper. There is an art to placing just the right amount of tobacco in the centre of the paper, and an even greater art in rolling the cigarette correctly. Roll it too tightly and you'll need the lungs of a bull elephant to get a draw. Roll it too loosely and the cigarette will burn down in seconds – that's if the contents don't tumble out of the paper first and burn holes in the knees of your trousers. Those who roll their own are bonded by a love not just of the effect, but also of the product itself.

Another method of imbibing tobacco – and one which, sadly, is on the wane – is the ancient and peculiar art of snuffing. At one time, inhaling snuff was as common as smoking a pipe.

What on earth has all this got to do with ghosts, you ask? Quite a lot, actually, for when a group of people are drawn together in commune, particularly by a shared love of a drink and a smoke, they will talk. This was the case centuries ago, when those who gathered in public houses would always enjoy the pleasure of a clay pipe. The supping, snuffing and the puffing were rituals which were punctuated by chatter. One would tell of a ship that had just come into port, another of a neighbour who had just developed black-lung after a surfeit of years down the pit. Fishermen would discuss the weather, farmers the crops. And all the while they would puff and sup and snuff, relaxing as they enjoyed the companionship of those with whom they worked or knew in some other capacity.

In the eighteenth and nineteenth centuries religion played a much greater part in the lives of the people. Superstitions were a daily facet of life, and those who ignored them were deemed crazy, not those who followed them. The existence of ghosts was not challenged, save by a few crusty intellectuals who had jumped on the Darwinistic bandwagon, and were revelling in the new-found fashion of dismissing anything which could not be touched or measured. That awful disease known as scepticism may have taken the scientific community, but those who supped and snuffed and puffed found themselves immune. In the drinking dens and alehouses, the old tales and yarns of yesteryear were recited with as much gusto as ever. Had it not been this way, they would not have survived to be included in this book. If you enjoy the tales you find in this volume, then it is not the authors you have to thank, but those who, in times past, puffed, snuffed, supped and told each other wonderful stories in their local watering holes.

So what were these drinking dens like? What sort of environment could pander to entirely physical passions like alcohol and tobacco, and yet, bizarrely, prove to be a breeding ground for philosophical discussions on the nature of the afterlife and those who inhabited it? To understand why so many inns and public houses have ghosts, we need to look at the environment in question.

In August 2000, something sad happened. The West End Vaults in Commercial Road, South Shields, was demolished. The pub had been closed for renovation, but was destroyed by a fire before the work could be completed. The West End Vaults was an old pub with an interesting history. Over the last century it was the haunt of shipwrights and sailors alike, and was the spawning ground for many ghost tales and strange stories. Now it is gone, and we have been cruelly robbed of a small but important slice of our historical heritage. No more will people sit in the lounge and ponder over their life and times. No longer will men gather in the bar and discuss the forthcoming football season. No longer will they sup, snuff and puff – at least not there – and no longer will the ambience of the place enchant others as it once did. The West End Vaults is gone, surviving only in the memories of those who once frequented it.

The West End Vaults was by no means the first public house to meet its demise by being engulfed in flames. In the mid-nineteenth century a similar fate met the Fox and Lamb situated in Wapping Street, South Shields. The Fox and Lamb's most notable character was its proprietor William Lamb, but like his alehouse he is now little more than a name found within the dusty tomes of South Tyneside's Central Library. One wonders if Mr Lamb's good lady was, in her maiden days, called Fox.

But aren't there legions of other pubs within the north-east of England? Aren't we spoilt for choice when it comes to finding a place to whet our collective whistles? Of course; but, slowly and surely, the old-style inns and alehouses are being lost. They belonged to a different age, one which was unspoilt by jukeboxes, gaming machines, topless barmaids and strobe lights. Sadly, the old-fashioned public house is dying a slow and lingering death. The fun-pubs and wine bars which are replacing them do not engender the telling of tales and the recital of legends. The noise often makes it difficult to think, let alone speak. True social commune has been replaced with an ersatz variety which involves nothing more intellectually challenging than working out what change you should get at the counter when you purchase your next exotically flavoured and overpriced drink.

Old pubs and inns exude charisma. It is as if the mindsets and personalities of the well-known characters who have drank there over the years have embedded themselves in the walls and ceilings. When you walk into such places, the past almost comes to life.

CHAPTER TWO

A Brief History of Drinking Houses

The history of drinking throughout the north-east of England has followed a reasonably uniform pattern over the centuries, although drinking in remote villages obviously was and is of a different character to that which takes place in towns and cities. To look at the alcohol-related history of every town, borough and county would be a vast exercise, and not really within the precincts of a gazetteer of this type. In the following chapters the authors will take a general look at the history of drinking in the North, but will focus by way of example upon a number of small towns and boroughs which were really microcosmic examples of the greater whole. Specifically, we'll look at South Shields and to a lesser extent Jarrow; two neighbouring towns on the south bank of the River Tyne which contained anything and everything that could be remotely connected to the manufacture, sale and consumption of alcoholic beverages. The reader should remember that the culture of drinking as it was in these localities was pretty similar to that elsewhere in the north of England. They are described in detail purely to give the reader a feel for the influence that the drinking of alcohol had on all levels of society.

To understand the nature of the tavern, even its very essence, we need to go back several centuries. Indeed, we are required to go back further still, perhaps to the time when this isle was governed by tribes of varying size, import and disposition. All of our ancient cultures, both indigenous and adopted (including the Celts, Picts, Britons, Romans, Angles, Saxons and, of course, the Vikings), seemed to have accepted communal drinking as a most natural and respectable pastime, particularly for the male of the species. If this communal imbibing did not take place out of doors, sitting around a roaring fire, it would certainly take place indoors, often in purpose-built huts. It is here, we would suggest, that we find the origin of the alehouse in Britain, although there is evidence that, in the Middle East, such establishments had existed almost since the dawn of human history.

The Norsemen took communal drinking very seriously indeed. They also took it to an entirely new level, supplementing their alcohol intake with good food (the original 'pub grub'?) and curvaceous serving girls (the first ever barmaids). Had the Vikings still been calling the shots today, it is unlikely that we would have seen anything as enlightened as votes for women or an equal opportunities policy, but that's another story. The term 'sexist' was not in the Norse vocabulary.

Of course, nowhere did the Danelaw have a greater impact culturally than in the north of England. Even today north-eastern dialects contains dozens of Norse words, and the area's cuisine has a faintly Scandinavian character. This is echoed in our love of fish, bread and pastry.

Another overspill from the Viking influence, as previously stated, is the fondness that people in this region have for good beer. Of course, it is a truism to say that people dislike bad beer, but at least since medieval times drinkers in this neck of the woods have been particularly fastidious regarding the quality of their ale.

Lest anyone be in any doubts about the seriousness with which the people here judge the contents of their tankards, the following should put them to rest. It is recorded in the South Shields Halmote (court) rolls that in the year 1380 one John Hilton[1] was fined, in the company of others, the sum of sixpence for selling ale of an inferior standard. They were also warned that a penalty of forty pence would be meted out unless they sold their beer by 'sealed measures'. This in itself needs some explanation.

Although we tend to think that it is only in recent times that the rights of the consumer have gained greater importance, this is actually not the case. In the fourteenth century, innkeepers were subject to severe penalties for short-changing their clientele. Goods were sold in two formats: by weight and by measure. Standard measures included bushels, gallons, quarts, tierce, pints and pottles. Any business found using defective measures would see the proprietor thereof hauled before the Halmote. In one year alone – 1424 – the following South Shields innkeepers were heavily fined for contravening weights and measures legislation:[2]

Will Michelson
Thomas Wavener
Rose Leg
Thomas Pinder
Nicholas Wode
Thomas Swethopp
John Wilson
Alicia Hertlaw
William Wryght
Alicia Alystyer

Throughout the North East, the enforcement of weights and measures legislation in inns and public houses was carried out by the ale-cunner. He was required to test the measures used every week, or 'fourteen days att furthest'. If an ale-cunner failed to carry out regular tests, he himself could be fined the sum of three shillings and fourpence. The office of ale-cunner was held for one year, which was probably the longest one could carry out the job without suffering irreversible liver damage.

The aforementioned list of offenders is, however, not a comprehensive one. Several other tradespersons also ran inns as a sideline, and they too found themselves in the dock for various measures offences. These included:

Robert Brown (Baker)
Henry Byng (trade unknown)
John Carleton (Baker)
Juliana Fleshewer (Baker)
Alexander Fleshewer (Butcher)
Henry Kyng (Baker)
William Potter (Corn merchant)
John Tosson (Baker)
Richard Waremouth (Baker)[3]

The lesson to be learned from the above list is, we would venture, that one should be very wary of trusting a baker who also moonlights as a taverner.

But it was not just weights and measures which were taken seriously, as much care had to be taken over where beer was purchased from, as well as its quality once it was poured. The term 'free trade' had a different connotation then, and local businesses were expected to support each other. Hence, in 1364, Richard de Byrden, Adam de Byrden, Richard Harpour and Robert Benedicite[4] were all fined for purchasing their ale at Newcastle instead of locally. Their motives are unclear. Perhaps they were offered it at a knockdown price, or perhaps they felt it was of superior quality to the ale produced locally. Whatever the truth, they were punished severely for breaking the rules.

A quaff of ale at the end of the day was seen as the right of all working men, and from time-to-time strict pricing controls were introduced to prevent unscrupulous publicans from ripping off their customers. In 1377, for example, innkeepers were forbidden from charging more than 'one pence ha'penny' for a tankard of ale.

Of course, what constitutes good ale and bad ale is subjective and purely a matter of opinion, but all landlords were expected to reach rigorous standards. To ensure that customers did not suffer in this respect, the Halmote Court of the Lord Prior also required ale-tasters to sample the beverages on sale and make sure they were palatable. In 1369, for example, two men – John Tyngring and Robert de Barthew – were employed in South Tyneside for just such a purpose, although we can be sure that there would have been no shortage of applicants.[5]

Another rule introduced around this time required landlords to sell their ale both on and off the premises. This was the beginning of the now largely defunct practice of pubs having a small window at the side of the inn where bottled beers could be sold to customers who, for whatever reason, did not want to drink inside.

By the seventeenth century, attention was being focussed not just on the quality and quantity of the beverage, but also on the premises from which they were sold. Moves were made to ensure that the drinking of ale in places to which the general public had access did not cause unnecessary offence to the more pious citizens in the locale. One local, by-law in South Shields stated:

> … that noe alehouse keeper sell any ale or beare in time of divine service, prayer and preaching, either before or after noon, or keep any guests in their houses above ten days, and lett itt be knowne to the Court and to the Constables and Churchwardens, whosoe offendeth shall fyne for every falt 3s 4d.[6]

By 1662 the ale-cunners were busier than ever. The records of the Halmote court show that, in that year, the 'West Panns' district of South Shields had two cunners appointed, Edward Killerly and Robert Bell, and 'Sheele' [essentially South Shields town centre] another two, namely, Thomas Haswell and Nicholas Wolfe. Their status was such that the by-laws also insisted that, 'all constables are to be their assistants'.[7]

By the nineteenth century, the number of cunners had reduced, although the matter of ale purity was taken just as seriously. In 1831 the service fell to the South Shields 'chymist' John Walker – a mischievous coincidence that his name is almost synonymous with a famous brand of whisky. Walker enjoyed the full support of constables Richard Bowman, Robert Mills, James Wardle and Matthew Sawkill. (Sawkill may well have been related to John Sawkill, proprietor of the Hope & Anchor, at 4, Long Row, South Shields).[8]

In 1842 a local brewer named John Jackson became the town's official bread taster (given almost as much importance as ale-tasting), whilst a former baker named John West was employed as the new ale-cunner. An interesting change of places if ever there was one.[9]

Recently there has been much criticism of the fact that South Shields has an unusually large number of inns and public houses, particularly near the town centre. Whilst sympathising wholeheartedly with residents who do not wish to be kept awake by louts winding their way home after 'a skin full', there are two salient facts which need to be remembered. Firstly, it is not the number of drinking establishments which is the problem, but rather the idiots who sometimes frequent them, almost always to the chagrin of the landlord. During literally years of research, the authors never once met the manager of a public house who took any pleasure at seeing customers drink themselves to oblivion. The reason? Their behaviour turns decent customers away, and is therefore bad for business. Secondly, much though this may come as a surprise, the situation now is nowhere near as bad as it used to be. To prove the point we need to go back to the year 1834.

At that time there was a directory kept at South Shields Town Hall which listed in excess of 150 watering holes in the town centre, the majority virtually within spitting distance of each other. This list did not include alehouses (which could only sell ales and beers, and not spirits), Letters (which we will explain presently), the retailers of beer, wines and spirits, or beer brewers, who would also sell liquor from their premises.

What follows in the next chapter is a complete list of all the drinking houses in South Shields in that year, and it makes fascinating reading. South Tyneside residents and others familiar with the locale may well recognise several of the names, as the establishments concerned are still in business. Others which are no longer with us will be remembered fondly, whilst yet others are now nothing but a name on a printed page, their history and character having been almost completely covered by the sands of time.

---

1 Hodgson, G. *The Borough of South Shields*, (South Tyneside Libraries, 1996) p. 56

2 Ibid, p.57

3 Ibid, p. 57

4 Ibid, p.50

5 Ibid, p.55

6 Ibid, p.107

7 Ibid, p.109

8 Ibid, p.161

9 Ibid, p.161

CHAPTER THREE

Public Houses in South Shields Circa 1834

ESTABLISHMENT	ADDRESS	OWNER OR MANAGER
The Adam & Eve	4, Laygate Lane	Archibald Steel
The Albion	Fairles's Quay	Solomon Jewson
The Alnwick Castle	4, East Holborn	Sarah Thompson
The Bamburgh Castle	35, Thrift Street	Ann Stobbs
The Barley Mow	63, Shadwell Street	bJohn Johnson
The Bay Horse	56, West Holborn	George Lowrey
The Beehive	6, Wellington Street	Richard Feard
The Beswick Arms	14, Long Row	Mary Paxton
The Black & Grey	21, Union Alley	Mary Lawson
The Black Bull	21, Shadwell Street	Elizabeth Davison
The Black Bull	55, East Holborn	Robert Stoker
The Black Bull	94, Wapping Street	Zechariah Winterburn
The Black Horse	6, Cookson's Quay	Alexander Wishart
The Black Swan	25, Thrift Street	John Briscoe
The Black Swan	88, Wapping Street	William Harrison
The Blacksmith's Arms	51, West Holborn	George Surtees
The Blue Gate	Claypath Lane	Thomas Purvis
The Brew House	22, Spring Lane	Grace Browll
The Brighton Beach	31, Coronation Street	John Strachan
The Britannia	84, Wapping Street	Elizabeth Gillespie
The Brunswick Arms	27, Brunswick Street	James Bulliwell
The Coble	58, Shadwell Street	David Craig
The Coble	Shadwell Street	Thomas Hindmarsh
The Coble	Coble Landing, Shadwell Street	Mary Young

The Comfortable & Bottle Houses	23, East Holborn	Elizabeth Mason
The Commercial	105, Wapping Street	William Laing
The Commercial	4, West Holborn	George Purvis
The Crane House	High Quay	Robert Jolly
The Cross Keys	32, Market Place	Robert Hodgson
The Cross Keys	12, West Holborn	William Kirton
The Crown	Westoe	Thomas Corry
The Crown	121, Wapping Street	John Cuthbert
The Crown	1, Lawe's Buildings	Mary Reed
The Crown & Anchor	24, West Holborn	John Bullock
The Crown & Anchor	100, Wapping Street	Walter Helm
The Crown & Anchor	7, Thrift Street	Elizabeth Robson
The Crown & Cannon	12, Laygate Street	Edward Smith
The Crown & Thistle	54, Wapping Street	Mary Ann Reed
The Crown & Thistle	Kirton's Quay	Robert Weatherburn
The Cumberland Arms	45, East Holborn	Thomas Nelson
The Deanmouth	Templetown	John Grey
The Dock House	High Dock, W. Holborn	Luke Blumer
The Dog & Duck	39, West Holborn	Barbara Kell
The Durham Arms	20, Market Place	Edward Young
The Earl St. Vincent	8, Dean Street	Joseph Tate
The Engine	107, Commercial Road	William Dand
The Fountain	48, West Holborn	James Clennet
The Fox & Lamb	48, Wapping Street	William Fryer
The Gardener's Arms	Westoe Lane	George Turner
The Globe	23, Laygate Street	Robert Bailey
The Grey Horse	Templetown	George Haddock
The Grey Horse	Harton	John Paxton
The Half Moon	Wapping Street	Susannah Atkinson
The Half Moon	34, Shadwell Street	Robert Jefferson
The Highlander	24, Market Place	Thomas Cubey
The Hop Pole	12, East Holborn	John Collier
The Hope & Anchor	4, Long Row	John Sawkill
The King William IV	22, East Street	William Surtees
The King's Head	32, East King Street	Elizabeth Jameson
The King's Head	15, West Holborn	Thomas Raffle
The King's Head	Market Place	William Guy Vennell
The Life Boat	5, Church Row	John Milbourne

The Lord Byron	East Holborn	Ann Anderton
The Lord Collingwood	81, King Street	John Dunn
The Lynn Arms	76, East Holborn	Sarah Patton
The Mariner's Arms	Market Place	Fraser Harrison
The Mariner's Arms	9, East Holborn	John Stoker
The Mariner's Arms	64, East King Street	Joseph Storey
The Market Place Tavern	20, The Market Place	William Cook
The Masonic Arms	West Holborn	Henry Darling
The Mason's Arms	72, King Street	John Hart
The Mechanics' Tavern	Hill Street	William Fowler
The Merchant Tailor's Arms	7, West Street	Robert Hewison
The Mill Dam House	1, East Holborn	Thomas Forrest
The Neptune	65, King Street	John Bains
The Noah's Ark	59, Wapping Street	Ann Mitchell
The Old Alnwick Castle	41, Commercial Road	John Major
The Old Greenland Fishery	36, Thrift Street	Elizabeth Parker
The Old Highlander	11, King Street	Richard Walton
The Phoenix	76, East Holborn	Sarah Patton
The Plough	Templetown	Thomas Harrison
The Queen's Head	Comical Corner, Wapping Street	Peter Henderson
The Queen's Head	8, Brunswick Street	Ann Pearson
The Railway	20, Long Row	John Wright
The Red Lion	26, East Holborn	Thomas Atkinson
The Rising Sun	81, East Holborn	John Todd
The Rose	Shadwell Street	Thomas Turner
The Rose & Crown	90, Wapping Street	John Gillis
The Rose & Crown	East Holborn	Jane Gray
The Rose & Crown	Shadwell Street	Isabella Purvis
The Rose & Crown	25, Market Place	James Young
The Scarborough Arms	1, West Holborn	Adam Oyston
The Scarborough Bridge	85, East Holborn	Paul Colledge
The Scarborough Castle	35, East Holborn	Dorothy Ridley
The Scarborough Spa	9, King Street	Mary Douglass
The Seven Stars	92, Wapping Street	William Ward
The Shakespeare	19, Heron Street	George Dowell
The Ship	Shadwell Street	Joseph Bell
The Ship	Heron Street	Margaret Brown
The Ship	7, Wapping Street	Jane Campbell

The Ship	43, Thrift Street	Thomas Charlton
The Ship	7, Dean Street	Ralph Dale
The Ship	High Quay, West Holborn	John Dodds
The Ship	60, West Holborn	Sarah Gladstone
The Ship	Narrow Landing	Edward Henderson
The Ship	Fairles's Quay	Margaret Liddell
The Ship	58, Wapping Street	George Morton
The Ship	Anderson's Lane	Sarah Paxton
The Ship	Hebburn Quay	William Redhead
The Ship	Harton	George Rippon
The Ship	40, West Holborn	Archibald Robertson
The Ship	14, West Holborn	Joseph Thompson
The Ship in Dock	West Docks	Hugh Rodham
The Ship Launch	31, Long Row	Henry Walton
The Shipwrights' Arms	29, Long Row	Sarah Dobby
The Shipwrights' Arms	29, East Holborn	Margaret Garthwaite
The Shoulder of Mutton	Spring Lane	Jonathan Slater
The Sportsman	Dockwray's Lane	Jonathan Clarkson
The Spotted Bull	Tyne Street	William Moscropp
The Stag	61, East Holborn	William Reay
The Star & Garter	East Holborn	Mary Payne
The Sun	Palatine Street	John Hart
The Sun	6, West Holborn	George Young
The Sussex Arms	25, East Holborn	Thomas Bate
The Three Horse Shoes	17, Laygate Street	Robert Reed
The Three Indian Kings	14, Market Place	John Hutchinson
The Three Mariners	Westoe	John Bell
The Three Tuns	88, Wapping Street	Elizabeth Henderson
The Three Tuns	50, West Holborn	John Peel
The Three Tuns	Pan-ash Quay	Thomas Stainton
The Travellers' Arms	Union Alley	John Tutin
The Turk's Head	21, Thrift Street	Margaret George
The Tyne End	8, Long Row	Jane Burnip
The United States of America	Hill Street	William Fowler
The Waggon	68, Commercial Road	Anthony Ewbank
The Waterloo	25, Coronation Street	Jane Dixon
The Westoe Tavern	Westoe	James Hobkirk

The Wheat Sheaf	Long Row	John Atkinson
The Wheat Sheaf	Comical Corner	Alice Todd
The Whitby Arms	Wellington Street	Jacob Storm
The White Swan	70, West Holborn	George Davison
The White Swan	45, Thrift Street	Barnabas Hindmarsh
The Yarmouth Arms	34, Wapping Street	William Inglis
The Yorkshire Tavern	99, Wapping Street	Thomas Brewster

There were also several drinking houses known as 'letters' in South Shields. These were pubs which seemingly had no name and were devoid of any sign outside the premises. The origin of the epithet 'letter' is obscure, but may have arisen through the business being referred to by local licensing officials simply by the initials of the proprietor. Hence, an inn owned by John Smith would be referred to as 'the JS'. Alternatively, we have also been told that a list was kept of all unnamed houses, and that each premises was listed a,b,c,d,e, etc, on the list, which eventually led to them being referred to as 'letters'. We would be interested to hear from readers who may have other explanations. The 'letters' in South Shields and surrounding areas during 1834 were:

89, Thrift Street	Elizabeth Lodge
Ferry Boat Landing, Wapping Street	Hannah Middleton
Hebburn (address unknown)	John Righton
11, Thrift Street	John Robinson
1, East Street	Hannah Tate
3, Dean Street	William Tate

The above lists throw up some interesting points and questions. Was Hannah Tate related to either Joseph Tate, the landlord of The Earl St. Vincent, or William Tate who managed a 'letter' house at number 3, Dean Street? The same question could be asked of William Surtees who ran the King William IV, and one George Surtees who was the proprietor of the Blacksmith's Arms. Also, may there have been a familial relationship between Richard Walton of the Old Highlander, and Henry Walton of The Ship? Several proprietors seem to have run more than one establishment, including John Hart, who ran both The Mason's Arms and The Sun. Sarah Patton was the landlady of both The Lynn Arms and The Phoenix, which at first glance, seem to be situated in the same street. Curiously, several inns are even registered at the same address, The Phoenix and The Lynn Arms being one example (76, East Holborn). This is due to the fact that, at least in some cases, local directories listed the proprietor's home or business address and not the address of the establishment, which were sometimes different. Not all proprietors lived 'on the premises'.

The list also throws up several names which were later reincarnated most famously. John Peel (the late radio presenter or the fox hunter, take your pick) was manager of The Three Tuns, whilst no less a personage than John Major looked after The Old Alnwick Castle! One or two landlords had names which most aptly fitted their trade, including Thomas Brewster, who was the proprietor of The Yorkshire Tavern.

Also of great interest are the first names which were popular during that period, but which are now only rarely used, whilst others give strong indication of the ethnic origins of the owner. These include Archibald Steel of The Adam & Eve, 4 Laygate Lane, Solomon Jewson (The Albion at Fairles's Quay) and Barnabas Hindmarch of The White Swan over on Thrift Street. Other characters, such as Zechariah Winterburn (The Black Bull) and Jacob Storm (The Whitby Arms) have names which are so wonderful they could have leaped straight from a Charles Dickens novel. Even without knowing anything about their life and times, it is still almost irresistible to conclude that, either in a negative or a positive way, they were people of rugged individuality.

A further perusal of the list shows that it must have been something of a nightmare if one wished to meet a friend for a drink. No less than fifteen inns were named The Ship, and to complicate matters further there were also two Shipwright's Arms, a Ship Launch and a Ship In Dock! Matters were further confused by the fact that some names, if not identical, were dangerously similar. If a drinking partner arranged to meet you at 'The Scarborough' where did they mean? Well, they could have meant The Scarborough Lighthouse, The Scarborough Spaw, The Scarborough Castle ...

To those who complain that South Shields currently suffers from an overload of public houses, the information provided above may give pause for thought!

Hodgson[1] makes mention of some of the more obscure names with which public houses were 'christened'. These included The Adam & Eve, The Hop Pole, The Yellow House, The Draw Well Inn, The Galvaniser, The Engine House, The Brighton Beach, The Alum House Ham [now the Alum Ale House], The Spotted Bull, The Shoulder of Mutton, The Greenland Fishery, The Silent Woman, The Burnt House, The Justice, The Noah's Ark, and so on and so forth. The origins of many of these strange epithets are now lost to us. Intriguingly, the old North Eastern public house in Mile End Road was later refurbished and renamed Ye Olde Sportsman. In fact, Ye Newe Sportsman may have been more appropriate, as an alehouse called The Sportsman once stood in Dockwray's Lane.

The reader needs to bear in mind that each of these drinking houses would have had its own loyal clientele. Each had its own origins, history and nuances, representing the dream of some entrepreneur to either earn money, own his own quaint inn or both. These characteristics echo through the years, reminding us of a bygone age. Who would we have found, on any given day – say, in the year 1845 – sitting in the corner of The Dog and Duck or The Burnt House? If we could travel back through time and be an invisible eavesdropper, what conversations would we hear? If only walls could talk. Sadly, most of the walls themselves disappeared many moons ago.

Some publicans gained a notorious reputation due to their persistently obnoxious behaviour and illicit dealings. Others could gain short-lived infamy through a single, well-meaning act which backfired with negative consequences. Such was the fate of one publican in South Shields, although the damage to his reputation was relatively slight.

In 1970, Mike visited the town of Epinay sur Seine in France as part of a 'town-twinning' exchange. He stayed with the Bodin family, with whom he became firm friends. He was still a pupil at the now-demolished Jarrow Central School, and every day he and his friends would eat in the dining area of the local school in Epinay. On the first day they were astonished (not to mention delighted) to find that they were served beer with their meal. It wasn't strong stuff, but they'd never have gotten away with this at home. The French pupils were used to it, and thought nothing of it. The English youngsters thought that all their Christmases had come at once. We don't know whether they still observe this practice in some French schools, but we doubt it somehow. We live in politically correct days.

Actually, it was serving alcohol to school children which nearly got one local publican into hot water. On October 25, 1809, the Jubilee of King George III was observed with gusto at South Shields. Known for their generosity, the folks o' Shields became even more philanthropic than usual and engaged in an amazing display of alms-giving. The magistrate Nicholas Fairles (for whose murder William Jobling was later hung and gibbeted) held a huge reception at his home for all the Charity School pupils of the borough. Present at the dinner was one H. R. Roddam, proprietor of a local watering hole called The Boar's Head Inn.

After the youngsters had eaten to their fill, Roddam presented them with a barrel of 'strong ale' with which they could round off the revelry. Fortunately for Roddam this was twenty-five years before the arrival of the Temperance Movement in the area, the members of which would undoubtedly have raised their hands in horror. As things turned out, one or two Methodists fired off a number of verbal broadsides, but it came to nothing.

---

1   Hodgson, G. *The Borough of South Shields*, (South Tyneside Libraries, 1996) p.135

THE BREWERS

However, it is not just the alehouse which plays a part in our story, but also the breweries which produced the ale which was quaffed in them. In the 1830s there were no less than ten breweries in operation within South Shields:

Thomas Bell & Co (Brewery Lane).
Edward Kent Fairless (Fairless [or Fairles] Quay)
Francis Garth (13, King Street).
Robert Jolly (High Quay, West Holborn).
James Kirkley (The Dean Brewery, Cookson Quay).
Lowes & Clay (The High Brewery, 43, East Holborn),
John Park & Son (33, Waterloo Vale),
Thomas Raffle (15, West Holborn).
John Strachan (31, Coronation Street).
Christopher Wood (The Market Place Brewery).

Robert 'Bobbie' Jolly was a real entrepreneur. Not only did he supply many of the pubs in the borough, he also ran a thriving one of his own – named The Crane House – adjacent to his brewing operation.

One of the partners at Lowes and Clay (The High Brewery) was none other that John Clay, the first mayor of South Shields. Clay later became involved in a bitter and protracted legal dispute with Peter Allan of The Marsden Grotto Inn, and, to put it mildly, did not act in a manner that one would expect of a man of his office.

In addition to the brewers, there were several 'retailers of beer' in the area, some of whom were also publicans. The retailers were generally reputable business people, but one or two were engaged in the supply of contraband liquor which, after being illegally imported, was stored at well-known 'smuggling pubs' like The Hop Pole before being fenced to the retailers themselves. This enabled them to sell liquor at cut price, often so cheaply that the publicans themselves would buy it in preference to that supplied by the local breweries. Hence, the retailers had some influence on the character and development of the drinking houses in the area.

In 1834 the beer retailers in South Shields were:

Thomas Blench, Commercial Road.
Margaret Charlton, 2, Laygate Lane.
Jonathan Grewcock, Templetown.

Francis Linyard, 19, Laygate Street.
John Maddison, Templetown.
Ann Mather, 12, Cone Street.
William Matthews, 2, Westoe Lane.
Robert Miller, 3, Nile Street.
John Moore, 72, East Holborn.
Mary Oyston, 7, Garden Lane.
William Purvis, 120, Commercial Road.
Hannah Stoker, 61, Commercial Road.
James Turner, Templetown.

Some beer retailers, like the Mather family, were also purveyors of wine and spirits. John Mather operated from 75, East Holborn. Other wine and spirit retailers included:

Andrew Bone & Co. of 70, Wapping Street.
Elliott & Hutchinson, of 12, Long Row.
Joseph Hargrave, of 82, King Street.
William McDonald, of 9, Dean Street.
Ann Mackay, of 2, Ferry Street.
Thomas Sharp, of 23, Market Place.

All of the facts listed above will give the reader some indication of the important cultural role which both ale and the alehouse played in the area now known as South Tyneside, and, of course, throughout the rest of the north-east region, particularly from the fourteenth century onwards. To our knowledge, the oldest inn within the borough's precincts dates back to the seventeenth century, and it is from this period onwards that public houses came to have a common association with apparitions and hauntings. Perhaps, then, it is not surprising that so many inns are haunted. Over the decades – nay, centuries – a succession of strong characters have frequented these taverns and, it seems, impressed their psyche indelibly upon them. The huge number of businesses discussed in this chapter are, in essence, the raw material with which we have had to work when researching the wonderful tales of ghosts and 'shades' which have been handed down from one generation to another. Any discussion of haunted inns and public houses would be futile without an explanation of the role such establishments played in the everyday life of the people who visited them.

CHAPTER FOUR

Old Inns Of Jarrow
Circa 1900

In the neighbouring town of Jarrow there were also many drinking establishments, although their history is not so well detailed in local history records. Some of these were run-down hovels that were not only frequented by drinkers but also local prostitutes. Bluntly speaking, they were not the sort of places where one would be inclined to celebrate a wedding anniversary or invite the local vicar for a dry sherry and salmon sandwich.

Not all the public houses in Jarrow were 'dives', though. Some were respectable establishments that had a good reputation for serving fine ales. Like most of the other pubs throughout the region, they also carried reputations for being haunted.

In 1900, at the end of the reign of Queen Victoria, alcoholism had become epidemic. The poor drowned their sorrows in cheap gin, the rich celebrated their wealth with fine wines and port. A comprehensive meander around Jarrow in that year would have revealed the following inns and alehouses:

Location	Establishment
Blackett Street	The White Lead
Western Road	The Western
Western Road	The Rolling Mill
Western Road	The Queen's (later renamed The Queen's Head)
Western Road	The Ellison Arms
Ormonde Street	The County
Ormonde Street	The Engineers
Ormonde Street	The Tinmouth Castle (later renamed The Tynemouth Castle)

Curlew Road	The Golden Lion
Curlew Road	The Rose & Crown
Curlew Road	The Foresters
Curlew Road	The Stirling Castle
Nixon Street	The Bell Rock
Ferry Street	The Golden Fleece
Pearson Place	The Prince of Wales
Tyne Street	The Commercial
Tyne Street	The Staith House
Station Street	The North Eastern
Grange Road	The Ben Lomond
Grange Road	The Station
Grange Road	The Alnwick Castle
Grange Road	The Cottage
Grange Road	The Grange
Grange Road	The Royal Oak
North Street	The Forge & Hammer
North Street	The Borough Arms
North Street	The Turf
North Street	The Victoria
North Street	The Harbour Light
Market Square	The Theatre Bar
Pitt Street	The Golden Fleece
Monkton Road	The Queen's Head
Chapel Row	The Crown & Anchor
Buddle Street	The Globe

Stead Street	The Oak
High Street	The Alexandria
High Street	The Telegraph
High Street	The Hylton Castle
High Street	The Duke of Wellington
Low Jarrow	The Allison Arms
Low Jarrow	The Alkali
Jarrow Slakes	The East Ferry Inn
Jarrow Slakes	The Spike
Cuthbert Terrace	McKechnie's Bar
Monkton Village	The Lord Nelson
Shields Road	The Prince of Wales
Shields Road	The Robin Hood
Shields Road	The Greyhound Inn

It is interesting to note how colloquial spellings were more common, even at the turn of the twentieth century. As time went on, however, things became standardised. 'The Tinmouth Castle' became The Tynemouth Castle, and, over in South Shields, 'The Gray Horse' became The Grey Horse.

The names may have changed but, as we shall see, the ghosts of these establishments stubbornly persisted.

PART TWO:

A Gazetteer of the North East's Most Famous Haunted Pubs

- **Pub:** THE ALBION INN
- **Location:** PELAW
- **Good Ghost Rating:** 5

The popular Albion Inn at Reay Street, Pelaw, is allegedly haunted by a well-liked customer of old known simply as 'Charlie'.

We don't know a lot about Charlie, except that he must have been a decent sort. Other customers referred to him fondly as, "The Gentleman of Bill Quay". For those who are not well versed in the local geography, Bill Quay and Pelaw are adjacent communities in the Gateshead area.

Charlie died sometime in the early 1960s, before the advent of our overly-technological society or the arrival of the dreaded wine bar. The Albion Inn was the less for his passing, but it seems that even the Grim Reaper could not dissuade old Charlie from visiting his favourite watering hole. Not long after his departure into the next world, his ghost was seen on numerous occasions in the bar.

A former landlady once saw Charlie in the pub and, not surprisingly, was a little disconcerted, as she was well aware that he was dead. Nevertheless, she plucked up the courage to approach him, but Charlie – perhaps not in a mood to talk – simply disappeared.

Later, another landlord arrived to manage the premises. To our knowledge he never had the privilege of seeing Charlie in spirit form, but he did have several rather strange experiences which led him to believe that the 'Gentleman of Bill Quay' was still around.

On several occasions he would hear the door to the bar open, followed by the eerie tap-tap-tap of a walking stick on the floor. Could this have been old Charlie's walking stick, or is it just possible that another spectre walked the floors of The Albion Inn in addition to himself?

Whether old Charlie has been seen recently or not we cannot say, but his character and personality obviously stamped themselves upon this friendly little bar in a way that the clientele should be thankful for.

In-depth Case Study: The Alum Ale House, South Shields
Good Ghost Rating: 9

Over 200 years ago, adjacent to the new ferry landing at South Shields, there stood a chemical factory known as the Alum Works or the Alum House. The businessman and creative entrepreneur Isaac Cookson opened his business, situated just around the corner from Thrift Street, sometime before 1760, although we cannot be sure exactly when. When Isaac retired it then passed in to the capable hands of his son John Cookson.

The south bank of the River Tyne, adjacent to the Alum Works, was a favourite spot for the scullermen to land their boats or cobles, and to this day their memory is echoed in local street names. The recently built housing estate below River Drive, for example, is called Coble Landing.

At some point the building now known as the Alum Ale House was erected, although we know little for certain about its early history. Regardless, it has provided refreshment for the local populace at least since the mid-nineteenth century.

There has always been 'something of the sea' about the Alum Ale House; perhaps it is the inn's close proximity to the river which leads out into the North Sea. A plaque once bolted to the outer wall of the pub bore an old poem which echoed seafaring days long gone:

> The ships lay off the Alum House ham,
> Awaiting the wind and tide,
> The Brotherly Love and Amphritite,
> And the Betsy Cairns so stout and tight,
> All floated side by side.

George B. Hodgson, in his classic work, The Borough Of South Shields, remarks that, 'The chief of the numerous public landing-places along the river-side was the Alum House Ham, from which plied a numerous array of scullermen. A race apart are these old scullermen, grizzled and weather-beaten sea-dogs every man of them, who had taken to the boats to earn a crust and a gill when too stiff in the joints to have any chance of signing on for another voyage.'[1]

On entering the Alum Ale House from Ferry Street – an area which itself has a hallowed place on the tapestry of South Shields history, and not always for the right reasons – one is struck by an almost tangible atmosphere of welcome and an aura of bygone days. There are no carpets in the main bar of the Alum House; only polished wooden boards which, could they speak, would undoubtedly have many a tale to tell.

Immediately north of the inn lies the aforementioned River Tyne, along which a variety of vessels still pass as they go about their business, both foreign and domestic. To the west sits the recently refurbished ferry landing which connects South Shields to its sister town of North Shields across the water. The new ferry landing serves its purpose well, but it is garish and modern and not at all in keeping with the character of the area. Regardless, the Alum Ale House stands aloof from such discussion and continues to bid welcome to those who wish to experience something of its charm and history.

Upstairs from the Alum Ale House bar is a flat occupied by the inn's proprietors. Over a drink one spring evening in 2000, Jenny Preston told Mike and his wife Jackie that those same living quarters were allegedly haunted by the presence of an Irish prostitute known as Giggly Meg. Meg, presumably, lived on the premises at one time. According to legend she also had a fondness – too much of a fondness, by all accounts – for the demon drink. There may be some truth in this rumour, as one of the signs of Meg's presence is the sound of a silly, giggly laugh that may well be precipitated by a state of intoxication.

Meg has other ways of making her presence felt. She can be incredibly noisy and is not averse to slamming doors when she wants to draw attention to herself. One previous manager even confessed to having remonstrated with Meg about this, after which she behaved in a more dignified fashion – at least for a while. On one particular occasion, Meg left the bedroom and walked into the bathroom, slamming the door behind her. The manager said that she was 'distinctly aware of Meg's presence' as she walked past.

Perhaps the most intriguing tale involving Meg revolves around yet another ex-landlady, who wishes to remain anonymous. One evening she took an apple pie out of the freezer and placed it on the kitchen bench to defrost overnight. Her intention was to cook it the next morning. Shortly afterwards she went to bed and never gave the pie another thought.

The following morning she entered the kitchen to make a cup of tea, and was astonished to find the alluring aroma of baking pastry filling the room. The pie was in the oven – which, thankfully, was lit – and was cooked to perfection.

---

1   Hodgson, G. *The Borough of South Shields*, (South Tyneside Libraries, 1996) p. 361

No one other than the landlady was in the flat at the time, and so, hard though it might be to believe, suspicion must inevitably fall upon giggly Meg.

Who was this saucy gal, Giggly Meg? We do not know, but as wraiths often tend to attach themselves to places which have witnessed tragedies of one kind or another, it is not unreasonable to assume that she may have met her end at the Alum Ale House. Perhaps she died suddenly on the premises, who knows.

There is a stairwell at the Alum Ale House which leads from the lounge to the residence above the inn. Here, on more than one occasion, a second spectre has made himself known to bar staff.

One day, a male employee who worked behind the bar was standing at the foot of the stairwell with a crate full of beer bottles in his hands. To his everlasting surprise he watched as a rather splendidly-dressed 'Victorian gentleman' walked down the steps towards him. The barman watched incredulously as the very bespoke chap walked past him, dressed in a long-tailed coat and carrying an expensive-looking top hat in his hand. The latter he gracefully placed upon his head before exiting through a none-existent doorway.

It's tempting to suggest that the man had, during his life, perhaps been a client of the aforementioned Giggly Meg; a mischievous notion, but an interesting possibility. Again, the identity of this gentleman has become totally obscured by the passage of time. All we know is that he apparently shared a fondness for the old Alum Ale House which persisted even after death.

Adjacent to the lounge in the Alum Ale House is the female toilet. Here, on numerous occasions, yet another female apparition has presented itself to unwary women as they powdered their nose.

Some years ago, an employee of the Alum Ale House and his friend were in the bar after hours, cleaning up, emptying ashtrays, etc. The friend decided to visit the toilet, but declined to use the Gents as, in the cold weather, it had a reputation for being a wee bit on the chilly side. (As all men know, a sudden drop in temperature has a most peculiar effect upon the male urinary tract, but we don't need to lower the tone any further by going into such matters just now.) And so, after gaining permission from his pal the barman, he used the Ladies instead as it had a far more ambient temperature.

On the face of it no harm was done; the inn had been cleared of both customers and staff with the exception of themselves, so the chap was hardly likely to disturb, or be disturbed by, a member of the fairer sex as he went about his business, so to speak.

Hindsight is a wonderful thing, and later the central character of our story probably regretted his decision, as he found that someone else was in the powder room beside himself. It was not, however, an inebriated good time gal who had simply fallen asleep in a cubicle due to a surfeit of alcohol, but a personage of an altogether more spectral nature. Although he may not have felt like it at the time, the man was extremely privileged; this was the ghost of the legendary Grey Lady, the appearance of whom suddenly removed any previously-held desire on the part of our friend to void his bladder. Discretion being the better part of valour, he quickly rejoined his friend in the bar.

Those who have seen the Grey Lady are unanimously consistent in their descriptions of her. They describe her as middle-aged, of proportionate build and quite attractive. The most noticeable feature is her rather elegant grey dress which has long, hanging sleeves. As her appearances usually only last for a few, fleeting seconds, more detailed descriptions do not exist.

Another appearance of the Grey Lady occurred some time later, when a friend of the (then) landlady Jenny Preston visited the female toilet. Previously having admitted to being 'something of a sceptic', she had no worries at all about entering the cubicle. In fact, just a minute or two later she was busy washing her hands in a washbasin before returning to the bar.

Ghosts come when you least expect them, and this one seemed quite happy to play by the rules.

Suddenly, without warning, the woman saw someone standing beside her. Or at least she saw something beside her; actually, a disembodied hand and forearm covered with a long, grey, hanging sleeve. (Later, Jenny remembers her friend saying that the arm and hand had a 'smoky' appearance, and other witnesses have commented on the same thing.) Suddenly the disembodied limb moved backwards, as if removing itself from the wash basin adjacent to the one Jenny's friend was using. And then, in the twinkling of an eye, it was gone.

Gail, another member of staff at the time, also saw the Grey Lady. Once again, though, she chose not to appear in conventional anthropomorphic form. This time she appeared as a dark shadow or silhouette which, unnervingly, followed Gail as she left the female toilet.

Unlike the aforementioned ghosts – those of the inebriated prostitute and the bespoke Victorian gentleman in a top hat – there is one sketchy clue to the identity of the Grey Lady. Some have identified her as a woman whose photograph hangs on the wall of the lounge. Jenny Preston showed Mike the picture one day when he visited the Alum Ale House, and pointed out the woman concerned.

The picture is certainly interesting. It shows a large group of dignitaries gathered for the launch of, 'The Railway Ferry Steamer, the Prince Edward Island. October 5th, 1914'. Towards the front is a rather stocky woman with something of a matronly demeanour. We do not know who she is exactly, but it is likely that she was a local civic dignitary or at least the wife of one. Further research may uncover some answers.

The fourth spectre known to haunt the Alum Ale House is affectionately called Charlie, or sometimes Old Charlie. Charlie lives in the cellar downstairs, or at least seems to spend most of his time there. Whether the epithet of 'Charlie' was foisted on him by the staff at some past time, or whether it has any basis in historical reality, we are unable to say.

Charlie can be something of a mischief-maker. On one occasion Jenny was down in the cellar preparing the wages for the bar staff when two strip lights directly above her head went out simultaneously. Annoyed, Jenny waited until her eyes became accustomed to the dark. Then she reached up and adjusted the bulbs slightly in their sockets. They came back on immediately, and that was that – or so she thought. Once again Jenny began to count out the wages, and once again the lights extinguished themselves. Now Jenny was extremely irritated. For a second time she fiddled with the bulbs until they came back on. But no sooner had she sat back down again when they went out for a third time. Jenny had had enough, and she shouted out to Charlie to leave her alone as she was busy and had no time to engage in fun and games. The lights stayed on after that. Charlie, it seems, had been suitably chastened.

Several other bar staff have felt Charlie's presence in the cellar, although significantly no one claims to have actually seen him. On a positive note, no one seems to have felt threatened by him in any way.

THE PHANTOM BARMAN

The fifth spectre to haunt the Alum Ale House has been dubbed the Phantom Barman, as he seems to restrict his activities to the area surrounding the counter in the main bar. The exact nature of this 'entity' is not easy to define, as his presence usually manifests itself with a variety of poltergeist-like symptoms.

Most experts recognise that poltergeists and apparitions are two entirely different phenomena, although they may sometimes appear together. When the Phantom Barman is present witnesses may report the sudden appearance and disappearance of objects, the apparent moving of items from one place to another or strange odours and sharp temperature changes which accompany polt activity.

The Phantom Barman – whatever type of phenomenon he may be – does not usually present himself visually. And yet, his presence and movements through the bar area can be 'sensed' by witnesses in a way that we cannot as yet explain. This is not an unusual aspect of hauntings. On several occasions the authors have spoken to witnesses who have said that they were able to 'follow' the path of an invisible spectre as it walked across a room without actually being able to see it. Some have even said that they could 'make out the shape' of the entity, even though it was entirely invisible. It was, said one, 'As if I was seeing it and yet not seeing it, both at the same time'.

The Phantom Barman seems to have a particular liking for an area at the back of the bar behind the counter. His favourite 'party piece' used to be removing bottles of beer from a shelf behind the bar and throwing them around, much to the consternation of the staff and customers. To put a stop to this a number of brass rails were bolted across the front of the shelf, necessitating a small amount of dexterity to remove the bottles from behind them. The Phantom Barman does not possess this, it seems, for since the addition of the rails he has left the bottles well alone.

There is a cupboard in the Alum Ale House that contains cleaning equipment and utensils. It is here where witnesses have detected the presence of the sixth spectre to haunt this curious old pub. Staff in the building have reported an 'uneasy feeling' whilst retrieving cleaning equipment from the cupboard, and one stated that 'it was not particularly pleasant'.

Mike first wrote up the ghost stories attached to the Alum Ale House in his book *Ales & Spirits*. Shortly after it was published he heard tales of a seventh spectre that was said to haunt the premises. This was the ghost of a Roman legionnaire which allegedly shared the cellar with Old Charlie, although whether these two wraiths have ever communicated with each other is unknown.

Two witnesses, to our knowledge, claim to have seen the soldier standing near the bar just inside the entrance. Readers unfamiliar with the inn may wonder what a bar is doing in the cellar. Many years ago a landlord felt that the room was being wasted, and invested a considerable amount of money in transforming it into a small lounge that could be hired for private parties. The low ceiling, iron beams and roughly plastered walls all added to the ambience, and before long folk groups, rock bands and others were entertaining the punters on a regular basis. Later the room was allowed to fall into disrepair again, but Jenny Preston and her partner John resurrected it, renamed it 'The Dungeon' and it immediately took on a new lease of life.

On one occasion a cleaner was mopping the floor when she suddenly felt as if someone was standing behind her. She turned, and for a fleeting second saw the ghostly legionnaire staring at her intently. There was a flash of light, and then he disappeared into the ether. Intriguingly, there was at one time a Roman quay situated near to where the Alum Ale House now stands. The authors know of witnesses who claim to have discovered a tunnel which leads from the river bank all the way to the Arbeia Roman fort on the nearby Lawe Top. Several Roman artefacts have been found near the site of the Alum Ale House, including some coins which were unearthed when some houses were being demolished nearby in the 1930s. Could the ghost of this legionnaire be connected to those finds? Did he once stand guard on the very spot where the Cellar Bar or 'Dungeon' now sits? We may never know.

The new residents at the Alum Ale House are currently resurrecting the Dungeon with gusto and seem set on returning it to its glory days. All power to their elbow, say we.

- Pub: THE ANCIENT UNICORN INN
- Location: BOWES
- Good Ghost Rating: 7

The Ancient Unicorn Inn is situated in the old village of Bowes which nestles high in the North Pennines. The area is one of natural outstanding beauty, and from the vantage point of the pub one can enjoy wonderful views of the surrounding countryside. The pub itself dates back to the sixteenth century and, like most old taverns and alehouses, it began its life as a coaching inn.

The Ancient Unicorn Inn is well and truly haunted and, by repute, houses a number of spectres and shades from past ages. A man with a bowler hat and a beard is alleged to haunt the pub along with the ghost of a young, unidentified boy who has been seen in the cellars. We were told that visiting patrons to the hotel have reported ghostly goings-on and other odd phenomena, and there are tales of people being touched, pushed by unseen hands and hearing strange noises in the dead of night.

By far the most famous ghost story attached to the Ancient Unicorn Inn is that of a young couple's love that was destined never to be. The story dates back to the early 1700s, when a young girl named Martha (more commonly known these days as Emma) fell in love with the son of the innkeepers at the village's other public house, which is now demolished. The relationship was frowned upon by both sets of parents and meetings between the two lovers were forbidden. However, a far worse fate was to befall them.

Not long after they began their love affair, Martha's' boyfriend fell seriously ill with a fever and died. Martha, (or Emma) is said to have passed away a few days later of a broken heart. Both were buried together in the local cemetery, where their graves can still be seen to this day.

Emma is reputed to haunt the Ancient Unicorn Inn and has been seen on countless occasions in different parts of the pub. She is said to be a 'sad but friendly' ghost.

- PUB: THE BAY HORSE
- LOCATION: STAMFORDHAM
- GOOD GHOST RATING: 7

The Bay Horse pub and hotel is located in the Northumbrian village of Stamfordham, between Newcastle and Hexham. The building was once a fortified farmhouse and coaching inn and dates back to the year 1590, making it nearly 420 years old. Now it is a fine hotel and public house with six comfortable en-suite bedrooms and a beautiful lounge area that was once, in fact, the original farmhouse.

The establishment is an awe-inspiring place with a wonderful ambience and has an almost palpable air of mystery about it. It is one of two pubs that sit gracefully in the heart of the village from which visitors can enjoy stunning views of the Northumbrian countryside that was once occupied by both the Romans and the Border Reivers.

Of course, The Bay Horse pub has a resident ghost or two, with apparitions regularly being seen in the restaurant area by numerous witnesses on different occasions. This leaves the patrons in no doubt that a spectre does indeed reside there. There are also reports of phantom footfalls being heard on one of the inner stairwells. Apparently, anomalous lights have been recorded on CCTV, and poltergeist-like activity has been reported in the kitchen areas. It has even been suggested that a mysterious tunnel lies beneath the pub, adding further to the charm which clings to this mysterious old inn.

- PUB: THE BEACON
- LOCATION: SOUTH SHIELDS
- GOOD GHOST RATING: 3

Towards the end of River Drive, on the Lawe Top area of South Shields, there sits The Beacon public house. The Beacon is an inn which at least dates back to the 1840s, and to our knowledge has always carried the name it is currently known by.

One Sunday evening Mike popped in for a pint, introduced himself to the manager and asked him if he knew of any ghost stories attached to the pub. Mike confessed that an old chap in another watering hole had let slip that The Beacon was supposedly haunted.

'Well, there is a story...there was a barmaid who worked here at one point, and she apparently fell down the steps into the cellar and died. I don't know anything else other than that, but I suspect it must have been a long time ago'.

And that was that, really, or at least the authors thought it was. Then they received a call from a former employee who told them that both she and her daughter had actually seen the spectre – the story was no romantic legend.

Maybe readers of this volume may know something about the tragic death of the young barmaid who fell down the stairs, or other spectres that supposedly haunt The Beacon. If so, please get in touch.

- PUB: THE BEEHIVE
- LOCATION: SOUTH SHIELDS
- GOOD GHOST RATING: 6

Pigot's Directory indicates the presence of a Beehive public house in Wellington Street, South Shields, in the early 1800s. The modern Beehive Inn is, however, only a namesake. Records indicate that it was built in the year 1953.

The architectural design of the modern Beehive is plain, almost utilitarian. It lacks the finesse of its Victorian and Edwardian neighbours and speaks of a time in our history when, to put it mildly, aesthetics were viewed to be of very little importance. None of this should be taken as a criticism of the inn itself, however, as visitors will find that it is one of the most welcoming pubs in the north-east of England.

A former manager of the pub happened to be drinking in the bar at the time we popped in to 'do some research' – a wonderful euphemism for drinking a pint of beer – and we asked him if the Beehive was, as legend had it, haunted.

'Definitely', he replied without hesitation. 'No one has ever actually seen anything, at least to my knowledge, but some very strange things have happened here.

'When I first took over the pub, I noticed a problem with the pumps down in the cellar. I'd switch them on, and by the time I got back upstairs they'd be switched off again. I'd go back down, and, sure enough, they'd be switched off. Then I'd turn them on again... they'd mysteriously turn off again...and so on'.

'Eventually things got so bad I had to get the technical people in from the brewery. They checked out everything, but couldn't find the problem. By the time we got back in the bar they'd been switched off again'.

The new Beehive may well be haunted then, just as its now-demolished namesake was reputed to be.

- **Pub:** THE BIRDS NEST
- **Location:** NEWCASTLE UPON TYNE
- **Good Ghost Rating:** 5

The Birds Nest public house was situated at the west end of Walker Road in St Anthony's Estate, Newcastle upon Tyne. It was just along the back lane from where its sister drinking establishment, The Birds Nest Social Club stood. Both buildings were eventually demolished. Several years after the social club accidentally burned down, the bar was unfortunately sacrificed for a new development in the St Anthony's area.

The bar itself was not that large, and consisted of two floors; the lower floor was the pub and the above floor was a private dwelling for those who ran the establishment. A plain, whitewashed building, the pub served as a drinking den for the 'Walker locals'.

During his childhood Darren spent a lot of time playing in the vicinity of the pub and its neighbourhood. That is where he lived as a boy, and for a short period of time he was friendly with Linda, the daughter of the pub's [then] owners.

As a friend of Linda, Darren was allowed into the flat above the pub to play on rainy days and these few occasions were the only times when Darren ventured into the premises. He vaguely remembers Linda telling him that while she was in bed at night she would often hear footsteps thumping across the floor when everyone else was fast asleep. The pub had been closed up by then and the bar was empty, so the noises could not have come from revellers downstairs. This frightened her somewhat. Along with the strange footfalls, she also mentioned that, on other occasions, glasses and bottles could be heard 'clinking' and 'tinkling' in the downstairs bar – as if being moved around or being collected by the glass collector, again through the night and when no one was down there. However, one has to take into account that Darren and his friend were quite young at the time and youngsters are renowned for telling each other 'spooky stories'. The authors suppose it would not be hard to imagine that both these episodes do indeed have rational explanations, but you never know. Kids' stories or real paranormal experiences? Darren can't say for sure, but the family didn't reside at this old pub for long ...

- PUB: THE BLACK BULL
- LOCATION: EAST BOLDON
- GOOD GHOST RATING: 6

During the course of our research for this volume, the authors spent many a wonderful hour visiting the north-east's finest haunted hostelries. They are not ashamed to admit that they took full advantage of the situation and sampled a wide variety of culinary delights and fine ales – all in moderation, mind you.

If you like good pub grub, you'll not be disappointed in what The Black Bull has to offer. Darren and Mike found this out when they carried out an impromptu on-site visit to find out about the numerous paranormal phenomena that are said to take place at this quaint village pub.

Actually, Mike has visited The Black Bull on dozens of occasions as he only lives half a mile away from the premises, but when he and Darren turned up a new manager had only recently been installed. The perfect opportunity arose to make sure that vigorous gastronomic standards were being maintained. Well, that's the authors' excuse and they're sticking to it. For the record, Mike had the steak and Darren had the fish.

There are numerous haunted pubs in the Boldons, but for some reason, the spectres that inhabit The Black Bull rarely have their praises sung publicly. Nevertheless, get chatting to the manager, staff and patrons and it probably won't be long before you realise that this welcoming little inn really is haunted.

The first story to draw itself to the authors' attention was a rather sad tale of a young toddler who was seen sitting at the bottom of the cellar steps by a pub employee. One minute he was there, the next he simply vanished into the ether, as if he'd never existed. We decided that an interview with the lady concerned would be absolutely necessary, and so made arrangements to go back for another visit. Meanwhile, the landlord immediately set about informing the authors about a strange incident that had occurred the previous evening.

Like most pubs, The Black Bull has a number of gaming machines installed for the enjoyment of its patrons. These machines have what is commonly called a 'jam alarm' which activates as soon as a coin becomes stuck in the delicate mechanism. In the early hours of one morning, one manager was in the bar alone when one of the jam alarms began to shriek with gusto. He deactivated the alarm, but was puzzled. They normally only sounded as soon as a coin became jammed, but as he was the only one in the bar at the time this seemed impossible.

Taken in isolation this incident cannot be seen as proof positive that the pub is haunted. However, when seen in the overall context of things, one certainly has to wonder.

In recent years there have been numerous peculiar incidents at The Black Bull. Gas taps attached to the beer pumping system have mysteriously turned themselves on and off. Bottles and glasses behind the bar have rattled violently without any observable reason. Lights have switched themselves on and off without human assistance and, on one occasion, seven ashtrays upon the bar counter suddenly took to the air and crashed to the floor unceremoniously without cause.

During one visit the authors turned their attention to the locals sitting at the bar. One chap, nursing a pint, told them that he had been good friends with two of the previous landlords. They in turn had told him about a number of things that had allegedly gone bump in the night, as they say. He even informed the authors that he had experienced one or two strange things himself whilst employed there. To be fair, the chap was still a bit sceptical about the paranormal and informed Darren and Mike that he didn't actually believe in ghosts.

Mind you, if seeing really is believing, then The Black Bull probably is a haunted pub as a number of landlords have readily admitted to having seen things out of the corner of their eye, particularly when alone in the bar.

'They're just fleeting wisps...you can't really focus on them; something off to the side will move, but when you instinctively turn to focus on it, it will be gone', said one.

Does the idea of The Black Bull being haunted trouble the staff and drinkers? It doesn't seem to; in fact, they seem to relish a dalliance or two with things beyond our senses. Once a month a resident clairvoyant even gives readings to a never-ending queue of patrons who want to know what the future holds. She has a good reputation, and no shortage of clients.

The Black Bull is a pub full of charm, character – and ghosts – and well worth a visit.

- **PUB:**   THE BLACK HORSE
- **LOCATION:**   WEST BOLDON
- **GOOD GHOST RATING:** 8

The Black Horse is situated next to Saint Nicholas's Church in West Boldon, and is one of South Tyneside's oldest pubs. Formerly a coaching inn, The Black Horse has character and is a wonderful reminder of bygone days.

The inn was built during the seventeenth century, although there may have been a pub on the same site even before that. Whether the previous establishment was haunted or not we cannot say, but the current building likely is.

One afternoon, Mike and his father popped in to The Black Horse for a lunchtime pint. Mike asked the (then) manager if he could tell them a little more about the spectres that reputedly still make their presence felt. The landlord confessed that he had been a sceptic concerning the paranormal – until he had moved to The Black Horse.

'I used to be a hardcore sceptic but all that changed about eighteen months ago. It was early one morning', he said. 'I was standing behind the bar when I happened to take a quick look up. There, sitting next to the window by the door, was a man dressed in dark, old-fashioned clothing.

'He wore tall boots, leggings and a wide-brimmed hat. I also noticed that his skin had a rather swarthy complexion.

'I said, 'Excuse me; can I help you?' He turned and looked at me for a second and then ... and then he turned away again and just disappeared into thin air ... right in front of me'.

The landlord admitted that the hairs on the back of his neck stood up, and that he left the bar in rather a hurry. Not wanting to alarm his staff, he kept his strange experience to himself. It is at this point that the story begins to take on a distinctly credible air.

Two other members of staff, who worked between the bar and the restaurant, also saw our mysterious phantom. They both thought there was something odd about the man, who was sitting on a stool at the bar, dressed in typical seventeenth-century clothing. Their suspicions were confirmed when he disappeared in a matter of seconds.

As you can imagine, the two women in question were somewhat relieved to find out later that they were not the only ones to have clapped eyes upon this spectral visitor.

The living quarters above The Black Horse are also rumoured to be haunted. The landlord stated that he'd heard the sound of a young child's voice in one of the bedrooms, only to find on entering that there was no one there.

Strangely, the ghost of a young girl aged around nine years has also been seen in the Gent's toilet. Unlike some spectres, her identity may not be so difficult to establish. In the 19th century a school stood adjacent to The Black Horse, and the playground apparently looked out over a quarried area of the steep bank at the rear, now known colloquially as The Leap. The young girl in question, who in her spectral appearances wears a white dress and sports long, blonde hair, allegedly toppled over the playground wall in a freak accident and died instantly after falling into The Leap below. Perhaps it is her apparition which haunts the inn today, who knows?

But there is yet another mystery attached to The Black Horse. There are rumours that an immense underground tunnel runs all the way from the inn to Cleadon Tower (or possibly the Toby Carvery Inn) at Cleadon Village. The landlord told Mike he'd located the entrance to this tunnel, although whether one could amble through it all the way to Cleadon is another question. Sadly the entrance is now blocked up, so we may never know unless excavations are carried out at some future time.

When one visits The Black Horse today, one is struck immediately by the warm, friendly atmosphere. The inn has a reputation for serving excellent food, and, as we found, visitors are made extremely welcome. So next time you visit West Boldon you could do worse than pop in to this fascinating little pub for some refreshment.

If you're having trouble telling the difference between the regular drinkers and those from a bygone age, the floppy hats and ruffled collars are usually a dead give-away ...

- PUB: THE BLACK HORSE INN
- LOCATION: WATERHOUSES
- GOOD GHOST RATING: 6

Haunted pubs are like fine wines; they mature with age. The Black Horse Inn at Waterhouses is said to be over 200 years old, but it wasn't till the 1970s that the [then] tenants made it public knowledge that the inn was allegedly haunted and possibly even infested by a poltergeist. Numerous eerie and unexplainable incidents had occurred there, such as newly fitted light bulbs mysteriously falling out of their sockets and shattering on the floor. The landlady recalled that during one such incident she walked into a room and two bulbs fell to the ground within a second of each another.

On another occasion, having swept up the shattered pieces of a bulb, another witness found that the fragments she'd just cleaned up had been returned to the very spot where she had found them. Very strange indeed!

During their research the authors also discovered that electric fires once had a tendency to behave in a most unreliable manner. One had a habit of switching itself on and off of its own volition. Tests showed that new wiring had only recently been fitted, and a 'natural' explanation was ultimately ruled out.

This phenomenon was just the beginning of the affair, and it was soon to get a lot worse. Darren and Mike were told that at one time alarm clocks had started to ring during the night, keeping all who heard them wide awake. More terrifyingly, the 13 year-old niece of the tenants once ran out of her room in sheer terror saying that a man was standing by her bed 'wearing a strange robe'.

It is interesting to note, however, that the only relevant historical story attached to the pub bares no relationship to a man, but rather to a woman who was allegedly pushed down the cellar stairs to her death. So did the youngster merely experience a bad dream? Or does the old Black Horse Inn also harbour the ghost of a man, too? Answers on a postcard please …

- PUB: THE BLACKIE BOY
- LOCATION: NEWCASTLE
- GOOD GHOST RATING: 8

The Black Boy Inn, or 'Blackie Boy' as it is more commonly known, is located in Newcastle city centre on the famous Bigg Market (sometimes called the Groat Market) and is one of the city's better-known haunted pubs. It is only a stone's throw away from The Old George Inn (mentioned later in this book) and, like The Old George, it too backs on to an old cobblestone yard. Established in 1823, The Blackie Boy pub currently serves food as well as the traditional alcoholic beverages.

The Blackie Boy has three levels, with a long bar on the ground floor – complete with an old library – and a clock behind the bar dating back to 1923. Upstairs there is a function room which is used for parties. The third or top level is currently used for storage. The ghost, it is said, resides on the second floor.

There are a few theories regarding whom or what the ghost of The Blackie Boy really is, and why it should haunt there; but in all honesty the authors think that no one currently knows the real truth behind the legend. During our research the authors spoke with the sub-manager. He informed them that he always knew the pub had a 'haunted reputation' and had heard strange stories from bar staff past and present.

Staff members have admitted to seeing dark shadows flitting about and an eerie sense of presence has been detected by a few. Of course this could be nothing more than auto-suggestion on the part of nervous and weary pub workers who are well aware of the bar's reputation.

The sub-manager also told us a few stories of ghostly phenomena that are a little harder to explain, including a chilling account from one former employee. While working on the second floor, this particular individual heard what can only be described as a 'harrowing scream' followed by a malevolent voice commanding her to 'Get out, get out!' Auto-suggestion? We don't think so.

The sub-manager also admitted to Darren and Mike that he had a paranormal experience of his own one day. One afternoon he was on his way to 'pay a visit' whilst working up on the second floor. As he strolled across the function room towards the loos he noticed that the door leading into the Gents was open. It then slammed shut in what seemed to be a controlled fashion. At first he wondered if a gust of wind, or a draught, could have been responsible. These solutions were ruled out when, on examination, the windows were found to be closed. Besides, the door was an old, heavy one of robust construction and it would have taken a gale force wind to move it.

Feeling quite scared, he retreated downstairs to think about what he had just witnessed and decided to 'pay his visit' on the first floor instead. After pondering over his encounter, he became convinced that it must have had a paranormal origin.

So there you have it; the second floor of The Blackie Boy continues to live up to its famous reputation, sometimes by scaring the staff witless!

- PUB: THE BLACKSMITH'S TABLE
- LOCATION: WASHINGTON
- GOOD GHOST RATING: 9

The Blacksmith's Table restaurant sits opposite the village green in the centre of Washington village, Tyne and Wear. It is a small, but quaint edifice steeped in history and legend. The building is over four hundred years old and was originally the local blacksmith's workshop. Now it is a privately owned restaurant and is reputedly haunted by a number of ghosts and spectres.

Ghost sightings have been reported from long ago right up to the present day, the most famous being that of a highwayman called Robert Hazlitt.

In the late eighteenth century Hazlitt 'worked' the roads in and around the Washington, Wrekenton and Long Bank areas. One day, after a coach robbery, he was seen galloping away on his trusty steed by a local boy. Some time after, the lad was walking past the Smithy, recognised the robber's horse from the robbery and notified the relevant authorities. The authorities approached the Blacksmith, and asked him if they could await his return. Permission was granted, and a number of armed men secreted themselves in the back of the workshop. Interestingly, it is this locale which now serves as the restaurant area. The idea was that they would both surprise and apprehend the highway robber on his return to collect the horse. When Robert Hazlitt turned up, he was promptly arrested and taken away.

As he was frog-marched to his day in court, Hazlitt was heard to curse the blacksmith for his betrayal and he undoubtedly knew of the fate that awaited him. Sentencing was remarkably quick in those days, and just a week later he was hanged on the gallows in Durham. His body was then brought back to the area in which he worked, and hung up in a gibbet cage as a warning to other would-be highwaymen. It is little surprise, then, that his restless spirit is said to haunt the cocktail bar of the restaurant and has reputedly been seen on a number of occasions.

The Blacksmith's Table is also haunted by several other ghosts, including a woman who has been seen materialising in the restaurant area. Seemingly she then walks straight through the wall where the entrance to the blacksmiths workshop used to be in days past.

In the top corner of the restaurant it is said that the old blacksmith himself sits at a table and observes the modern day comings and goings of the restaurant's patrons.

Finally, the ghost of 'an unknown soul' is said to stand facing one of the walls, motionless, looking over his left shoulder. No one knows who he is.

- PUB: BOB TROLLOP'S
- LOCATION: NEWCASTLE UPON TYNE
- GOOD GHOST RATING: 8

Bob Trollop's is an aged traditional black-timber framed Newcastle alehouse. It is located on the Sandhill area of the Quayside, and is part of the Wessex Taverns chain of public houses – as are the neighbouring Red House and

Offshore 44, which are also mentioned in this volume. This charismatic and most welcoming inn has wooden beams on the ceiling and a sturdy wooden floor, giving the pub it's much ancient and olde worlde feel.

A colleague of the authors, Steve Taylor, who is the man behind Newcastle's very successful ghost walks, tells the authors that at one time Bob Trollop's pub was once a house of ill-repute and that it was owned by one Margaret Reay in 1840. It appears that the basement area of the pub was used as the 'knocking shop' for four women, and it is said that one of the girls had brought back a man for some illegal night-time fun when an argument broke out – but over what he couldn't say. It then got out of hand. The drunken man in question is believed to have picked up an oil lamp that was used to light up the cellars and smashed it over the young prostitute, thus setting fire to her. This wicked act resulted in the burning to death of the young lady of the night.

Yet it is not the murder victim that is said to haunt Bob Trollop's but actually a former landlady.

Steve went on to say, 'In the pub at the back there is a boarded-up stairwell of which the last few stairs can clearly be seen. They come down from the above floor and protrude into the bar area, and it is these stairs where the ghost of the landlady can be heard as she paces down them to enter the room'.

The manager, Joyce Wemyss confirmed this as true when the authors visited the pub during their research. She had heard the footsteps on occasions, as have a number of the bar staff whom the authors spoke to whilst researching this book.

Other mysterious phenomena have been reported there too. The room above Bob Trollops, where the blocked-off stairwell leads to the upper floor, is the function room that belongs to the Quilted Camel club. It is in this room from which thumps and bangs have been heard to emanate when no one is up there.

'It's as though someone was stomping around up there with boots on', the authors were told.

The authors had an interesting time down at Bob Trollop's, researching the ghosts and having a good look around. During their time there, they were also able to visit and learn about another two wonderfully haunted inns – Offshore 44 and The Red House. They are right beside one another and they are all ran by the same manager, Joyce Wemyss. Those ghosts can be read about later in this volume.

- **Pub:**   THE BRIDGE HOTEL
- **Location:**   NEWCASTLE UPON TYNE
- **Good Ghost Rating:** 7

The Bridge Hotel stands next to the Castle Garth and has a special place in the hearts of both authors, for it was there where a paranormal research society that they were both once affiliated to would meet, once a week, to discuss topics of a preternatural kind and arrange investigations. It was through this research society that the authors met and, quite frankly, they have not looked back since.

The pub commands spectacular views across the River Tyne and Newcastle Quayside from the beer garden out back, which is situated precisely in the middle of the ruined and gaunt Newcastle city walls. The land the pub is built upon was once was a medieval site and housed both a Saxon burial ground and a Roman fortress. Stories persist of a tunnel leading from the pub cellars under the now cobbled car park and into the neighbouring castle keep, but the authors can't find any evidence to corroborate this. Both stewards at the Pub and at Newcastle Keep know nothing about this, and suggest that it would not be plausible for the area between the two buildings to contain such a tunnel. However, Castle Keep curator Paul McDonald told Darren that the pub in question over the road 'had been investigated' by a local research team after hearing that mysterious 'dark figures had been seen and later reported in the ladies loos' that are situated downstairs near the cellars.

On checking to see if anyone was there at the time, the witnesses found they were on their own. The function rooms upstairs are also reputed to be haunted (if the psychics from the society that once met here are to be believed) by a dark figure of a man that has been both sensed and seen standing behind the counter in the bar.

Regardless of whether the pub is haunted or not, the land it is built upon most certainly is. A well known and respected TV medium, and friend of the authors, once visited the site and subsequently saw the ghost of a Roman soldier standing outside the castle at the precise area where the main settlement once stood!

- **PUB:** THE BRIDGE HOTEL
- **LOCATION:** SOUTH SHIELDS
- **GOOD GHOST RATING:** 8

The Bridge Hotel – or what's left of it – is situated in Queen Street, South Shields. Many moons ago the inn had its back entrance in Queen Street and its front entrance in the parallel King Street. The King Street entrance was known as the 'respectable' door, and was utilised by white-collar workers, 'professional' people and those who had a few bob in their pocket. The 'tradesman's entrance' in Queen Street, was utilised by labourers, shipyard workers and others who, quite wrongly, were seen as being on a lower rung of the social ladder simply because they got their hands dirty when they worked.

The front part of The Bridge Hotel was on a raised platform and surrounded by a fancy railing. No queuing at the bar in this part of the pub; for an extra penny you could get 'service' and have your ale brought directly to your table by the barmaid.

One morning in the early 1900s – we can't be exactly sure when – a cleaning lady of Gallic extraction opened up the premises early and, to her horror, found dirty footprints in the respectable end of the pub. Mon Dieu! Or even Zut Alors! Had a common labourer dared to set foot in the posh bit of The Bridge Hotel? The mystery was never solved, but the appearance of the dirty footsteps became a regular thing and even after the manager kept watch one night he still found them on the floor the next day at dawn. Pretty soon The Bridge Hotel was reputed to be haunted by a deceased drinker who had once been refused a drink in the 'respectable' end of the pub. In death he came back to do what he wasn't allowed to do in life; go into the posh end.

Alas, The Bridge Hotel closed many years ago and what used to be the front of the pub at the 'respectable' end is now a shop front. Nip round the back into Queen Street, however, and the last vestiges of the 'tradesman's' end can still be seen. The pub no longer exists, merely the frontage; but it serves as an eerie reminder of the cheeky ghost who once caused quite a bit of mischief inside.

- **PUB:**   THE BUFFALO INN / BUFFALO CENTRE
- **LOCATION:**   BLYTH
- **GOOD GHOST RATING:** 9

Midway along Regent Street in Cowpen, Blyth, stands the Buffalo Community Centre. In a previous incarnation the building was once The Buffalo Inn, and records show the structure on this spot dates back to the year 1841. Pigots' Trade Directory for 1834 lists an inn or a tavern on Keelman's Row called The Red Bull. It is possible that this is the original Buffalo Inn building.

Darren first became aware of the Buffalo Centre after a good friend of his, Cindy Nunn – founder of the respected research team API (Anomalous Phenomena Investigations) – informed him of the alleged ghostly goings-on inside the former drinking hole. Cindy and her team had spent a night investigating the premises and found the place to be very interesting indeed. Darren then decided it would be in his best interests if he interviewed the young lady who actually lived in the private flat above. He also spoke to her colleague who had worked at this venue for some years. Darren found out that nothing paranormal had occurred inside the actual private flat on the top floor – even though rumours persisted of a suicide by hanging in there. To the best of our knowledge such a tragic event never actually occurred, although noises – like the chairs in the meeting room under the flat moving around – had been heard. Knowing that the Buffalo Centre was completely locked up and no one was in the building at time of the alleged psychic disturbances, this concerned them somewhat as you can imagine.

It appears that whoever is residing in the former alehouse likes to play about and does so by opening and closing the doors and, as previously mentioned, re-arranging the chairs. In regards the rather negative histories that a lot of haunted venues seem to have, The Buffalo is quite different as there are no records of murders, deaths, or any nasty business at all having occurred on the premises. The thought occurs that if any ghosts do indeed reside here, they may just be sticking around simply because they like the place! (A cliché the authors know, but hey … it happens.)

During Darren's visit he was also informed about two apparitions that have allegedly been seen in the Centre. One was described to him as an old man in a black coat and was said to have been seen standing next to the fire doors on the lower level of the building.

The other is another man who has been seen in the hallway. No one knows whom they may be.

On his visit to the Buffalo Centre Darren took with him a psychic medium called Glenn Hall – a good friend of the authors and a member of the North East Ghost Research Team. It must be understood that during the interviews Glenn sat in the office downstairs out of earshot and did not hear the results of the chat Darren had with the witnesses. Nor did he know the building's history or what was alleged to have happened there previously. Glenn subsequently 'picked up' on the two apparitions, specifying exactly where they stood; pretty impressive stuff considering Cindy Nunn said to Darren regarding the ghost; 'A shadowy male figure is often seen in that location. The lady that lives here has mentioned it too. I have seen it myself while visiting at The Buffalo Centre on other business'.

The story does not end there, as Glenn also relayed the account of the moving chairs. Glenn's reading continued in the old stables outside – now a workshop and part of the Buffalo Centre property.

The first thing Glenn said was, 'It will be worthwhile investigating here'.

'Why is that?' Darren asked.

'I don't know,' he said. 'I just get the impression of heavy footsteps being heard in here by someone … there is something about this workshop'.

Darren later found out that Cindy Nunn and her team, while in that location, had heard footfalls in that very room.

She said, 'They paced back and forth and around the team members while we were in the dark, and we were all perfectly still'.

That was something else that Glenn could not have known.

The investigators then decided to try an EVP experiment in the workshop. They made themselves comfortable and began the tests. Darren 'called out to the atmosphere' in the hope that any of the alleged residing spirits would make contact via the EVP machines. He called out for approximately 10 minutes, asking certain questions, and then everyone present gathered around the machines to listen. To their utter surprise – and shock – they all heard a voice on the recording that did not belong to any of the 'living' people present. The voice simply said, 'Help Me!'

Quite odd to say the least, and very similar to another EVP recording Darren has in his possession; a recording that was made on an investigation in Durham where the disembodied voice said, 'Can you help me?'

Perhaps in a few cases there are spirits out there on another plane of existence that are indeed trapped, for whatever reason, and are in need of help to move them on. The evidence for this seems to be steadily accumulating.

Whatever is going on at the Buffalo Centre in Blyth is truly astonishing to say the least and the authors are pretty confident that genuine psychic or spiritual activity is occurring there on a regular basis. Of course more investigations are needed in order to determine if it is anything substantial in terms of objective evidence, and the authors will be making a return visit. We will also be interested to know what other investigators may find there during their research.

- PUB: THE CHAIN LOCKER
- LOCATION: NORTH SHIELDS
- GOOD GHOST RATING: 5

The building formerly known as The Chain Locker was renamed in 1986 after originally being called The Crane Hotel. The building is not a public house any more and has been converted into luxury apartments which face the ferry landing at North Shields; such a shame really, as the pub that once occupied this site was a fine drinking den which boasted character, charm, and, allegedly, a ghost.

Many years ago Darren would have a quiet pint there before venturing over to South Shields for a 'night on the tiles' and spent many a happy hour – pardon the pun – whetting his whistle before the main event, so to speak.

We were chatting with the [then] landlord about life in general, as you do, when the subject of ghosts arose. Darren was informed about a weird incident that once occurred in the bar.

After last orders had been called and the pub had emptied, the bar manager was cleaning up on his own when the distinct sound of footfalls were heard clumping across the wooden floor. Accompanying these strange footsteps was a whistling sound. Upon each note that was whistled there was what musicians would call a vibrato, leading the authors to think that whatever, or whoever it was – if indeed it was a ghost at all – would in all probability be that of an old man! After all, most old men warble when they whistle a tune. The mystery was never solved, and the identity of the phantom whistler has never been ascertained.

It was an isolated event and it appears that nothing of the sort has ever happened again. Well, not to our knowledge.

IN-DEPTH CASE STUDY: THE CITY HOTEL, DURHAM
Good Ghost Rating: 7

On a dark, cold January night – all good ghost stories are supposed to start like this – Darren and the Ghost and Hauntings, Overnight Surveillance Team (GHOST) arrived at the 500 year-old former manor house that is now known as The City Hotel. It is situated in Durham City itself, and is just around the corner from another famously haunted pub called Jimmy Allen's [see page 92]

It was with this north-east-based research team that Darren and his friends decided to carry out the investigation. They brought with them two guests; the famous ghost-hunters Ralph Keeton and Nikki Austwicke. Darren and the team had met Ralph and Nikki during another investigation at The McOrville Inn at Elwick (more about which later in this book), and it was decided that an invite to the City Hotel would be appropriate.

Not much is known about the history of the City Hotel. Truth to tell, there was even considerable debate about whether or not it was haunted. Not knowing, Darren had earmarked the night simply as a 'diagnostic', during which efforts would be made to determine whether there were indeed any spectres present. A more detailed investigation, to determine their exact nature or who they may have been, could be carried out later.

The team arrived in Durham at about 10.30pm and immediately made their way to the hotel where the [then] owner, Paul, met them. After offloading their equipment they made themselves comfortable and awaited the arrival of Ralph and Nikki. The celebrity guests turned up just before 11pm. The assembled ghost hunters chatted for about an hour while waiting for the pub to empty, and when it did they set about carrying out their usual pre-investigation tasks. The 'baseline' tests were carried out first, which involved taking temperature readings, along with EMF (electromagnetic field) sweeps, to determine the normal 'baseline' readings of the rooms and other locations. Should any anomalies be traced and picked up during the investigation itself, researchers will have detailed accounts and records of these readings to compare, so they can determine what is normal and what is paranormal. During a baseline test good researchers will also determine the location of creaky floorboards, draughty rooms and corridors, faulty doors, which may close on their own and other common, natural occurrences that are often mistaken for paranormal activity. These tests were followed by a 'reading' from the guest medium Ralph Keeton.

For our investigation we were allowed into six of the hotel rooms, the 200-year-old listed grand staircase and the main bar downstairs. Throughout the baseline tests Darren determined that no areas showed anomalous readings in regards to the EMF sweeps, and the average temperature of the rooms was 18-19°. A few windows were subject to slight draughts coming from outside and one or two rooms had some very squeaky floorboards, so care was taken not to misinterpret any possible phenomena that really would have had a natural cause. However the bar showed a temperature of 24° simply because not less than 20 minutes earlier it was full of revellers and their body heat would have accounted for this.

Ralph Keeton began his psychic reading at the City Hotel at about 1.00am and this was filmed and recorded for documentation purposes. Our first area for investigation was the front of the bar and this is what Ralph told us:

> In this area I am standing in now there is a young girl. She is about 13-14 years old ... and she has very long hair – very, very long hair indeed. She would have been reported, if anyone had seen her, as what is called a white ghost! While chatting to you guys she literally floated in here and it is this area in which she wanders. Rather then make the area go cold, this girl does the opposite and makes people feel rather hot and sweaty – it's a bit like a hot spot rather than a cold spot. I think one or two may have seen her and she is going to come through tonight. She either lived here or has been associated with this building somehow as she knows it quite well and we may see a flash of white light in this area as this is how she will show herself to us.

The team then relocated to the bar and assembled in the area where the darts board was situated. Ralph continued with his reading, and picked up on the fact that the building was actually two structures rather than one. Paul, the [then] owner confirmed that this was true. Ralph then went on to ask if a chimney or an open fire had been taken out of this area. This too was confirmed by the owner. Ralph continued:

'This is going to sound pretty obvious, but you are going to have movement around this bar area and wisps of smoke and mist have occurred here. You also have a door that needs slammed closed at times'.

Again, the owner confirmed that this was true, as the fire exit door sticks and has to be closed with some force.

'Is there a recurring problem in the ladies' loos?' Ralph asked.

'No', came the reply.

At this point the owner and his friends began to smile and laugh.

'So why are you laughing?' Darren asked them.

'Because we have the problem with the ghost in the gents'!' they said.

'You see', Ralph added, 'I am getting the ladies…with me it's the ladies' loos… I am going to go down there, I need to see what I sense when I go down there'.

The team walked to the bottom of the corridor and immediately Ralph turned to the wall on the left- hand side and said, 'I want to go that way'.

'You can't,' said Paul. 'We don't know what is in there, but we do know it used to be part of this building'.

'Yes, I can feel it,' Ralph said. 'I feel like a want to walk that way. I also feel sick down here too, because I have the feeling that anyone coming down this way may indeed feel sick and that is due to the presence that is down here. He is a prankster and likes to joke around by making people feel ill-at-ease and it is this guy that blocks up the loos. He is a total joker and we are going to have some fun down here later on'.

'It's quite interesting that you used the word 'he',' Nikki said.

'Did I?' said Ralph. 'That is interesting, I must be subconsciously picking up that this is a male, then'.

The team then ventured back into the main bar, and Ralph picked up on a spirit presence that had just presented itself. As it transpired, in this section of the reading the spirit presence turned out to be all too significant to the pub, the owners, bar staff and locals. Due to personal reasons the authors do not wish to elaborate upon, the information psychically gleaned by Ralph Keeton, and the identity of the spirit-person who 'came through' to him, must remain confidential.

Darren commented later, 'What I will say is that this reading was almost perfect in every way, and things were sensed and picked up on that no one could have known except the pub owners and one barman. The look on the barman's face after the reading said it all'.

Ralph then picked up on the period 1840-1842, and told the investigators that a hangman or executioner once stayed or lived on the premises. Then he began to talk about three creaky steps on an upper level and asked if there were any. He felt someone walking on the stairs, and determined that when the spirits actually trod on the three stairs in question, people became aware of their presence.

Ralph then asked to go upstairs to continue his reading. When the team reached the 200-year-old listed stairwell, almost immediately he decided that 'everything was all wrong'.

'I'm all disjointed…' said Ralph, 'I don't feel right here. The layout, the walls… are all in the wrong place and I feel that the grand staircase should go down where the floor is now situated… and again I just want to go this way', he added, pointing to the wall.

Again, Paul the owner confirmed that this was correct. He told the team that there were indeed more stairs that led down to where the investigators were standing. There had also been another area of building during that period, which had subsequently been demolished. This was the area where Ralph then wanted to go.

'Beeston or Beaston' he then said, 'Who is Beeston?'

He then told the researchers that they would get 'some activity down the corridor' which led to rooms 4-6, so they all headed off in that direction. He subsequently mentioned the presence of a large, slightly deaf woman who was very domineering and bossy to say the least. He also stated that the level of the floor was not at its original height and said it should be 'far higher up'. Then he said that there was a weird, ghostly smell connected to that area and at that point Darren felt a cold draught or breeze blow right across his face. Another investigator, Drew Bartley, who was sitting nearby in Room 4, then felt the same, cold draught as it passed him also.

Later, Darren would comment that it was at this juncture that the reading started to become 'rather odd' for him in more ways than one. Ralph explained that the 'domineering woman' had an affinity for Darren and was drawn forwards when she heard his voice. He said there was a 'Scottish connection' with her, and she would attach herself to Darren when he ventured into this area. Darren later said that at that point he felt dizzy and disorientated and found it hard to focus but said nothing to the others at that time.

'I thought it might have just been me feeling odd, yet in the same respect I thought maybe this was the spirit woman making me feel this way, as it had happened before on other investigations. Ralph then said, to my utter astonishment, that people would feel disorientated and dizzy while up in that area!'

Then Ralph said, 'I've got swords…two swords crossed over'.

Darren added, 'I began to think for some strange reason that Ralph was beginning to 'read me' because I actually own two swords; a wooden one, called a bocken, and a steel Samurai sword from Japan. When Ralph mentioned the 'two swords' I told him about the ones I owned'.

'You have two swords?' he said, surprised. 'Do you have problems with your jaw or a tooth, or some problem inside your mouth at the minute?'

'I do indeed', said Darren, and he went on to tell him what he had been experiencing recently.

'Right', said Ralph, 'we are going somewhere with this. The woman we have with us here recognises these similarities between you and herself, and that is why she likes you. So this hand [Ralph held up his left hand at that point] ... I am talking about this finger, which is the middle finger on your left hand ... is sore. A joint or knuckle that has been broken or dislocated and is now painful'.

Darren told him that this very knuckle had been broken during some martial arts training a few years previously. It all seemed surreal to Darren, as what Ralph was saying tied in with lots of different aspects of his life, even though they were essentially trivial ones.

'So why has she latched onto Darren?' someone asked.

After a few seconds of deep thought and concentration Ralph said, 'It's his voice... she's recognising Darren's voice. The more he speaks the more she will come forward as she finds him very interesting'.

'If you do a vigil up here later on and you ask for phenomena you will get them, that I promise', he said.

At that point Darren become rather dizzy again and nearly lost his balance. He felt nauseous also, and this time he told everyone.

'That's what I felt too', Ralph said. 'This lady has made a very strong connection with you; the more you speak the more she comes forwards towards you', he said.

At that point in the proceedings Darren decided to leave the area because he could now barely string a sentence together through being disorientated and dizzy, combined with feeling apprehensive and unnerved. The investigators left the area and, for the time being, brought Ralph's reading to an end.

After a short break the team decided it was time to split into groups and investigate the building further in an effort to see if they could experience – and subsequently document – any paranormal phenomena. Darren's group went back to the corridor, adjacent to rooms 4-6, to see if they could indeed get any signs of paranormal activity. Another group went to rooms 2 and 3, whilst Ralph, Nikki and the rest of their group went along another corridor towards the loos. Since time was getting on the teams designated themselves 30 minutes in each location.

As soon as Darren's team arrived at their location back upstairs he immediately began to feel disorientated and dizzy again. He called out to the 'spirit lady' in the hope she would give those present a sign. Nothing happened for a while, so he tried again. It was then that a fellow investigator 'swept' Darren with his EMF meter and ascertained a reading of 2 MG (milligaus).

Darren's team then relocated to Room 4 and sat down for a while. He again called out to the 'spirit woman' and asked if she would be prepared to give out any other signs of her presence. It was at this point, 2.49am, that both Darren and a fellow investigator, Drew Bartley, clearly heard someone whistling down the corridor.

Darren later commented, 'Now we knew for a fact that no one was down there at that time, so who whistled we could not say...yet! The rest of the vigil was quite interesting, as we all heard a loud bang followed by a series of bangs. It sounded like a rumbling noise which we were really at a loss to explain. Our guest described it as sounding like furniture being dragged across the floor. It seems Ralph's prediction for phenomena occurring in that area due to my being there was proved correct! We then ventured into Room 6 along the corridor and held a small séance, during which one or two light anomalies were caught on night-vision video camera. After the vigil had finished we returned down stairs for a short break.

'After the break we returned to the same location... only this time we decided to bring Ralph with us to see if he could continue his reading of the area...and maybe me. At 3.30am, Ralph began to tell us that the 'spirit lady' was only coming forward that night because I was present. He told us that this was her area, and that this was where she would stay. In other words she would not be coming home with me after the investigation, which in all honesty I was rather pleased to hear. At this point I was leaning against the wall with my right arm while listening to Ralph, when suddenly it was pushed from behind at the elbow making me stumble forward a little'.

Ralph saw this and asked, 'You were just pushed there?'

'It sure felt like it', Darren said.

Within the space of five minutes the same thing happened to Darren again, only this time it felt a little harder. At the same time a light anomaly was filmed behind him at that crucial moment. Darren then felt weirdly exhilarated and later said that a 'feeling of delight came all over' him for he simply could not explain. The researchers then moved back into Room 6, and both the reading and the investigation continued.

Ralph paused briefly and then said, 'Now, I am going to tell you what I got when I was talking to the others downstairs. I am getting the impression that this building was used by pirates, now when I say pirates I don't mean the seafaring, swashbuckling vagabonds that sailed the high seas in search of treasures... no! I mean it was a place for storage of illegal things, and I must stress that it's not recent. We are going back a good few years here...'

At this point Darren decided to 'call out to the atmosphere' in the hope that the elusive 'spirit lady' would give them another sign'. Almost immediately he started to see small 'light anomalies' floating about the room. These anomalies were similar to the kind usually referred to as 'orbs', but in some ways markedly different.

'They weren't white, or bright, but rather the opposite. These little orbs of energy I was seeing were actually black in colour. I thought it may have been my eyes playing tricks in the dark, but Ralph assured me that there were such things as 'black orbs'. Black orbs, he went on to say were actually a negative form of energy'.

Ralph then said that the 'spirit lady' who had an affinity with Darren was standing close by and seemed to be leaning over him as though she was pressing herself upon the investigator. Without warning Darren then experienced what he later described as 'a sensation of absolute pain and agony' emanating from her, and Ralph said that this pain 'went back to about 1827'. Darren actually felt the woman standing next to him and touching his head.

'Fish, fish...she hates fish', Ralph said, as he began to hold his throat. 'Why is she telling me to tell you that?'

At that point in the reading Darren went white and later conceded to having been 'overcome with surprise and shock'. That day, whilst eating his lunch – which consisted of a scabby portion of chips, a pile of mush vaguely masquerading as a portion of peas and a battered fish – a large fishbone had lodged in his throat.

'I honestly thought I was going to choke to death', Darren recalled. 'Although I could still breathe – just – it was lodged there for about 25 minutes until I swallowed some dry bread which I was encouraged to do by a fellow diner. I subsequently left the rest of my lunch and decided I was going to give fish a wide birth from that point on!'

'Well', said Ralph, 'she simply told me to tell you this; she wanted you to know this'.

Ralph then said the strangest thing:

'Why have you cried? Have you been crying?'

Darren later recalled, 'Again you could have knocked me down with a feather. Just that morning before I went to work there was an incident at our home involving our [then] seven-month-old daughter Abbey. The incident resulted in myself and my partner Jayne shedding a few tears. I will not elaborate on what actually happened, but I did indeed cry that morning. I had never cried or shed tears for a good few years, and for Ralph to pick up on that really did astound me'.

'I am seeing through your crying eyes', Ralph added, almost poetically.

Darren elaborated further: 'I explained what had happened, and he went on to say that this woman knew I had been crying when I came into her domain that evening. She wanted me to know that everything would be alright concerning the situation with my daughter at home. Now, after the event, I can say that I'm glad to know that Ralph and the lady in question were indeed right and that my daughter is absolutely fine, as are myself and Jayne.

'In retrospect, pondering over everything that went on in that corridor makes me really think about the whole 'psychic' thing and convinces me even more than ever that there is indeed something in it'.

The vigil at that location eventually came to an end, and they all regrouped in the bar downstairs for a break.

That evening's investigation is one that Darren will not forget in a hurry. His experiences during Ralph Keeton's reading, combined with his ill-at-ease feelings earlier on, really made him think hard about everything and had a very profound effect upon the investigator.

But the night was not yet over. The researchers still had one more location to stake out, and that was the corridor that leads to both the male and female toilets. After the final break of the vigil the researchers headed off to their last location. They made themselves comfortable and again started to 'call out to the atmosphere' in the hope that they might witness some 'good paranormal activity'.

'It was so dark down there you could not see your hand in front of your face', recalled Darren, and as he made a determined attempt at spirit communication all those present became aware of what sounded like 'a man's guttural breath' or, perhaps, someone clearing their throat. It was certainly not one of the investigators, they all knew, as it seemed to come from directly behind where Darren was positioned. Darren was actually standing with his back facing into the male toilets, and was peering around the corner along the corridor.

The investigators seemed to agree unanimously that there was a 'male spirit' present, and after a brief discussion regarding who he may have been the researchers 'called out to him'.

Darren later said that, 'It was interesting to note that when Ralph was 'reading' that area earlier on, he claimed that the spirit down there was indeed a man. It looks like he was right again'.

As time went by during the latter part of the investigation, nothing else seemed to be happening until the team all heard the sound of shuffling of footsteps coming from the opposite end of the corridor. Upon inspection of the area they found nothing untoward, and no one was around to account for the anomalous noises. Overall, it seemed that the vigil was producing some good results.

Earlier the investigators had placed a 'trigger object' – a wooden crucifix – in the corridor but it had failed to move and the EMF and temperature surveys provided no anomalous readings. At the end of that particular vigil the entire investigation quickly came to an end; experiments were finished off, equipment gathered up and the researchers headed off home for some well-deserved rest.

'In summary', Darren said later, 'the investigation as a whole was rather good for me personally as I was subjected to what I believe to be some very strange phenomena. Along with the reading from Ralph, it certainly made this an investigation to remember.

Unfortunately, the other groups' investigations provided me with very little in the way of information as a quiet night was had by them. They reported the occasional knock and bump, sensations of coldness and so on, but nothing that could have been deemed as irrefutable proof paranormal phenomena.

I guess working with a medium most of the night does break the monotony of what may otherwise be a dull and long evening with only few random phenomena encountered. Having said that, working without a medium can be just as rewarding if one is patient, and tenacious'.

- PUB: THE CLOCK HOTEL
- LOCATION: HEBBURN
- GOOD GHOST RATING: 7

The Clock Hotel stands on the corner of Albert Road and Black Road in Hebburn. There are several services which will take you past the Clock from Jarrow bus station, although it isn't really that far to walk if you fancy the exercise.

The Clock Hotel is a pleasant pub. In the summer it is fronted by a number of vivid floral displays and several chalked boards advertising the pub's beers, provisions and forthcoming attractions. There isn't another pub near the Clock Hotel, so it provides a welcome for many locals who wish to whet their whistle. The Clock Hotel was built in 1934, although it certainly presents a more modern visage that could fool you into thinking that its origin was much more recent. The first owner was the brewing company of Steel & Coulson, and the first tenant was, we are led to believe, a certain Mr James Underwood.

The inn has been refurbished on numerous occasions. In 1998 the interior was finished entirely with mid-to-dark oak fittings and tables. The optics and bottles behind the bar were set within a quite grandiose backdrop which is thoroughly Victorian. Drinkers can sample a variety of popular beers, including, of course, the legendary Newcastle Brown Ale. The Clock is also well known for holding parties, the hosts of which are advised to book up well in advance.

As a child Mike lived only a short distance from the Clock Hotel, and even then he remembers hearing tales of a ghost which had, on at least one occasion to his knowledge, discomfited an unwary patron or two. The details were always vague. The apparition was supposedly female, and had a habit of appearing outside the inn underneath the porch which leads into the lounge.

Of course, the appearance of a ghost can be somewhat disconcerting at the best of times. This one, however, apparently upped the ante a bit by screaming like an Irish banshee and scaring the living daylights out of all and sundry. This is not the sort of thing that normally happens when you pop in to your local for a quiet pint, we'll grant you. In any event, that at least was the tale, and one local said, 'She appeared in front of me one night when I was on my way home and let out the most unearthly wail. It chilled me to the marrow, and I never went near the place for ages after that'.

Of course, this was too good a story to ignore, so one overcast Saturday morning in August, 2000, Mike paid the Clock Hotel a visit. The manager was away on vacation at the time, but an assistant told Mike that she would do her best to get some information for him.

Two weeks after Mike first visited the Clock Hotel, Elaine Armstrong rang him. She'd managed to glean some information about the apparition which allegedly haunts this comfortable inn, and the tale was intriguing.

Rumours that the Clock Hotel was haunted can be traced back several decades. During the 1970s one manager claimed to have seen a 'black shadow' following him in the cellar, and it was weeks before he plucked up the courage to venture downstairs again. The black shadow reared its head – or should we say its silhouette – several times during our research in relation to the Clock, so we suspect there may be some truth to it.

But what about the apparition of the screaming woman? We were told that, possibly during the 1970s, a local woman had committed two murders; specifically upon two successive spouses. For this she allegedly served time in Durham jail. As far as the staff were able to tell it was the spectre of this multiple-murderess which supposedly haunted the Clock Hotel. If this is true then we must presume that she too has gone to meet her Maker. The only other snippet of information which became available was that the woman in question was apparently given the nick-name of 'the Merry Widow of Windy Nook'.

To try and put some flesh on the bones of this interesting story, we spoke to both the Northumbria and Durham Constabularies, several local historians and numerous other people. Just who was the Merry Widow, and why had she dispatched her husbands? Before we attempted to answer these questions we were conscious of the need to be careful: If indeed the murders had been committed in the 1970s, it was possible – indeed almost certain – that relatives of both the victims and the perpetrator would still be living in the area. We had no desire to open old wounds or cause any distress to their families, and so decided to tread with caution.

Mike was initially sceptical about the time-frame. Despite living near the Clock Hotel during the 1970s, he could not remember any incidents involving a serial killer. This led him to believe that the murders must have taken place much earlier, and this assumption proved to be correct. The true story is as follows.

In August 1955, Mary Elizabeth Wilson married an elderly chap by the name of John Knowles. He died not long after. In January 1956 she took in a lodger, John Russell, and he died not long after. In September of the same year Mary Elizabeth Wilson married James Leonard. He too apparently found this mortal coil a bit boring, and was dispatched to the afterlife within two short weeks. In October 1957 Lizzie got herself hitched to Ernie Wilson. Within another two weeks he'd gone to join the rest on the other side of the veil.

By this time, of course, locals were becoming a tad suspicious. Tests showed that all of Lizzie's deceased companions had unusually high levels of phosphorous in their system. Lizzie was arrested, and the elderly bachelors of the area could rest easy.

At the trial, the prosecution was in no doubt that Wilson had fed her men rat poison. The defence apparently argued – if you can believe this – that they had all been stuffing themselves full of aphrodisiacs in order to keep up with Lizzie's voracious, and apparently insatiable, sexual appetite. As some aphrodisiacs contain phosphorous, there was no need to blame Lizzie for anything, it was argued. The men had effectively poisoned themselves. The jury didn't buy it, and she spent the rest of her days in clink. She finally passed over to the other side herself in 1962.

Lizzie Wilson was, as previously stated, known as the Merry Widow of Windy Nook. She was also known to frequent the Clock Hotel in Hebburn, where she resided for some time, and hence it is believed that it is her spectre which, from time to time, stands in the porch of the Clock Hotel and screams.

Are the stories true? To our knowledge she hasn't been seen for a good number of years, and the Clock Hotel is still a favourite watering hole for the good folk of Hebburn.

- PUB: THE COOPERAGE
- LOCATION: NEWCASTLE UPON TYNE
- GOOD GHOST RATING: 9

The Cooperage is located on Newcastle upon Tyne's historic quayside and is by far the oldest pub in the city, dating back to the 1300s. This magnificent old building was a cooper's workshop in the nineteenth century, hence the current name of this charming old drinking house.

The beams on the exterior of the building give the pub a classical Tudor look, and, when one steps inside, the 'olde worlde' feel springs to life allowing the past to greet you like a warm breeze. Like many ancient taverns and inns, the Cooperage sells some of the best real ales available, making it a popular attraction for locals, quayside revellers, and students.

Of course, although this beautiful old pub holds its original charm, character, and ambience, some say it retains more than that. The building itself is soaked with local folklore and superstition, and the authors admit that when one steps inside one cannot help but feel the atmosphere change; not for the worse, they hasten to add, but there is a palpable change in the atmosphere nonetheless.

Rumour has it that many, many years ago a visiting sailor whose ship was birthed at Newcastle quayside was accosted by some locals (or according to some, other visiting sailors – no one knows). For whatever reason, the man was actually nailed to the side door of the pub that leads out onto the old stone stairwell that runs up past the Cooperage itself. It is alleged that the original door still occupies the current door aperture, and it is said you can still see the original nail holes. The authors ventured down to the Cooperage for a peek, but, alas, could find no trace of the aforementioned nail holes in the door, which is now not in use and may not be the original fixture anyway.

Needless to say, this unfortunate chap died due to his injuries and it is said his ghost has been seen both inside the pub and outside on the stone stairwell where he was so brutally murdered.

Another, better-known spectre was seen in the 1970s on the upper floor of the inn, in what now serves as the function room. Apparently, the cleaner reported for work one morning and was eager to get on with her duties. The bar had been busy the night before as there has been a function on, so where better to start than at the top in the function room and work her way down? She meandered into the function room, cloth in hand, and began to pick up the empty bottles whilst cleaning the tables and emptying the ashtrays. During her work she became aware that someone was in the room with her, so she looked up across the room and saw a 'white, misty cloud' floating over by one of the tables. Shaking with fear, she stood fixed to the spot watching this misty apparition until it began to move across the floor towards her, all the while becoming larger and more human-shaped. Not surprisingly, she dropped her cleaning gear and ran like never before down the stairs and out the building. She never returned.

This is by far the most famous ghost story attached to the Cooperage, but there are persisting rumours that poltergeist-like activity occurs in the bars on the ground floor. Lights switch themselves on and off, glasses are sometimes thrown around with and witnesses often mention feeling a 'sense of presence'. Perhaps it is the unfortunate sailor who was nailed to the door, who knows?

Regardless of who the ghosts are or why they remain here, we can safely say that the Cooperage pub has to be one of the finest haunted establishments we've visited during our research. The authors must also pay tribute to the friendly landlord whose hospitality we enjoyed whilst supping a pint of his finest.

- **PUB:** THE COUNTY INN
- **LOCATION:** AYCLIFFE VILLAGE
- **GOOD GHOST RATING:** 6

According to a former manager of this establishment, the County Inn 'is most definitely haunted', and he draws this conclusion from the most telling of evidences; his own personal experience. On occasions, after locking up for the night, he would be lying in his bed and suddenly, from out of the darkness, he would hear the sound of voices coming from inside his building. Knowing for a fact he was in the building alone he initially surmised that he had intruders on his premises, which of course most people would. At first he would go downstairs to investigate these disturbances only to find the bar completely empty and with no sign of any forcible entry. After a few months he gave up trying to track down the eerie voices, knowing that, upon investigation, he would inevitably find nothing, or no one around.

At other times he would hear the bar piano being played; yet strangely, nobody was to be seen sitting at it. The cause of these ghostly occurrences and strange incidents? Well, the former manager puts them down to the fact that at one time the inn had been used as the local morgue. When anyone died locally their bodies were left in what is now the inn cellar, as it was once the coldest spot in the village. This practice enabled the corpses to be kept nice and fresh for the undertaker.

From what we can tell the shades of these unfortunates have not been as active as late, but the County Inn is still a wonderful pub filled with a plentiful supply of ales...and spirits.

- PUB: THE CROSS HOUSE
- LOCATION: EASINGTON LANE
- GOOD GHOST RATING: 6

The Cross House is no longer an inn, which is a pity as it had a wonderful reputation for being haunted. The tale of the Cross House ghost first arose in 1981, when a family took over the derelict establishment that was situated on Pemberton Bank. While they were busy renovating the property they discovered that they had a sitting tenant, a ghost, whose presence was confirmed by a number of local folk who once drank on the premises when it had been an inn.

These former drinkers at the late, lamented hostelry stated that the ghost would flick lights off and on – but only when a party was being held. The locals apparently warned the family against taking over the property, but they were down to earth, no-nonsense folk, and not easily scared by such talk.

Once they had settled in, the talk of a ghost only came about when their four-year-old daughter made a telling comment some six months later. The family was watching television one evening when the young girl suddenly said, "Mummy, please don't be frightened...we have a new friend, and we are not alone".

All the while she clenched her hand and held out her arm as if holding onto some unseen person.

'What are you talking about?' asked her mother, 'There's nobody there.'

These words were spoken too soon, as the increasingly doubting mother soon began to revise her opinion regarding the idea of a ghost haunting the property. One night, whilst lying in bed, she was shocked to see the image of a woman move across the ceiling. She came to believe that, in the light of these incidents and other unexplained occurrences, she and others in her family must be psychic. Interestingly, she also added that her grandmother had once made a strange comment, warning the family that one day they would 'move into a building filled with many beds'. They did – the Cross House. When exploring the old cellar the family discovered that it was filled with old, iron bed frames.

As to who the ghosts are – or rather, were – no one really knows. Some claimed that one spectre was that of an old villager who once made tin hot water bottles. Other folk believe it was a poltergeist, or some sort of evil spirit. We may never know for sure.

* PUB: THE CROSS KEYS
* LOCATION: WASHINGTON VILLAGE
* GOOD GHOST RATING: 6

The Cross Keys public house is situated in Washington, Tyne and Wear and stands across the village green from the town's wonderful Old Hall and the Blacksmith's Table restaurant – both delightfully haunted venues themselves. During the course of Darren's ghost investigation career he has spent time researching the aforementioned venues in an effort to track down and document the resident denizens of the other world. Overnight vigils have been held in the Old Hall and the restaurant on a number of occasions.

Prior to these overnight investigations Darren would occasionally spend a little time in the Cross Keys public house, winding down and preparing for the investigations to come, although due to strict adherence to the author's overnight investigation rules and protocols, no alcohol was ingested. Of course, being in an old, eerie pub stirred up the investigator within, and Darren was compelled to ask a barman about any resident ghosts the pub may have had.

'I don't know much about the pub', the barman told Darren, 'but I do know odd things occur here once in a while; things move on their own, doors have been found open when previously closed…and bar staff have, on occasion felt an eerie sensation that they are not alone in the pub'.

* PUB: THE DUN COW
* LOCATION: WITTON LE WEAR
* GOOD GHOST RATING: 5

The Dun Cow was constructed around 1799, and thus has had time to build up a decent collection of ghosts over the centuries. Sightings by managers and recent staff seem to be thin on the ground, although we were assured by some locals and former staff members that a spectre does indeed haunt this charming little inn.

The spectre, we were told, is said to be that of a former landlord who makes his presence felt by moving the bar accoutrements about, and generally making a nuisance of himself in a poltergeist–like fashion. The authors prefer to use the term 'poltergeist–like', as the ghost at the Dun Cow is certainly not a true polt. Rather, it is a playful and interactive spirit. Believe us when we say there is a difference!

We also managed to ascertain that in times past a number of customers were most reluctant to occupy or pass through a certain passageway inside this old boozer, for it is there that the ghostly landlord apparently likes to pace back and forth. Unfortunately, and quite typically, he failed to make an appearance during our visit.

- **PUB:** THE EDEN ARMS
- **LOCATION:** RUSHYFORD
- **GOOD GHOST RATING:** 8

The Eden Arms, formerly a coaching inn, has throughout its illustrious history played host to many a famous personage, the Lord Byron and his wife being just two examples. Annabella Millbanke of Seaham Hall stayed at the inn on January 2, 1815, while another famous guest was Lord Eldon, who was the [then] Tory High Chancellor.

During the course of his many stays at the Eden Arms – then called the Wheatsheaf – Lord Eldon would partake of his favourite tipple which was stored in his own, private cellar. (Being High Chancellor brought enormous privileges then; some in Parliament, but most in your local boozer). The Chancellor's cellar was stocked with "Carbonell's Fine Old Military Port". Sadly to the authors' knowledge this beverage is no longer in production. However, should the current landlord find any old bottles downstairs we would be quite happy to test them – all of them – for authenticity. As evening drew on and the sky dulled, Lord Eldon would sup a few pints with the landlord – a Mr Holt – before cracking open a bottle of Carbonell's or three.

In such a convivial atmosphere it should come as no surprise to find that this pleasant roadside stop has its own ghost. Allegedly, it is that of Lady Eden after whom the inn now seemingly takes its name.

Lady Eden was a kindly soul and much given to charitable deeds. She had great compassion for the poor of the parish and was devoted to her property until her death in 1587. However, to her chagrin she never lived on the premises, but many years after her death it seems her ghost took up residence in the inn.

The figure of Lady Eden, wearing a long cloak, has reportedly been seen on a number of occasions in the corridor outside rooms 1 to 6. It has also been reported that sharp, clear knocks and bumps in rooms 18 and 19 have paved the way for her entry. One startled guest, in one of these rooms, after sensing that some unseen person was staring at him, quickly insisted on a change of residence.

Her Ladyship has also been seen in the cellars, so one must respect her wish to haunt after death an area she so cherished in life.

An odd postscript to this ghost story ties up this section well... rather oddly! Close to the Eden Arms lies the road to Coundon and a number of drivers have seen the spectre of a pig suddenly run across the road and vanish. Brilliant! It's amazing what one learns when out and about during this sort of research.

- **PUB:** THE FERRY TAVERN
- **LOCATION:** SOUTH SHIELDS
- **GOOD GHOST RATING:** 8

Adjacent to the ferry landing in River Drive, South Shields, and merely a few yards from the Alum Ale House, there used to stand an old, boarded-up inn which was known as the Ferry Tavern. It is sad indeed that this well-known pub is now demolished. The area has been redeveloped, and the hammer of progress has now razed to the ground one of South Tyneside's most interesting watering holes.

The Ferry Tavern had an extremely chequered history. In its halcyon days it was a lively pub, frequented by merchant seamen and visitors from both sides of the Tyne, as it stood directly next to the new ferry landing. There were times when the Ferry Tavern was known for good music. There were even times when it was known for good food. And yet, for some reason, the ups were always interspersed with lengthy downs. Periodically the owners would refit the premises and its fortunes would revive for a while. Inevitably, however, such times were followed by periods of decay when the paint would fade and the carpets would start to look a little threadbare.

The Ferry Tavern seems always to have been well managed, and we have seen nothing which indicates that any of its landlords ever neglected the place. Rather, it seems that the inn merely reflected the economic and social circumstances of the day. When times were hard, they were hard at the Ferry Tavern, too.

Contrary to popular opinion, landlords do not have the degree of influence over their clientele that those outside the pub trade may assume. True, a landlord can, theoretically, admit or banish whomsoever he or she wishes. However, at the end of the day the books have to balance in the black, and the only way to achieve this is to open the doors to all who wish to enter, save for a small number whose behaviour simply cannot be tolerated.

At some point in its history, the Ferry Tavern started to attract the wrong type of clientele. Even though only for a short while, it gained a reputation for being an ideal place to carry out business meetings. Men would go there and meet with women, who, in exchange for a small fee, would then do the business, if you catch our drift. Such assignations were never carried out on the premises, you understand; well, at least not the physical aspect of them anyway. Rather, ladies of the night would meet with the punters for a discreet drink before engaging in more earthy pleasures elsewhere. This sort of situation is virtually beyond the control of the landlord, for it is not as if anything untoward is taking place on the premises. Ironically, the Ferry Tavern had recovered its good reputation long before the decision was made to close it in line with the redevelopment of the town centre. Some of the more questionable visitors now having moved on to other premises, or, alternatively – having found that the passage of the years had reduced their powers of seduction somewhat – hung up their stilettos for good. Its latter years were lively ones, echoing happier times.

When we began to research this book, several people told us that the Ferry Tavern had been haunted. One story concerned a 'shadowy but solid' figure of a young teenage girl, dressed in a shawl, who could be seen just after dark standing on the corner near the entrance. She was thin, and sported long, blond hair which looked either greasy or wet. Her facial expression indicated that she was 'totally fed up and depressed', according to one informant. Her clothing had a distinctly Victorian set, and it is possible that she may have been one of the beggars or prostitutes who frequented the riverside at that time. As she appears outside of the Ferry Tavern as opposed to indoors, it is entirely possible that she has no connection with the pub whatsoever.

Another story concerning the Ferry Tavern is that several bar staff saw the apparition of an old man sitting in the corner of the bar, apparently smiling to himself as if he had just heard something funny. Whether this tale is true or not we are unable to say, but the same informant told us that the Ferry Tavern was also subjected to a mild amount of poltergeistry. Electric equipment would switch itself on and off, and the pumps would frequently be disengaged too. This latter feature crops up with unerring regularity in haunted pubs, as you will discover throughout this volume.

Time has overtaken the Ferry Tavern, but not its memory.

- PUB: THE FISHING BOAT INN
- LOCATION: BOULMER
- GOOD GHOST RATING: 8

The Fishing Boat Inn is situated in the fishing village of Boulmer, Northumberland, and is approximately three to four miles north of Alnmouth. This fine pub is the only one in Boulmer village, with the nearest inn being in the small hamlet of Lesbury four miles away. One can imagine the uproar from the locals when the authorities decided it was time to call 'last orders' on the pub itself. The feud was eventually resolved, the pub re-opened and is still a fine drinking establishment to this day with some of the best views of the North Sea and the north-east coastline.

During the compilation of this book the authors were contacted by an individual after he read a feature in the *Northumberland Gazette* about their ghost hunting work. This is what he had to say:

Hi Darren and Mike.

I read the Northumberland Gazette today – about your ghost hunting work – and would like to share with you a few stories of my upbringing in the Fishing Boat Inn, in the small coastal village of Boulmer in Northumberland.

I was born and raised in the village from birth to the age of 13. My father lived at the Fishing Boat Inn with my mother and grandparents. My grandparents ran the pub – which had been run by my father's family for decades – and my parents were living there while looking for a place of their own.

A story my dad used to tell me was that on one occasion, while lying in his bed, he woke up felling terribly cold. Then, all of a sudden and out of the blue, he felt what he described as a cold hand take hold of him around the neck, but not in a malicious way. Within seconds the feeling went. He then woke my mum to tell her that the gentleman that lived down the road, had passed away through the night and that they would get the house. Sure enough the next day, this story was confirmed and they moved to the house soon after.

We lived there until I was one year-old and then moved back to the pub when my grandfather moved to a house along the row where the pub is situated. The pub has over three floors with the bottom floor above a cellar in which a tunnel used to run to the north of the village where smugglers used to bring their illicit goods and contraband. The bottom floor was the floor space for the bar and lounge area as well as our living room at the back and kitchen. On the next level my dad had a sitting room where he used to entertain his 'posh guests', as well as my two sisters' bedroom, my parents' bedroom and the bathroom.

There were two attics, with one converted to a bedroom for myself and my older brother. I hated the attic as I always found it spooky, so I slept in the bedroom with my sisters. One night, when I was about 5, I could not get to sleep (it was probably about 10pm and the pub was still open downstairs) so I came to the foot of the stairs to the attic where my brother was sleeping. I called for him two or three times and got no answer so I picked up a small piece of track from a racing car game and threw it to the top of the landing between the two attic doors. To my amazement it stopped in mid-flight and flew back down the stairs at me. I ran into my sister's bedroom and stayed there, terrified.

On another occasion I was running a bath and went to pay a visit to the 'little boys' room, when the plug shot out of the bath and hit the wall beside me. I was 7-8 feet away from the bath. Another time I turned the taps off on the bath only to look at the sink at the same time to see the taps on the sink turn on. I ran out of the bathroom terrified and caught my little toe on the doorframe of the bathroom and broke it!

The last occasion, in regards to strange goings on, was the night before we left the pub. In the spring of 1986 my father went bankrupt and we were going to move to the nearby village of Longhoughton. Myself and my brother shared a mattress on the floor of the posh sitting room which was situated directly above the bar area. The floor of the bar was covered by slate-like tiles of blue and red. I awoke in the early hours of the morning with everyone in bed asleep. I could hear a sound coming from the bar below. Frozen to the spot I listened and could hear a sound like a walking stick striking the tiled floor and the sound of a foot dragging behind, then another strike of the walking stick and again a foot dragging behind. This sound must have lasted for maybe 30 seconds or so which may have been the time it would take for someone to cover the distance from one end of the bar to the other. I woke my brother, but by this time the noise had ceased. I was led to believe by my father that a phantom 'grey lady' was resident in the pub and that she would not harm anyone.

This was no consolation when I was younger. I can't ever remember any of my three siblings having encounters like the ones I had and I always wondered if I had a screw loose or maybe imagined it all.

I also remember my uncle came to live with us when he left his wife and he told me that on one occasion he was sitting on his bed deep in thought when he felt a cold hand upon his shoulder. So maybe, it wasn't just me after all!

Kind Regards

Rory Lane.

So, it seems that this nice old pub does indeed seem to be haunted by maybe more than one ghost. Having more than one person witness odd phenomena at the same place does indeed support the theory that strange occurrences are happening. Our thanks go to Rory Lane for contacting us and allowing us to publish his accounts.

- PUB: THE GLOBE
- LOCATION: SUNDERLAND
- GOOD GHOST RATING: 8

The Globe in High Street East, Sunderland, was a well-liked pub by locals. Guaranteed to be heaving on a Saturday night, the bar played host to young lads and lasses whilst the lounge was usually in the possession of married couples playing dominoes. Everyone in Sunderland either frequented the Globe or at least knew of it.

Alas, all good things come to an end. In February 1956, a fire broke out and before long the dried-out timbers were roaring.

Initially we were unable to find any ghost stories attached to the Globe, which is highly unusual for a pub of that age, character and reputation. Then the authors were informed by an old patron – now a grand old 91 years of age – that there had indeed been one or two spooky goings-on there.

'I can't remember too much about the tales, but I do recall that the place was haunted. The ghost was supposed to be a woman who died in the toilets…that's all I know.'

As the flames took hold and threatened other buildings nearby, the fire engines arrived and the fire fighters made valiant efforts to save the 100-year-old bar from extinction. Here the story takes on another curious aspect, for to contain the blaze they found it necessary to break down a partition wall in the music room. To their bafflement they discovered a hidden staircase. Where did it lead? For how long had it been sealed up? Alas, we'll never know. The Globe is no more, and its secrets have died with it.

- PUB: THE GREEN TREE
- LOCATION: TUDHOE VILLAGE
- GOOD GHOST RATING: 5

Tudhoe is a delightful village that lies to the south of Durham City. The Green Tree is the last remaining pub in the village, and looks out over the idyllic village green. It is said to be haunted, but the truly paranormal occurrences are those which are said to have taken place immediately around it and not within the premises itself.

The most famous of the Tudhoe apparitions is said to be that of a black horse. In some versions of the tale the horse is said to be headless. In others it is aid to be ridden by a horseman who is also without a head. In either event, something decidedly odd seems to traipse around the village after the hours of darkness.

According to legend, the horse used to emerge from the old village pond in Tudhoe. The pond is gone now, having been filled in and turfed over, but even after the pond was naught but a distant memory the horse would still emerge from the same spot.

The black horse only appeared, so it is said, when a death was about to occur or disaster was about to strike the village. It would emerge at dusk and clip-clop around the village until dawn when, so they say, it would disappear back into the pond – or later, the ground – from whence it first emerged.

The famous naturalist Charles Waterton, who was schooled in Tudhoe as a youth, claimed to have seen the fabled black horse on more than one occasion.

The inn itself is said to be haunted by the shade of 'The Blue Lady'. Little is known of her, although some say she was a wicked mother who, in a fit of the most diabolical pique, poisoned her entire family.

The pub is also said to be haunted by the ghost of a young boy. On one occasion he crept into the bedroom of one of the resident staff members who woke up with a start just before he disappeared. The blankets, she noticed, contained two small indentations where his little hands had rested as he peered down at the unsuspecting barmaid.

- Pub: THE GREY HORSE
- Location: WHITBURN
- Good Ghost Rating: 5

The Grey Horse stands in Mill Lane, Whitburn. It is a pleasant inn and quite spacious. After Mike received a tip-off from a WraithScape reader that the place was haunted, he popped along to see if he could uncover the truth.

It was a Saturday lunch time when he called, and was surprised to find the pub quite quiet. The manager was away on holiday, but one of the barmaids sat and listened patiently whilst he explained the purpose of his visit.

'I haven't actually heard any ghost stories, to be honest, but then again the manager may not have told us about them so we don't get frightened!' she grinned. She did suggest that some of the long-time patrons of the pub may know more, and Mike happened to glance at a couple sitting at a nearby table. He could tell by looking at them that they were not first-time visitors. The two looked to be what a publican friend of ours calls 'fixtures and fittings', so Mike decided to play bold and introduce himself.

The gentleman was sucking contemplatively on a pipe – this was before the dastardly no-smoking ban was introduced, you understand – and at first said nothing. His wife simply shook her head.

'I'm sorry, I don't recall any ghost tales at all from here … none that I can think of…although they do say that the Jolly Sailor down the street is haunted'.

Mike told the lady that the Jolly Sailor would be his next port of call, but confessed his disappointment at finding that the Grey Horse was essentially ghostless.

'Mind you, there was that incident with the cleaner …' said the man as he re-lit the bowl of his pipe.

'But that was nothing…I'm sure it wasn't', his wife replied.

Sensing an upturn in his luck, Mike said, 'Tell me about it'.

And so they did. The story was short on detail, but fascinating nonetheless. It seems that, about thirty years ago, a cleaning lady worked at the Grey Horse who was much loved and respected by all who knew her. She was devoted to her job, and apparently kept the place shining like a new pin. Then, suddenly, she died. Some time later occasional knocking and creaking sounds would be heard, to which the other staff would respond, 'Oh, there she goes again! Mrs T is doing her rounds'.

So was the Grey Horse haunted? The lady Mike spoke to says not.

'All old pubs make creaking sounds and things like that', she rightly said. 'I just used to put it down to the building settling…never really thought it was a ghost'.

Mike finished his drink and said farewell. The visit had been worthwhile after all, because there was still a glimmer of a chance that this pleasant little pub may be haunted. It would be a shame if it wasn't, really.

- PUB: THE HALF MOON
- LOCATION: GATESHEAD
- GOOD GHOST RATING: 7

One of the most renowned inns in Gateshead was the Half Moon. The property stood on the corner of Half Moon Lane and Bottle Bank, and dated back to the eighteenth century. Originally built in 1782, the pub was partially demolished in 1891 when a runaway tram ploughed into the frontage. Generously compensated, the owner ensured that the pub was quickly rebuilt.

Like all pubs with an air of history it boasted a resident ghost. It is said that a Blue Lady was occasionally seen in the bar and other locations. She seemingly took her name from the fact that she was adorned in a long, blue dress, which in her day must have been the very height of fashion.

The exact identity of the Blue Lady is something of a mystery, but locals say she was called Lucinda. As to whom she really was and why she haunted this particular property we still aren't sure, but she certainly had a good sense of humour. Apparently, when the mood took her she liked to spend her time switching off beer supplies in the inn's two cellars.

Alas, the old Half Moon Inn was demolished in the latter half of 2001 and is now nought more than a pleasant memory.

Legend has it that there used to be a monastery situated on the site where the Half Moon later stood. Mind you, what a woman in an outrageous blue dress would be doing in a religious building full of men is anybody's guess, but the authors can think of at least one possibility; and no, we aren't saying what it is.

IN-DEPTH CASE STUDY: THE HOP POLE, SOUTH SHIELDS
Good Ghost Rating: 10

Some years ago Mike told the readers of his WraithScape column about a ghostly apparition – that of an elderly lady – which had been spotted in South Shields market place. The following tale concerns yet another elderly woman who allegedly haunted the Holborn area of High Shields. She was known – intriguingly – as 'the Red Lady of the Hop Pool', but more about that presently.

Strangely, fifteen years ago Mike had a Christmas ghost story published which bears some curious parallels to the Red Lady tale. In his fictional account, a late-night reveller bumps into the ghost of a long-dead sailor in River Drive, South Shields. The sailor is waiting to board a ghostly vessel called the Aggie, a contraband ship headed for some distant port or other. Now, it seems, the tie-in between ghosts, smugglers and pirates may have some basis in reality.

According to Ivor, the Hop Pool was a public house of some notoriety, and its reputation and atmosphere were only enhanced by the presence of the spectral Red Lady. The problem is that South Shields has never, during its history, played host to an inn called the Hop Pool. However, some research by another devout WraithScape reader may have shed some light on the mystery.

Apparently, there was an alehouse called not the Hop Pool but the Hop 'Pole', which stood in East Holborn near the Middle Docks. It was first mentioned in a directory published in 1834, which listed over 150 alehouses, inns and bars in the South Shields area. When the Hop Pole was demolished we have no idea, but we've been told that an inn already stood on the site in the early eighteenth century.

The Hop Pole stood at 12, East Holborn, a well-known area frequented by shipwrights and sailors alike. To say that the area was 'quaint' would be to give it a historical gloss which would really be more of a whitewash. Holborn was, generally speaking, a rough area, although it did have one or two nice parts. During the 1830s the inn was managed by one John Collier, of whom we know relatively little. What we can say with a fair degree of certainty is that the manager of an inn in that particular locale would not be of the gentry.

So now we know something about the public house, but who was the mysterious Red Lady?

Britain has always had a problem with smugglers and still has today. Despite the fact that the old sailing ships have been replaced by container lorries and the stripy shirts and eye-patches have given way to Armani suits and designer sun glasses, every day tons of illicit goods are smuggled into the country to avoid the paying of customs duty.

Of course, ports and docks were then, as now, favourite places through which the contraband could be routed. Once unloaded, the goods had to be 'stashed' in a secure hiding place until they could be 'fenced' to traders who could be counted on not to ask too many searching questions about where the dodgy produce had came from.

Rumour has it that the Hop Pole was a 'warehouse' in which smugglers stored their goods before distribution. Another WraithScape accomplice, Ian, tells us that were stories about hidden rooms, underground tunnels and false wall cavities being used for this very purpose. In an era when the concept of sniffer dogs and hi-tech surveillance equipment hadn't even been considered, a little ingenuity may well have been all that was needed to fool the excise men into thinking that the Hop Pole contained nothing more sinful than barrels of grog and a few crates of cheap beer.

But of course, it didn't harm to have a little extra help, and our correspondent told us that the Red Lady was a formidable apparition who had a reputation for scaring the breeches off all but the most stout-hearted. Quite convenient, really, when you think about it, and this may provide a more mundane explanation for the presence of this female phantom.

Apparently, some kill-joys began to suggest that the Red Lady of the Hop Pole didn't actually exist at all, but was merely an invention of the smugglers to frighten off curiosity-seekers, nosey-parkers and those scaredy-cat customs officials who didn't feel like tangling with spirits from the Other Side.

But let us assume for a moment that the stories about the awesome Red Lady are true. What has history told us about her?

It was around the 1830s that the first tales of the spectral Red Lady, or Lady in Red, started to circulate. According to stories handed down, she would appear at a window in one of the upper storey of the inn, always wearing a red dress of particularly good quality. By all accounts she was seductively beautiful, and was said to lure the unwary close to the inn by ample use of her female charms. And then, according to legend, the trouble would start. Her beautiful face would suddenly transform itself into a mask of pure hatred. Her eyes would become twin orbs of cold menace, and she would bare her teeth in a manner not unlike that of a wolf. Then – horror of horrors – she would 'point' the poor chap concerned and curse him. Those who were so treated by the Red Lady were doomed to lead the most miserable existence imaginable until the end of their days.

'Pointing' someone – the simple gesture of extending the forefinger of your hand towards an enemy, but with evil intent – was an old form of cursing which was widely used in certain areas. Certainly it would have been understood by foreign sailors from Eastern Europe. So seriously was the story of the Lady in Red taken, that ships passing by would steer to the north bank of the river so that as much distance as possible was put between the Hop Pole and the vessel concerned.

A wonderful tale, except for the rumours that the Red Lady was simply an artifice designed to frighten away the excise men. But can we be absolutely certain that the ghostly legends regarding the Hop Pole were entirely fictitious? Not quite. There is a further tale connected with the Hop Pole, although we've also heard the same story attached to another pub which stood nearby, so we cannot be sure with any degree of certainty that what we are about to relate really did take place at the Hop Pole itself. Nevertheless, for what it's worth we'll relate the story as it came to us.

At some time before the Hop Pole closed, drinkers and bar staff alike were apparently plagued by an increasing number of 'paranormal incidents'. These involved objects moving around, glasses levitating and unearthly footsteps walking across the floor when no one was there. At first the staff treated it as a joke, but as both the intensity and frequency of the incidents escalated, they became afraid. Several barmaids refused to work in the place alone, and one or two resigned completely.

No longer able to see the funny side, the manager decided to call on the services of a local Catholic priest. The cleric – whose name is now lost to us – was unequivocal in stating that the ghostly goings-on and poltergeist-like activity were undoubtedly the work of the Devil, and that the power of the Almighty was required to 'drive him out'. The priest, it seemed, almost relished the opportunity to do battle with the Adversary. One Sunday afternoon, the Father and a goodly number of his parishioners made their way to the Hop Pole in an ostentatious procession. With open hymnbooks they sung at the top of their voices as they wound their way to the entrance of this rather notorious inn.

On entering the Hop Pole, the manager escorted the priest and his flock up the stairs to a room which, it was claimed, was the epicentre of the paranormality. As the singing exorcists approached the door leading into the room they could hear all manner of bangs, bumps and shrieks coming from within. True to his convictions, the old priest firmly took hold of the handle and attempted to open the door. Despite his best efforts, however, it refused to budge. His reaction was to urge those gathered to sing louder in an effort to 'drown out the Devil'. After much persistence the door eventually opened, and the priest informed those with him that he intended to go in alone, at least initially, to carry out a part of the cleansing ritual.

Exactly what happened next is a little confused, but it seems that before the priest had the opportunity to close the door behind him naturally it slammed shut of its own accord. Almost immediately the parishioners and the staff of the Hop Pole heard the old cleric shouting for help. To his credit, the owner attempted to shoulder-charge the door and help the priest, but the wood was too solid. As the priest's screams grew worse the landlord became more alarmed, and eventually brought a huge hammer to the door. It splintered instantly, and he dashed in to find the priest slumped in the corner, gibbering.

According to the story as it was related to us, the priest recovered his sensibilities after two weeks, and his faith in God remained undiminished. However, he did relate that he had witnessed something in that upper room which was so terrifying it could barely be described. Till the day he died he refused to divulge the nature of the apparition which frightened him so.

- **Pub:**   **Jimmy Allen's**
- **Location:**   **Durham City**
- **Good Ghost Rating:** 9

Jimmy Allen's is tucked away under Elvet Bridge in Durham City centre and is a modern pub that could, more or less, be classed as a wine bar. Jimmy Allen's has a number of floors, the top one actually coming out onto Elvet Bridge itself.

Having visited the pub on a number of occasions, the authors came to the conclusion that although there is indeed a certain 'atmosphere' within its walls it is not your stereotypical haunted inn. That's not to say we don't think it is haunted – on the contrary, we do.

On the lower level of the premises the phantom of the legendary 'Jimmy Allen' is said to reside. Jimmy was the official Northumbrian piper to the Duchess of Northumberland and, for the last seven years of his life, for crimes such as hustling and theft, he spent it locked up in a cell there. The premises that is now Jimmy Allen's you see, once housed the old Durham Prison.

Initially Jimmy was sentenced to death for his crimes but his sentence was later reduced to life imprisonment by the Prince Regent. However, fate would deal him a vicious blow for his sentence was only commuted the day after he was executed in 1810.

It is said that if you listen carefully you can hear the ghost of Jimmy Allen playing on his Northumbrian pipes, the melodic sounds reverberating around the old, lower levels of this one-time gaol-house.

In-depth Case Study: The Jolly Sailor, Whitburn
Good Ghost Rating: 9

The Jolly Sailor public house is located on East Street, adjacent to the main road between South Shields and the city of Sunderland. A former coaching inn, the premises were already in existence in the mid-eighteenth century.

When you walk into 'The Jolly' as locals call it – via the side entrance – one immediately becomes insulated from the traffic and other unwelcome signs of life in the twenty-first century. Visitors are plunged into a quaint, old world of yesterday where the past greets you like a warm breeze.

On entering the bar Mike ordered half a pint of bitter and introduced himself. The landlady, Julie Knox, had just taken over the inn a few weeks previously along with her husband Simon, and had only heard fleeting rumours about the ghost. But what she had heard was enough to convince her that 'there may be something in it'.

'There was a chap in here the other evening, and he seemed to know something about the ghost stories attached to the pub. The previous manager also knows quite a bit about it too. In fact, I think she researched the history of the Jolly Sailor and managed to get a considerable amount of information'.

He asked Julie if she would pass on his telephone number and ask them to ring him. She said she would.

Just before Mike left, he asked Julie if she'd had any problem with the beer pumps or any trouble with 'the electrics'. Just once, she replied, when the pumps mysteriously went off. As she told him this she was pulling a pint of beer for another customer. Or at least she was trying to, for the beer refused to leave the tap.

'Maybe it's the ghost', Mike said, only half joking.

Then the telephone rang. No one there. Then it rang again, and again. Each time Julie picked it up it went dead.

'You've done it now!' joked one of the regulars. 'That's with talkin' aboot that ghost!'

Mike spoke to several of the drinkers in the bar, but they hadn't heard anything specific about the spectre which allegedly haunted their favourite watering hole.

'I remember many years ago', one old chap told him, '…there were some people – from Durham, I think, but I could be wrong – who came down here to try and catch the ghost. Experts of some kind, they were…and they brought all sorts of gizmos and bits of equipment; stayed overnight, upstairs, they did. Never saw anything as far as I recall…'

Mike concluded that the experts would probably have been from the Society for Psychical Research or some similar body, although the trail would probably be quite cold by now.

On the wall by the bar was a poster. It was advertising a Psychic Fair that was to be held on Monday, 5th September. The fair would include Tarot card reading and rune-casting, and would be held in the Jolly Sailor itself. He wondered what effect this might have, if any, on the resident ghosts! Julie later told him it had been a complete success.

Mike left the Jolly Sailor in the hope that it wouldn't be too long before he received a telephone call from someone about the mysterious spectres who, allegedly, haunted it.

It took about three weeks for Julie and Simon to find out some details about the ghosts of the Jolly Sailor, although Mike sincerely appreciated their detective work. Busy publicans have far more pressing things to do than act as unpaid researchers for paranormal investigators! When Mike did speak to them, the story they told him was a fascinating one.

On the negative side, very little in the way of solid information was forthcoming about exactly whom the ghosts may have been. He was, however, given further leads which allowed him to put some metaphorical meat on the bones. What Julie and Simon did unearth – and Mike will be eternally grateful to them for it – were two cracking yarns which would do justice to any book of ghost stories.

The first tale concerned a previous landlady who looked after the Jolly Sailor in the mid-90s. One evening she was busy keeping the patrons happy by serving drinks in one of the bars downstairs, when someone asked for a drink of Southern Comfort. This immediately sent Mike on a nostalgia trip, for Southern Comfort was the favourite tipple of his first stepfather, Tommy, who had died several years previously. He introduced Mike to its seductive charms one Christmas Eve, and he was just fortunate enough to have recovered sufficiently by the following day to still interface with the turkey and trimmings enthusiastically. Mind you, it was a close thing – he had considerable difficulty keeping his paper hat on, and the peas seemed to move around the plate of their own accord. The borderline between merriment and inebriation is dangerously thin, as we all know.

Anyway, back to the Jolly Sailor. Having been asked for a shot of Southern Comfort by a customer, the landlady discovered that the bottle was empty. Not to worry, she told her patron, for another bottle could easily be brought down from the bar upstairs. She then promptly went to retrieve said bottle as quickly as possible.

Now when the landlady got to the top of the stairs she had an option. She could, had she so desired, switched on the lights in the bar and illuminated the entire room. However, the intense glow from the street lights outside made this unnecessary. She could see her way around the bar quite clearly, and hence decided to leave the lights off. Blissfully ignorant of what was about to happen next, she put one foot before the other and headed for the bottle shelf.

Most of us – if we could but admit it – talk to ourselves from time to time. When dialling a telephone number we've just been given and are unable to write it down, who doesn't repeat the number continuously until we've dialled it? The landlady apparently did something similar as she walked across the bar, whispering to herself, 'Southern Comfort…Southern Comfort…'

Someone – or perhaps something – evidently heard her, for suddenly, and without warning, a bottle of Southern Comfort leaped from the shelf and deposited itself in the arms of the bemused publican. Her reaction to this incident is not recorded, but one supposes that she would certainly have raised an eyebrow to say the very least.

This incident is intriguing, for it opens up the very real possibility that what we have here is not a conventional, common-or-garden apparition, but a poltergeist.

The word 'poltergeist' is German, and basically means 'rowdy spirit'. Of course, this is a subjective definition, for a poltergeist may not be a spirit at all. In fact, the authors believe that there is overwhelming evidence to suggest that almost all poltergeists have no consciousness or sentience; they are not 'aware' and do not 'think'. So, what is a poltergeist, then? There is a theory that certain environments – particularly ones to which the public have access – are 'psychically charged', and that some people have the ability to 'activate' such a building when they enter it. Through a process of telekinesis (the ability to move things at a distance through the power of the mind, and without touching them), some people can actually create poltergeist activity without realising it. Subconsciously, the busy landlady may have 'commanded' the bottle of Southern Comfort to come to her, but because she was unaware of her own abilities she may very well have assumed that an invisible entity was present and playing tricks on her. When psychic individuals enter a building which is conducive to hauntings, they may trigger off all sorts of paranormal, activity without being conscious of it. It's a bit like lighting the blue touch-paper on a firework without realising it. You may not realise you're responsible and you'll still get a terrible fright when it bursts into life.

But not all poltergeist activity can be explained so easily. Stress can also cause people to subconsciously create poltergeist activity, although this must remain another subject for another book, for it is complex indeed.

But could some poltergeists be caused by 'spirits' – discarnate entities who will, for purposes we can only muse upon, move objects around and apparently tease the life out of the living? The authors have to concede that they cannot rule it out, and the following story from the Jolly Sailor illustrates this all too well.

There is a theory, held by many sincere Christians, that ghosts, poltergeists and other manifestations of paranormality are actually the work of wicked spirits who are masquerading as the dead to deceive people. In other words, when a spiritualist medium tells you that your late aunt Maud is 'coming through' with a message from the other side, it is really not Maud at all, but Old Nick or one of his demonic minions. In one sense, such a theory is hard to disprove. All humans are imperfect, and we can all be hoodwinked. If the Devil and his foot-soldiers are of an infinitely superior intellect to ourselves, then fooling us will be easy. On the other hand, just because something is possible it doesn't mean that its necessarily so. We must concede that, at least hypothetically, apparitions which appear and act like deceased persons may be just that – the discarnate spirits of the dead who are still meandering round this mortal pasturage.

In the final analysis, we must concede that each individual must be left to make up his or her mind on the matter. However, what we can say with conviction is that, whatever poltergeists may be in reality, they certainly act and behave like deceased persons from time to time.

There is a tradition in haunted public houses that the ghosts which inhabit them are often those of previous owners, tenants, managers, bar staff and, of course, customers. Bar staff in particular seem to have, at least ostensibly, a reluctance to leave their place of employment merely because they are dead. Those of you who have read this book systematically from the first page will undoubtedly be aware of this.

According to fellow researcher Alan Tedder, a young couple ran the inn from 1984 to 1986, but, seemingly owing to 'the jinxes' attached to the pub, they eventually left. During their tenancy a fire had occurred in the upstairs flat which caused over £2,000 pounds worth of damage. Tragically, the blaze killed their pet dog and cat.

For several months 'the jinx' seemed to bring nothing but bad luck, for beer taps were turned on by unseen hands, a bathroom cabinet fell off the wall and a heavy lampshade gave Bill a nasty head
wound when it crashed down upon him without reason. Bill also told Alan that he blamed 'the ghost' for the damage caused when a room was flooded out by a burst pipe.

In September 1998 there was a cleaner employed at the Jolly Sailor. By all accounts she was pleasant and conscientious, and went about her duties vigorously. The authors know the name of this lady, but will refrain from printing it so as not to cause her further distress. Early one morning – she started at 7am – she happened to be in the Jolly Sailor on her own, the landlord having left earlier to attend to some business.

At some point the cleaner turned her attention to the upstairs bar. This was the same bar in which, the year previously, the now infamous bottle of Southern Comfort had caused such a stir. On entering the bar she saw that there were still a number of glasses scattered around from the previous evening's revelries. Simon told Mike that there was around eight pint and half-pint beer glasses and approximately four wine glasses.

The domestic decided to make the cleaning of the glasses her first task. She quickly gathered them up and stacked them on the bar, and then began to wash them one by one. As each glass was cleaned and left sparkling to

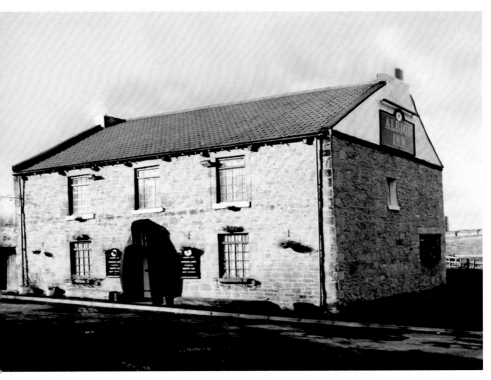

1 *The Albion Inn, Pelaw:* Home of a spectre known as "Charlie". (Courtesy of Walter Ritson).

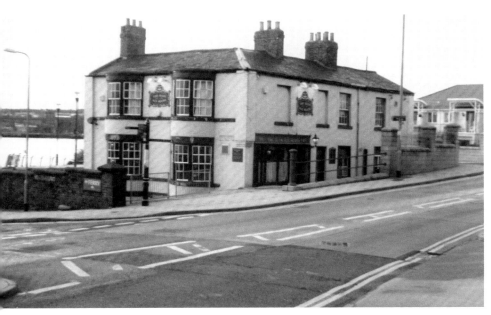

2 *The Alum Ale House, South Shields:* A quaint pub said to play host to the shade of an Irish prostitute known as "Giggly Meg".

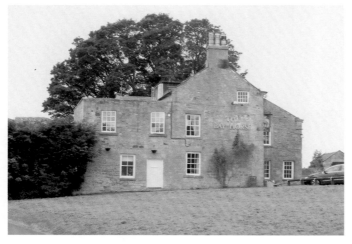

3 *The Bay Horse, Stamfordham:* Phantom footfalls have been recorded by patrons in this picturesque watering hole.

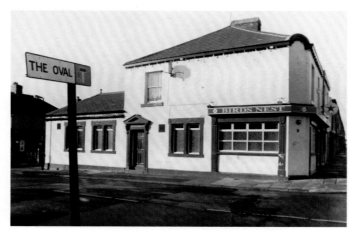

4 *The Birds Nest, Walker:* Eerie footsteps and the sound of clinking glasses were heard on numerous occasions in this old bar.

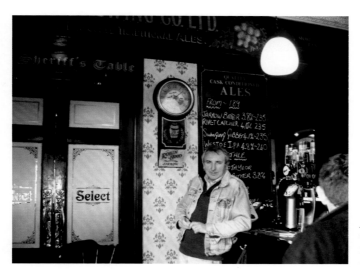

5 *The Robin Hood, Jarrow:* The "haunted clock" with the proprietor, Jess McConnell, underneath.

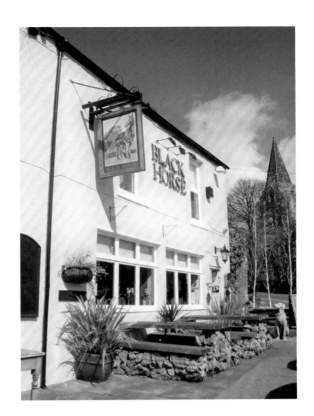

6 *The Black Horse, West Boldon:*
Home of a spectral cavalier and a
ghostly schoolgirl who died in an
accident.

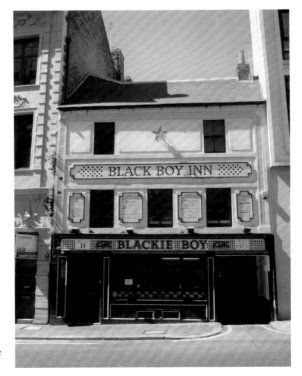

7 *The Blackie Boy Inn, Newcastle
upon Tyne:* Dark shadows have been
seen flitting about in the corners
of this pub, and an eerie "sense of
presence" has been described by some
experients.

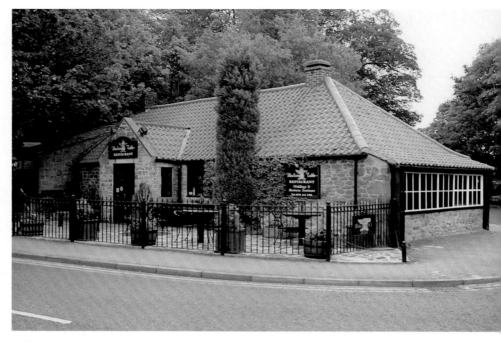

8 *The Blacksmith's Table, Washington:* Allegedly haunted by the ghost of an old highwayman called Robert Hazlitt.

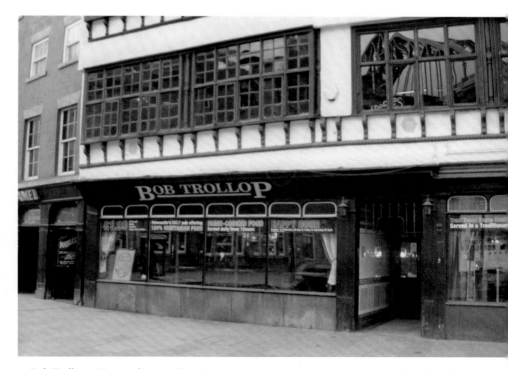

9 *Bob Trollop's, Newcastle upon Tyne:* A young prostitute was burnt to death in the pub in the nineteenth century, and the inn is supposedly haunted by the spectre of a former landlady.

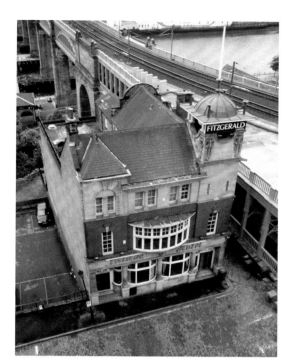

Right: 10 *The Bridge Hotel, Newcastle upon Tyne:* Dark figures have been seen in the pub, and the shade of a Roman legionnaire has been seen nearby.

Below: 11 *The Bridge Hotel, South Shields:* Closed many moons ago, The Bridge Hotel was supposedly haunted by the ghost of a disgruntled patron who left muddy footprints in the bar overnight.

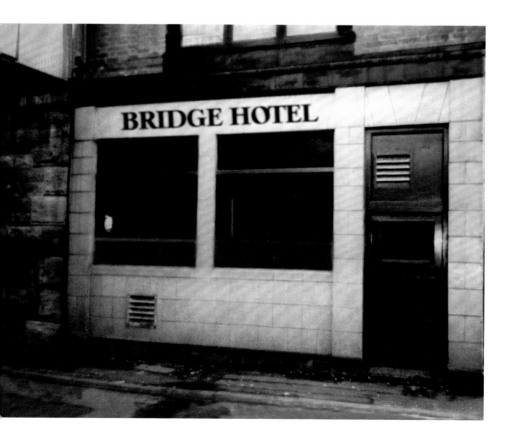

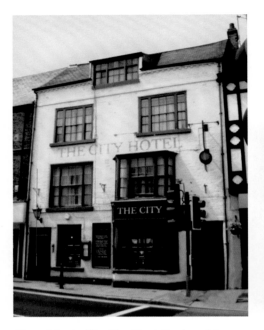
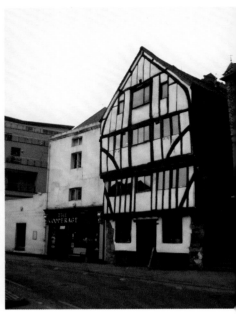

Above left: 12 *The City Hotel, Durham:* Numerous ghosts are reported to haunt this old inn, including one which inhabits the gents' toilet.

Above right: 13 *The Cooperage, Newcastle upon Tyne:* A white, misty cloud has been known to float over tables in The Cooperage and frighten staff.

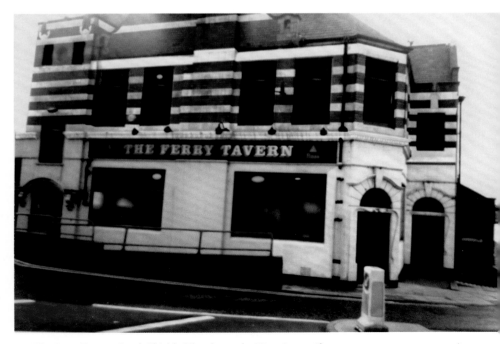

14 *The Ferry Tavern, South Shields:* The ghost of a Victorian waif was seen on numerous occasions outside this now-demolished pub.

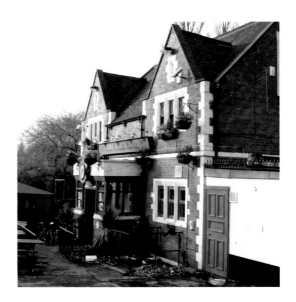

15 *The Robin Hood, Jarrow:* Home of the haunted clock.

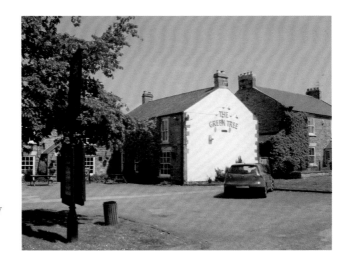

16 *The Green Tree, Tudhoe Village:* Allegedly haunted by The Blue Lady – a wicked mother who is said to have poisoned her children.

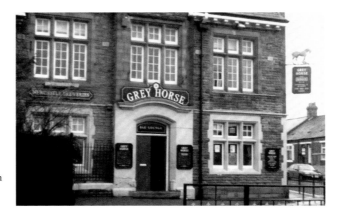

17 *The Grey Horse, Whitburn:* A cleaner known as "Mrs. T" is said to be responsible for groaning and creaking noises that have been heard in the pub when it is empty.

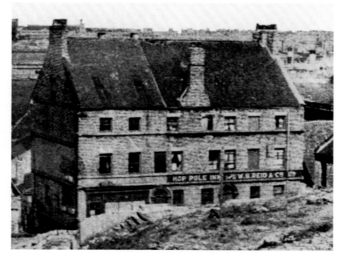

18 *The Hop Pole, South Shields:* A rare photograph of The Hop Pole, a smugglers' pub demolished many decades ago and said to be haunted by the spectral Red Lady, who was believed to curse passing ships. (Courtesy of Ivor Muncey).

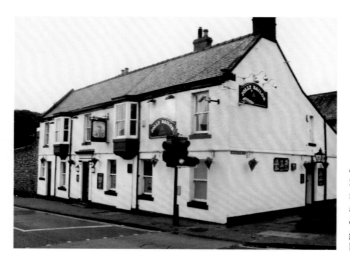

19 *The Jolly Sailor, Whitburn:* Haunted from cellar to rafters, The Jolly Sailor has a ghost that moves glasses and bottles about and has on several occasions sent eerie winds gushing through the building.

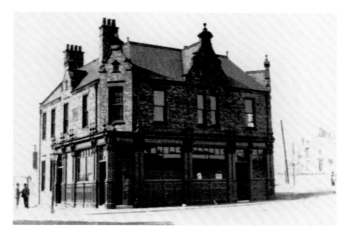

20 *Kennedy's Bar, Tyne Dock:* Formerly known as The Tyne Dock Hotel, this superb bar was once said to be haunted by the ghost of an old security guard and a motorcyclist who died in an accident. The authors know of no recent sightings.

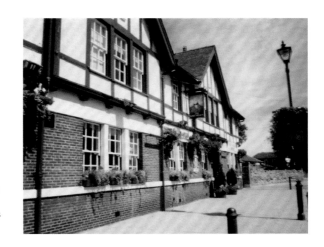

21 *The Lord Nelson, Monkton Village:* A phantom barman in an open-necked shirt and slacks has been seen in the pub, although his identity remains a mystery.

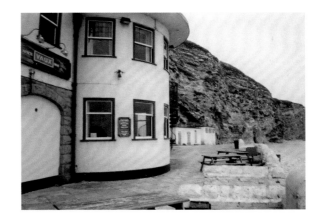

22 *The Marsden Grotto, Marsden Bay:* Home of spectral smugglers and phantom cats...

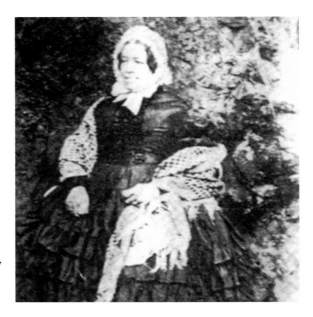

23 *Lizzie Allan*, wife of former Marsden Grotto patron Peter Allan, whose ghost has been seen in the Cave Bar sitting in an old rocking chair as she smokes her clay pipe.

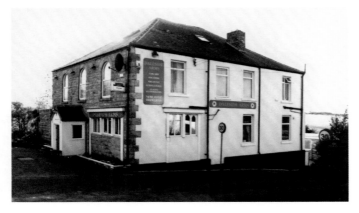

24 *The Nicky Nack Pub, Croxdale*; Now known as The Daleside Arms, the inn was visited by a local farmhand just before his terrifying encounter with a "black ghost".

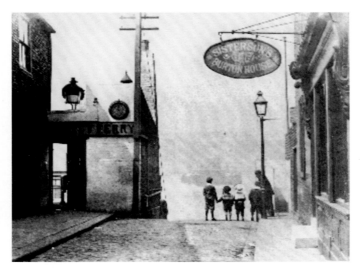

25 *The Noah's Ark, South Shields*; The road leading to the now-demolished Noah's Ark pub (just out of view on the right) which was said to be haunted by a local character known as Jack the Hammer.

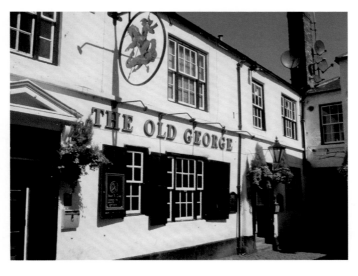

26 *The Old George, Newcastle upon Tyne:* Allegedly haunted by no less a personage than King Charles I.

27 The Old Ship, Harton Village: The pub has now changed locations, and there is a sliver of doubt whether this is the original building, but the modern inn is said to be haunted by a man who appears as a dark silhouette.

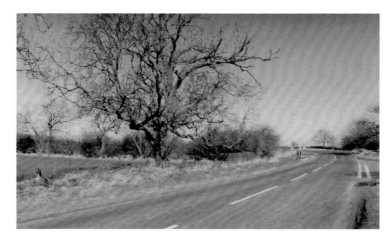

28 Patie's Inn, Darlington: Sometimes called "Patie's Inn of Horror", the pub stood just to the right of the tree in this picture.

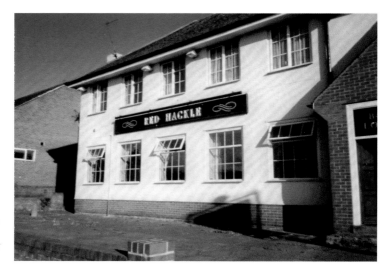

29 The Red Hackle, Jarrow; Haunted by numerous spectres, one of which addressed a former landlord by name.

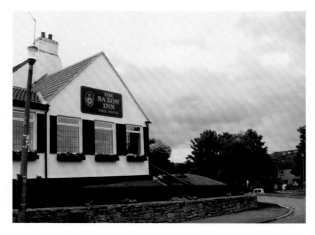

30 *The Saxon Inn, Escombe:* The resident spectre of this delightful pub is said to wash and dry glasses left on the bar.

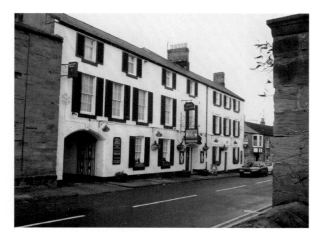

31 *The Schooner, Alnmouth:* A young widow is said to have taken her life in this pub, and still haunts the premises to this day.

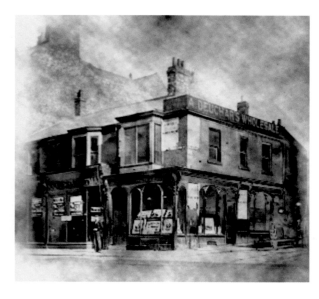

32 *The Scotia Hotel, South Shields:* Haunted by the ghost of a former barman who has been heard walking up and down the steps which lead to the cellar.

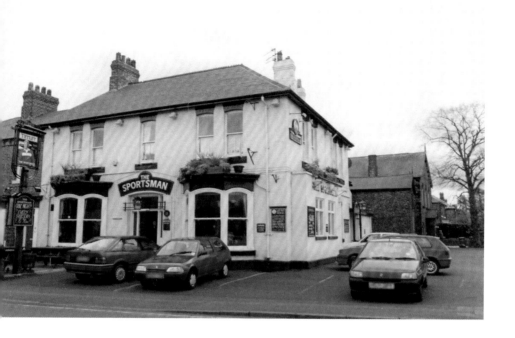

Above: 33 *The Sportsman, Eaglescliffe:* The ghosts of this old inn only appear on Wednesdays – the local market day...

Right: 34 *The Steamboat, South Shields:* Haunted by the ghost of an old sea captain who has been seen sitting in a leather armchair in the lounge.

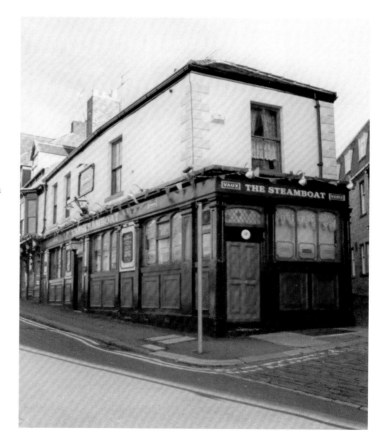

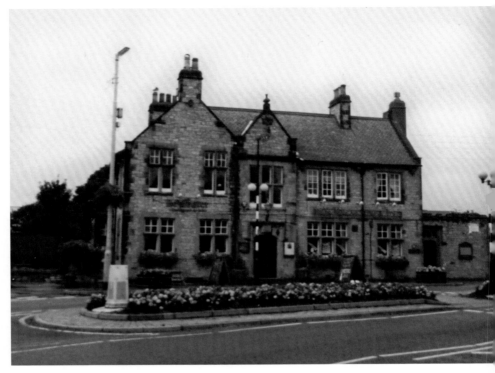

35 *The Toby Carvery, Cleadon Village:* A spectral coach and horses has been seen driving away from the inn at Christmas.

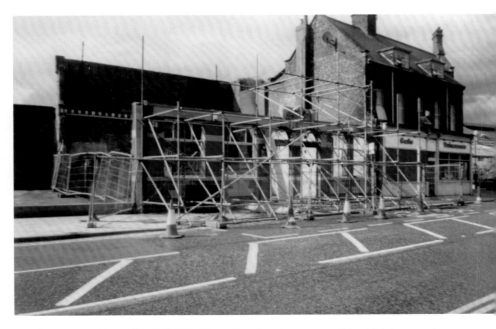

36 *The Trimmers' Arms, South Shields:* The only pub to have never sold a drink between its opening and its demise.

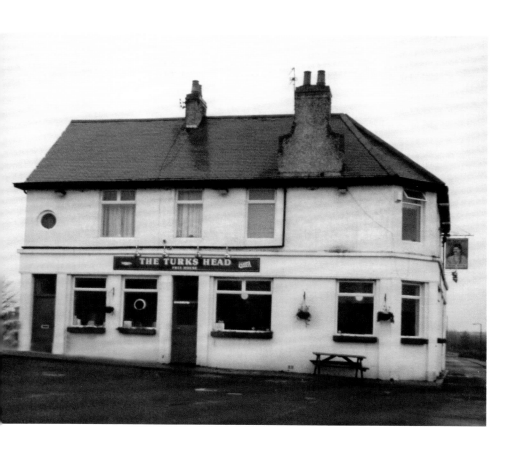

Above: 37 *The Turk's Head, South Shields:* Mysterious tunnels are said to run under the ground beneath the site of the Turk's Head, now demolished.

Right: 38 *The Tynemouth Lodge Hotel, Tynemouth:* The ghost of a woman in Georgian attire has been seen chasing two spectral children from a room on the upper level of the pub.

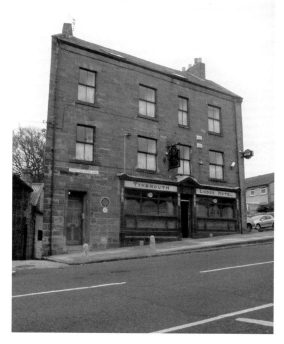

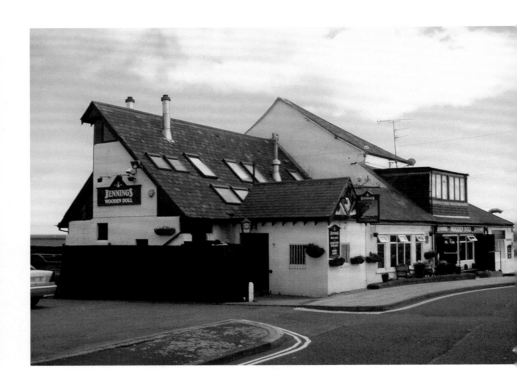

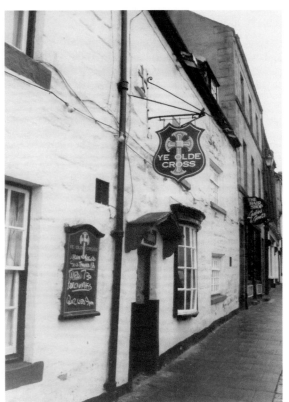

Above: 39 The Wooden Doll, North Shields: Darren W. Ritson, one of the authors, had an unnerving experience in the pub where he felt that he was being watched by one of the ghosts said to inhabit the premises.

Left: 40 Ye Olde Cross, Alnwick: Moving a collection of old bottles in the window is said to activate a deadly curse.

her satisfaction, the lady placed it upside-down on a drip tray to drain dry. Before long her task was completed, and then a call of nature dictated that she visit the toilet in the corridor adjacent to the bar.

And this is when the fun started – if you can call it that – for the cleaner apparently didn't find what happened very funny at all. Just as she left the bar, she heard the most horrendous smashing of glass. It sounded as if all of the glasses she had washed so carefully were being picked up and thrown around the room. There was no doubt in her mind that someone or something was breaking the glasses, as she could actually hear them smashing. Startled, she immediately went back into the bar to see what had happened. The place was in silence now, but resolutely she decided to find the broken drinking vessels or at least their remains.

The problem was that she couldn't find them at all. There was no broken glass, no sign of damage. Everything, in fact, looked perfectly hunky-dory. Except for one thing, that is. The glasses she had washed and placed upon the drip trays had disappeared. Bemused, she walked behind the bar to see if she could see them. She was not to be disappointed, for the glasses were there, alright. Unseen hands had picked them up and placed them, the right way up, in the basin and on the draining board.

The cleaner knew that she was in the public house on her own. Hence she also knew that whatever had picked up the glasses and moved them was not of human origin. The authors have been told that she ran from the Jolly Sailor in an extremely distressed state, too traumatised to close the doors behind her, even, and never set foot in the place again.

What are we to make of this? The simple answer, bizarre though it will seem to some, is that an invisible entity – or spirit, if you will – was not happy with the way the domestic had cleaned the glasses and put them back in the sink for her to do again. This conjures up pictures of, perhaps, the shade of a previous bar person who is still attempting to impose his or her standards on the place, and who is unaware or unable to accept the fact that they are dead.

But what of the sound of breaking glass? The cleaner was apparently adamant that what she heard was not the sound of glasses being clashed together – something which may have occurred when the entity transferred them from the drip trays to the basin – but of glasses breaking. The fact that no broken glass was ever found is curious, and opens up the possibility that the cleaner may have been listening to a ghostly echo of a past incident which took place in the bar, one in which glasses really were broken.

But other ghost tales connect themselves to the Jolly Sailor. Some years ago, a team of painters and decorators were working in the pub. One morning they were sitting having their bait, when a 'wind' suddenly came out of nowhere. All gathered then heard the distinct sound of the door nearby, which led out into the yard, clashing as the breeze slammed it shut. The problem was that the door didn't clash shut at all. It couldn't have done, because it was locked shut. Again, we must consider the possibility that the painters heard an 'echo from the past'. What they heard was the wind blowing the door shut alright, but in a different time. Other accounts of strange 'breezes' in the Jolly Sailor have also been recorded, as will be made clear presently.

Another peculiar tale associated with the Jolly Sailor is that a tunnel leads underground from the pub to the Marsden Grotto Inn several miles up the road. There is good reason to suggest that this is not a flight of fancy, and Mike's own research into the mysterious tunnel network under the Whitburn and Marsden area has borne this out.

And what of the Green Lady, a spectre whom the authors have heard mentioned on several occasions, but about whom there seems to be little information? Their quest goes on. If she is responsible for the paranormal activity at the Jolly Sailor then she is doing it as anonymously as possible. Ghosts can be shy too, one supposes, but more information about the Green Lady was to be forthcoming, as you will see.

In October 2006, Darren took part in an overnight investigation at The Jolly Sailor. Entering the pub was, he said, 'like stepping back in time'.

That's an understandable reaction, for the ceilings are decorated with oak beams and mock-Georgian and Edwardian memorabilia tastefully line the walls, along with old photographs of Whitburn taken in bygone days. The icing on the proverbial cake is a roaring fire at which visitors can warm themselves when the weather outside is inclement.

Darren and the rest of the team made themselves comfortable, and after a short wait the manager and several members of staff came to see them. The investigation was actually being led by a team other than Darren's, (G.HO.S.T), of which Darren was a team member. The staff members were actually going to join them in their investigative efforts, swelling the numbers even further.

Darren first spoke to the [then] manager Beverley Jackson, who informed him about an incident that occurred one evening whilst she was at the pub alone. Beverley had been in the kitchen attending to her duties when, suddenly; she heard the refrigerator door open. As she glanced up she saw the door slowly swinging open. Incredibly, a man's hand seemed to be holding the door from behind. Whoever had opened the door was now standing behind it. However, when Beverley looked down there were no legs protruding from underneath the bottom of the door. Suddenly the refrigerator door closed again, and no one was behind it at all. The only visible part of the spectre had been the strange, disembodied hand which then disappeared.

Beverley then informed Darren of another encounter that she'd experienced on the first floor of the pub.

'It appears that there's a playful ghost who likes to toy around with peoples possessions,' she said.

Getting ready to leave the pub, she was putting on her coat and had a large bunch of keys in her hand. She put down the bunch of keys for a moment while she inserted an arm into a sleeve, but when she went to pick her keys back up they had gone. Beverley scoured the room high and low before widening her search to include the rest of the building. She even asked a colleague who was downstairs at the time to help her locate her keys, and they both searched – to no avail. The two women were just about to give up on their search when they glanced down and noticed that the keys were in exactly the same place she'd originally left them before putting on her coat. Beverley was adamant that they were not there previously during the search, and is convinced that their disappearance was the action of the mischievous ghost.

Now more about 'The Green Lady'. She has been seen on occasion wondering around the upper floor of the inn wearing a long, flowing, green-tinted dress. She is believed to be the ghost of a woman who once lived at the pub and was rumoured to have been courting a coach driver from Newcastle upon Tyne. Seemingly she'd had big plans for the future – a future that included her coach-driver lover until one day he abandoned her for another woman. This devastated her of course, and legend has it that, in a state of heartbreak and anguish, she locked herself in her room and subsequently starved herself to death. The legend of the Green Lady dates back to about 1770 and a number of different versions are in circulation. According to some she did not passively starve herself to death, but proactively committed suicide by some other method. In some versions she was a buxom young maid, in others an old hag.

Her favoured spot for haunting the inn is seemingly the back lounge, but on one occasion, quite spectacularly, she was said to have stepped out of the pub during the night and took the inn sign down!'

The manager told Darren of another experience she'd had one night while working in the main bar. Standing behind the counter and chatting to three of her regulars at last orders, the rest of the pub cleared as, one by one, the patrons left for their homes. After the rest of the pub had been vacated Beverley and the three regulars continued to chat as they finished off their drinks, the conversation only being broken momentarily when she went to lock the door. Before coming back to the bar she made sure no one else was left on the premises. As nothing seemed untoward she rejoined her friends and continued chatting.

The three friends drained the last drops from their glasses, and Beverley was just about to let them out when she suddenly saw a figure walk past the door and along the corridor.

'It happened so quickly', she said.

Beverley told Darren that her first thought had been that it must have been another customer whom she'd forgotten about or missed when emptying the pub at last orders. That is, until she walked into the corridor to greet this person only to find that there was no one there. She looked in the lavatories, in the snug and all around the pub but could find no one – no one except her three friends who were in the bar all the time.

'It must just be another of the Jolly Sailor's ghosts,' she said.

After listening to their encounters, and after reading Mike Hallowell's' chapter on the pub in his book *Ales & Spirits*, Darren became convinced that the pub was haunted and was looking forward to see what the investigation would uncover. The 'team psychic' was not available for the investigation, so the vigil would be limited purely to scientific evidence-gathering. 'Had the psychic been there', Darren said later, 'all available knowledge of the establishment and the ghostly encounters that had taken place there would have kept from her. It would have been interesting to see what she would have 'picked up' during the 'reading' phase of the event. I guess her reading will have to wait for another time, but it will indeed be interesting to see what she comes up with'.

After the pub had closed its doors the team was ready to begin the investigation in earnest. The first job was to conduct a thorough baseline test in all locations. This took quite a while, as there were at least 16 places to test for average room temperatures, EMFs and the rest of the usual array of data. Draughts were located and squeaky floorboards tracked down so that the investigators knew exactly 'what was what', so to speak. If anything did occur, they would have baseline readings to compare in order to determine if any peculiarities were potentially of paranormal origin. As usual, trigger objects were placed in various locations around the pub – upstairs and down. These included a crucifix in the function room, a flour tray containing some objects in the snug area and a doll left in the private flat on the very top level of the pub. Motion sensors were also placed on either side of the corridor where the ghost had been seen walking. The team was then ready to split into three small groups and begin the investigation.

Darren was working with a fellow investigator, Lee Stephenson, and their first location was the bar-cum-pool room on the ground floor. They ventured in at 2.00am, and it wasn't long before they caught a light anomaly on night vision video camera. Darren took some digital stills in the hope that they'd 'catch something paranormal' but to no avail.

At 2.05am Darren 'called out to the atmosphere' to see if any spirits would give a sign of their presence, and almost immediately both investigators heard the sound of a footsteps coming from along the corridor near the main bar. Upon inspection they found no one there – no one of this world anyway!

The investigators returned to their station, and before too long an ice-cold breeze suddenly rushed through the room at head height. Both Darren and Lee were unable to work out where this breeze had come from. During the baseline tests in this area the windows were checked for draughts and nothing was found, so the origin of the breeze remains a mystery. Was it the denizens of the other world trying to make themselves known? Who knows. Then, suddenly, a loud crash was heard – as if a tin tray had been dropped in the snug (which was empty at this point). Again, on checking it out the researchers found nothing out of place.

At the same time, the other group of investigators, including Drew Bartley and Fiona Vipond, were in the function room on the next level up at the other end of the building. When they swept the area with the EMF meter it seemed to go off for no apparent reason. One of the guests during the vigil, a barman, stated that he felt a breeze on his left-hand side. Curiously, at the same time another light anomaly was caught on video camera in the same location as the breeze.

At 2.25am a séance was carried out and the researchers filmed the proceedings. Nothing seemed to happen during the séance, or so they thought, until they checked the trigger object – the crucifix – that had been placed on the table prior to the beginning of the investigation. The team had checked this object before they started the séance and it was in place, but when they looked at it afterwards, to their astonishment, it had been moved. The barman, although already a believer in the paranormal, confessed to being 'absolutely blown away' by this and found it hard to believe what he'd witnessed.

The other 'guests' at the vigil were assigned to the mid-section of the building to investigate three of the rooms. The results were negative. The manager and her friend Beverley Jackson were based in the courtyard, and they too experienced nothing.

The second location was the upstairs function room, where not less then 20 minutes earlier the trigger object had been moved. When the researchers ventured inside, Darren noticed that the serving hatch doors between the room and the other bar were fully open. Earlier he'd noticed they were completely closed, so he radioed down to ask the last group in there whether the doors had been touched.

'Those doors were closed when we left' came the firm reply.

'Closed?' Darren replied, 'Are you sure?'

'Of course I am' said the researcher downstairs.

'Well the bleedin' things are wide open now!'

At that point Darren decided to 'play' with the doors to see if the hinges were broken. He also wanted to see if the doors would somehow open on their own. He could find nothing wrong with them, and when they were moved to the closed position they stayed that way. After 30 minutes of sitting in silence – observing, waiting and monitoring – the investigators left the room and headed 'back to base' for a break.

By this time the second group was investigating the downstairs bar. An EMF reading was taken in the adjacent corridor, and although it was normal something very interesting happened at the same time. The entire group heard a creaking noise and what they described as footfalls emanating from within the corridor just near the main bar – exactly where the first group had heard them earlier during the vigil. It seemed that at least one phantom liked to walk around that particular location in the pub at any rate, but who it was they were unable to determine.

Groups 2 and 3 once more failed to experience anything untoward during the next stage of the vigil – not that this bothered Beverley and her colleague, as they'd had plenty experiences of their own in the past. However, for the others it was proving to be a relatively quiet night.

The researchers eventually joined together as one group and ventured upstairs to hold a large séance in the function room. They prepared by placing the seats in a circle and then set up the video cameras to record the proceedings.

The séance lasted for about 20 minutes, and the phenomena experienced by the sitters, was in all honesty 'subjective'. Different techniques were tried to 'entice spirits in' and attempt communication with them, but nothing much happened. During the séance Darren 'picked up' the name Elizabeth and thought that it might be connected to the Green Lady said to haunt the inn. Suddenly Darren saw a brief flash of light, but suspected it might have come from another investigator who was taking notes whilst holding a torch. However, the investigator later stated that at that time the torch was actually turned off. After the séance the team headed back downstairs for another break.

At this point in the investigation Lee Stephenson had to go home, so Darren joined up with another group.

One of the 'guest investigators' had agreed to stake out the cellars – on his own – so the others decided to make camp in the snug area. The snug is actually reputed to play host to another female spectre in addition to the Green Lady, but if she was present she didn't put in an appearance. Neither did the guest investigator see anything remotely spooky during his vigil in the cellar. The other two groups, however, did observe some odd light anomalies whilst out in the courtyard and actually managed to film them. The manager Beverley, and her colleague added that although they felt they 'were not alone' and 'were being watched' while staking out the flat on the second floor, said very little had happened in reality. The last phases of the investigation were then got underway as the cleaners were due in to get on with their work. It was 5.10am, and Darren decided to spend the last portion of time alone in the cellar.

'I was feeling brave', he mused later, 'and although I was beginning to tire I knew the ice-cold atmosphere would wake me up. It certainly did! Along with the deafening noise of the generators pumping away in the darkness, and my only source of light being the LCD screen from the video camera, I 'called out' to see if could get any results. I was rewarded with several reasonably good light anomalies, but that was it. After 10 minutes the batteries ran out throwing me into total darkness. At that point I climbed up the ladders and made my exit. The rest of the vigils were pretty quiet'.

The team decided that there was still time for one, last séance in the snug area. As the researchers preceded they all heard noises and movement coming from along the corridor. Every investigator was accounted for in the snug, and an air of excitement was being generated when, alas, they realised it was simply the cleaners arriving. Nothing paranormal there, but it did signify the end of our investigation. The researchers packed up their equipment, said thank you to the manager for her hospitality and departed.

- PUB: KENNEDY'S BAR (THE TYNE DOCK HOTEL)
- LOCATION: TYNE DOCK
- GOOD GHOST RATING: 5

Notorious for flooding even to this day, the low area of Tyne Dock has as its most pivotal landmark a pub called Kennedy's, formerly known (and still often called) the Tyne Dock Hotel.

In past decades the inn was a favourite meeting place for sailors of all nationalities, and many stories must have been swapped over a pint of ale. The name 'Kennedy's' is not a slick epithet designed to give the pub a wine-bar image. The triangle of land on which it stands was originally known as Kennedy's Corner, and we have been told that the original name of the establishment was Kennedy's Bar.

Several stories of ghosts at the inn have come to the authors' attention, all of them irritatingly vague. One tells of a security guard who was murdered just after leaving the premises, although this was almost certainly a tale imported from another pub nearby, called The Grapes, now demolished.

Another story concerns a young motorcyclist who died outside the entrance in an accident during the early 1960s. Both are said to visit the pub as apparitions, but the patrons whom we spoke to had never heard either tale before. The story regarding the murdered security guard is true – we've seen the newspaper cuttings – but his alleged haunting activities remain unverified. Both tales may therefore be apocryphal, but you never can tell.

- **PUB:**   THE KING'S HEAD
- **LOCATION:**   SUNDERLAND
- **GOOD GHOST RATING:** 4

The King's Head Pub once lay on The Durham Road, a convenient stopping-off point for thirsty wayfarers. Recollections of the ghost stories attached to the inn are sketchy, but enough to whet the appetite.

According to legend, many moons ago a new landlord moved into the premises. He hadn't long settled in before he realised that the place was haunted by the spirit of another former landlord, who – most curiously – seemed most disapproving of the new landlord's liking for a drink. It is said that when he sat in the bar his glass of beer would slide across the table and crash onto the floor.

For those of fainter heart that alone would have been cause enough to vacate the premises immediately, but there was more to come. Persistent, eerie sounds were also heard to emanate from the dumb waiter that served the upstairs function room. Perhaps the noises were coming from the room itself rather than the dumb waiter, as on one occasion the room was actually locked up when a host of musical instruments that were being stored there could be heard playing, apparently on their own.

Even the time-honoured custom of ringing the bell for "Time, gentlemen please!" had been left to the ghostly landlord of yesteryear, who appears to be a stickler for the rules as the bell was often heard to ring at closing time, also of its own volition.

- PUB: THE LOOK-OUT
- LOCATION: SOUTH SHIELDS
- GOOD GHOST RATING: 8

In Fort Street, South Shields, you will find one of the most fascinating public houses in the area – the Look-Out Inn.

Mike had planned to take Mrs H. with him on a visit to the Look-Out one Wednesday evening, but she was busy. Fancying a pint, he went anyway. As soon as he walked through the door he was pleasantly surprised to see Fred, a chap who'd befriended him when he'd once visited the Beacon not too far away. He was, as it transpired, in the middle of telling the tenant of the inn, Hilary Gavin, about Mike's research. He was sure the words 'speak of the devil' must have popped into his mind.

Hilary Gavin was what feature writers, journalists and reporters call a 'gift'. Not only did she tell you what you wanted to know, she also told you dozens of other things which you weren't even aware of and which proved to be far more interesting. Hilary had done a great deal of research into the history of the Look-Out – a sure indicator that a landlord doesn't just see what they do as a job, but that they have a true affinity with the place. From the outset, Hilary proved to be a great help, and the authors owe her a debt which they will never be able to repay for her assistance.

The Look-Out is thoroughly Victorian in its ambience, and has a most wonderful atmosphere. At lunchtime it is quiet, serene even. The bar stools are filled with regulars engaged in deep conversation – on this occasion it was local politics and the rising crime rate, if Mike remembers rightly – but it is also quite possible to lose yourself in a corner and contemplate your navel if you wish to do so.

On an evening the atmosphere changes. As dusk falls, local couples start to pop in, along with one or two small groups of women having 'a night out'. Something prodded Mike mentally, bringing forth a buried childhood memory. After pondering for a few minutes he remembered what it was. The Look-Out, of an evening, is very reminiscent of the way public houses used to be back in the early and mid-sixties before the advent of wine bars and the explosion of night clubs into the public's cultural consciousness took place. He remembered visiting the Ben Lomond in Jarrow (later renamed the Viking for several years, before reverting to its former epithet in 1999) at New Year, watching crowds of revellers enjoying themselves without the deafening accompaniment of popular music. The Ben Lomond was noisy alright, but the noise consisted entirely of laughter, banter and up-beat conversation. The Look-Out, Mike thought, was exactly the same, and he pointed this out to Hilary.

'That's because the Look-Out is a family pub', she explained. 'Do you see those people drinking at the bar? Their parents drink here, and their parents drank here before them. It's been like that for generations, ever since the pub opened. They see the Look-Out very much as their pub. People meet here to talk and socialise – like I say, it's a family thing'.

The oldest reference to the Look-Out in local literature hails from 1849, but the pub may have existed in some form before that. The story is that the inn was rebuilt, but whether on the same site as an earlier tavern of the same name or not the authors have not been able to determine.

The oldest character connected with the inn of which we know anything – and that is precious little – is Sarah Stevenson. She was, we are led to believe, a doughty character who ran an orderly house. In 1871 or thereabouts the inn was sold in auction. And the new owners were licensed to sell 'beers and provisions'. This reveals that it was a traditional ale house, and that its license to sell wines and spirits must have been granted later.

Until relatively recently the first floor of the building was also part of the inn itself, whereas now it is the living quarters of the tenant. Hilary showed Mike her living room, and told him that there was an interesting story attached to it.

'At one time the window looked over the river – you can't see it now – and the Tyne Pilots used to have their meetings here. The pub actually stood in St. Stephen's Street then, not Fort Street, as it does now. The legend is that it was in this room where the Tyne Pilots first made their plans for a lifeboat service, but I've seen nothing to substantiate it'.

Nevertheless, the fact that the Tyne Pilots met there at all is interesting in itself, for, in the nineteenth century, some of them carried out what we may call 'unofficial' excavations at the site of Arbeia, the Roman fort, nearby. What happened to any finds they may have made may or may not be recorded, but there were rumours that some of them were spirited away under cover of darkness. One archaeologist at Arbeia told Mike that he had heard of 'a substantial amount of excavated material' being taken away in a basket, but there is no proof. Roman antiquities fetched a huge price at that time, particularly in London, but whether monetary gain was their motive is unclear.

The layout of the Look-Out has changed over the years. Initially, the ground floor seems to have been divided into four separate rooms; the lounge, the bar, a 'snug', and an incredibly small room commonly referred to as the 'Winky Room', although no one now seems to know why. The first alteration seems to have been the removal of the wall between the bar and the snug. At a later stage the walls of the Winky Room were pulled down, which effectively incorporated the space into the main bar. Latterly, the wall between the snug and the bar was removed too, thus creating an L-shaped open-plan bar. The lounge is still a lounge, but now an area as opposed to a separate room. The alcove which contains the pool table is referred to – with tongue placed firmly in cheek – as 'the Games Room.'

The rush towards open-plan public houses was largely fuelled by a desire to cut overheads. When an inn is open-plan, one bar serves the entire establishment. This cuts down on the number of bar staff required, and the owners have less to pay out in wages.

Despite the alterations, the Look-Out retains much of its original character and charm.

Hilary Gavin took over the running of the Look-Out in 1998, but she was aware of the inn long before then, being 'a local', as they say. She didn't claim to have seen any apparitions in the anthropomorphic sense, but had nevertheless endured several strange encounters.

'The first thing to mention is the atmosphere', she told Mike. 'This is a really friendly pub, but sometimes you do get the feeling that there's something here. I don't mind coming into the bar at any time, but I must admit that I always feel a bit strange when it's quiet. That's when it hits you – when there's no noise. That feeling is strongest in the Gents' Toilet. You definitely feel as if someone's there, watching'.

Mike asked Hilary if she'd had any strange experiences in the main bar, and she answered in the affirmative. Firstly, she related an unnerving experience when, one evening, she was locking up after the last drinkers had departed. She found that the jukebox had switched itself off at the wall socket without any human assistance. (A similar experience was reported by one of the barmaids in the Red Hackle, as we will relate later, and in other haunted pubs the authors have investigated). It is a common feature of pub ghosts that they often give the impression of being 'helpful'; for example, turning equipment on and off as if to save you the bother. Then again, some landlords and landladies will testify that such interference is anything but helpful.

And then there were the noises. Hilary and others had heard strange, knocking noises in the Look-Out. Interestingly, they came from one location; the north-easterly corner of the main bar.

'It sounded as if someone was knocking on a window', said Hilary, 'but we could see that no one was there'. The noise seemed to have a certain 'unearthly' quality about it, for it disturbed those who heard it to a fair degree.

Hilary's daughter Helen supported the veracity of Hilary's experiences. She told Mike that she'd often 'seen something out of the corner of her eye' – a routine experience with those who see apparitions – but, when she turns to focus on it, it has already disappeared. She too had heard the odd noise, and felt uncomfortable when the bar was quiet and she was there on her own. She had also seen 'fleeting shadows' which appeared and disappeared in a moment, but which were there just long enough to be noticed.

Another phenomenon which Hilary had encountered is known to paranormal researchers as TOS, or Transient Olfactory Stimulation. This is a sophisticated way of describing strange smells which seem to have no rational explanation or logical origin, and may therefore be classed as 'paranormal'. The majority of TOS phenomena fall into one of three categories; cooking smells, fragrances (lavender is the most popular) and tobacco odours. It was the latter two which Hilary had noticed. The odour of tobacco was particularly strong in the bar area. The location may be significant, for this part of the Look-Out is still sometimes referred to as 'the Men's Bar', and it is also true that the vast majority of those who frequent it are males.

'Its pipe tobacco I can smell', said Hilary. 'Sometimes I'll come down the stairs, walk in the bar, and there it is – the strong aroma of a lit pipe'.

This is interesting, for there is a faint hope that, one day, we may be able to establish exactly which of the Look-Out's past characters the pipe-smoke phenomenon is connected to. We say this because it is undoubtedly connected to an apparition which has been seen on the first floor, then Hilary's accommodation. This ghost was seen not by Hilary herself, but by a past landlady, and consisted of an elderly gentleman sitting in a chair smoking a pipe.

Hilary Gavin also smelt the fragrance of flowers in the public area of the Look-Out, too, but had no idea what generated it.

Another feature of the Look-Out is that, although the structure of the building has changed internally, it has retained its distinctive Victorian style. However, over the years the owners have accommodated one or two other changes to make life easier for patrons. The westerly aspect of the lounge, for example, contains a quite ornate window of patterned glass. This window at one time looked out upon a yard. Members of the fairer sex were forced to traverse this yard if they wished to visit their powder room, to put it politely. Eventually, a corridor was built outside which stretched from the door in the lounge to the toilet. In one fell swoop, then, the toilet became an interior fixture instead of an exterior one, and so did the window.

At this point in our narrative we must return to the aforementioned Fred, for on one occasion he had a strange experience indeed. Some time ago the interior décor of the Look-Out needed freshened up, and Fred agreed to do the job. So as to cause a minimum of disruption to clients, he was asked to do the work during the night so that the paint would be virtually dry by the time the inn opened for business the next day.

On the night in question, Fred waited till the pub was cleared before he started work. At least he thought the pub was empty. Now, with hindsight, he's not so sure. Something unnerved Fred as he painted. He had a strange feeling he was being watched, and as a consequence he looked behind him. What he saw affected him profoundly, and he remembered it vividly. There was no one actually in the bar, but, looking through the frosted glass of the window which looked into the 'ladies corridor', as it was named, he could see several figures – two, possibly three. The opaque nature of the glass made it difficult to see any detail – they appeared like silhouettes – but Fred watched incredulously as, without so much as a word, they walked along the ladies' corridor and into oblivion.

He found it hard to concentrate on his painting for the rest of the night.

Hilary told Mike an amusing postscript to this story – although Fred may have disagreed. One evening, shortly after the incident aforementioned, Hilary hung a large, ornamental mirror in the corner of the lounge. Fred came in later, passed through the bar and was about to turn left into the Gents' Toilet, when he happened to glance across the lounge and became aware of a figure staring at him.

'He nearly had a heart attack', said Hilary. 'He was staring into the mirror and at himself'.

The cellar beneath the Look-Out is probably the most intensely haunted area of the pub, and for several reasons. The first story relates to the death of a person on the cellar steps – or more precisely, at the bottom of them – although details of the event seen incredibly difficult to get hold of. This indicates strongly that the event must have occurred very early on in the pub's history, because had it happened in even relatively recent times some of the old-timers who drink in the Look-Out would undoubtedly remember it.

On the night that Mike visited, an old chap sitting in the bar ventured forth with what little information he knew.

'I heard the story some forty years ago', he said, 'and the chap who told me was an old man then'.

It seems that, at some time in the past, a landlady of the Look-Out fell headlong down the cellar steps. Her injuries were so serious that she died, although whether she expired immediately we cannot say. There are, of course, several possibilities. She may have thrown herself down the steps, although this is unlikely in the extreme. She may have been inebriated and fallen down the steps – a fate which befell another drinker in the 1800s just down the road at the Steamboat Inn. Is this likely? At best we can say that it is not impossible. The third possibility is that the she was the victim of murder most foul, and pushed down the steps by person or persons unknown. Again, it's possible, but highly unlikely. Finally, we may consider the possibility that the landlady accidentally tripped and fell, which we must confess is the most likely explanation. As with all early Victorian public houses, the Look-Out's cellar steps are steep, narrow and cramped. It doesn't take much imagination to picture an accident.

Other than this we know very little, and a trawl of newspaper and library archives with so little information to go on would be an impossible task.

The next logical question, of course, is whether this tragedy has increased or enhanced the haunting phenomena at the inn. It could very well be, for the cellar has developed a reputation for playing host to a 'presence' of some kind. Hilary had, on many occasions, felt as if she was being watched whilst downstairs. Her daughter Helen had similar experiences, as have other members of staff. Curiously, the reluctance of some to go down into the cellar was borne out by something which happened whilst Mike was there.

The barmaid on duty on the evening Mike visited had, just a week previously, been in a nasty car accident, and suffered injuries to her leg or foot. Walking was obviously a painful exercise, and she asked Hilary's daughter if she would go down into the cellar and fetch up some bottles of a particular bottled lager which had been requested by a customer. Helen looked distinctly uncomfortable, and only agreed to do so if someone would stand at the top of the cellar steps and watch her as she descended.

Another feature of the cellar in the Look-Out is that it is subject to sudden and unexplained temperature changes. One minute it can be almost unbearably warm, the next freezing cold. Those who have experienced such changes say that they do not seem natural. They are too rapid and too sharp. Of course, it is tempting to suggest that the anomalous phenomena in the cellar and the sense of unease that pervades the atmosphere could be connected in some way to the death of the landlady who fell down the steps all those years ago. Without denying that this may indeed be the case, we must not ignore another aspect of the Look-Out haunting – one which we have hitherto refrained from mentioning, but which must rate as one of the most fascinating apparitional phenomena we have encountered during our research for this book.

The Arbeia Roman fort – or at least, that portion of it which has been either wholly or partially excavated – is only a fraction of the original complex of buildings. At one time, what is now Fort Street would have fallen within the perimeter of Arbeia itself. In short, the Look-Out Inn is now standing within what used to be the confines of a Roman Fort, and on top of goodness-knows-what in the way of ancient artefacts. Until such times as the houses and buildings which now stand on the site are demolished, the Roman remains underneath must remain buried and untouched.

Of course, the Arbeia ruins have been covered with the detritus of succeeding generations. What is now the cellar in the Look-Out, for example, will have been at ground level at some stage of the Roman occupation. Working on the principle that apparitions tend to appear at the same spacial co-ordinates as their flesh-and-blood originals did during their lives – and there is evidence to this effect – then we would not expect an apparition of a Roman soldier, say, to appear at ground level today. Rather, he would appear at the ground-level of the era he inhabited, which may be several feet below the soles of our shoes.

There is a fascinating example of this at the medieval Treasurer's House in York, where a troop of legionnaires appeared to a rather frightened apprentice plumber, Harry Martindale, some years ago. Later, he stated that these spectral legionnaires seemed to be walking with the lower part of their legs beneath the ground. Further investigation showed that they were actually walking on an old Roman road buried beneath the floor, and 'ignoring' the two feet or so of construction materials which had been placed on top of it during the next sixteen hundred years, or whatever.

All of this may go to explain why, on several occasions, the spectre of a Roman legionnaire has actually appeared in the cellar of the Look-Out Inn at South Shields.

Mike first heard the story of the ghostly Roman soldier in the Beehive, and was glad when Hilary Gavin confirmed it to him during his visit. Yes, she said, she was aware of such stories, but none of the witnesses to these apparitions came in to the Look-Out now. This was frustrating, because it meant that tracking down these witnesses would be an almost impossible task. She didn't know any names, addresses or details, for all the sightings had occurred before her tenancy there. Mike decided to tackle this problem later, and concentrate on gleaning what few details she knew from Hilary.

The Roman soldier has appeared on more than one occasion. On each showing he apparently does the same thing; he stands and stares, his face devoid of emotion. His thoughts, if there are any, are locked inside a mind which has its proper home in a different time.

What do we know about this soldier? Indeed, what can we know?

The Romans came to South Shields in 80 AD or thereabouts. It is possible therefore that the apparition which appears in the cellar of the Look-Out could be from either the 1st. Asturians, or ala I Asturum (a cavalry regiment), the 5th. Gaulish Cohort or cohors quinta Gallorum, or, later, the Barcariorum Tigrisiensium or Tigris Bargemen, all of whom were stationed at Arbeia over the centuries. Unless at some future time we can trace witnesses to these dramatic appearances, and perhaps get a more detailed description of the soldier's appearance, it has to be said that we are simply guessing.

In the final analysis we think we can agree that there is something intensely sad – and moving – about the apparition of a Roman soldier, standing guard for untold aeons, eternally protecting an outpost of an empire which crumbled into the dust many, many years ago.

Mike left the Look-Out. Sitting at a table near the door were members of the Ladies Darts Team. They seemed in good spirits. Mike walked across the road and began to take photographs. A group of women saw the camera and raised their legs in Tiller Girl fashion, laughing and smiling. In a flash he was back in the 60s once again, remembering good times, innocent times. As he walked back down Fort Street the sounds faded, replaced by the roar of the sea.

And still he felt sad when he thought about that lonely legionnaire.

- **PUB:**   THE LORD CREWE ARMS
- **LOCATION:**   BLANCHLAND
- **GOOD GHOST RATING:**   10

Possibly the most famous 'pub ghost' in the whole of the north-east of England is that of Lady Dorothy Forster – the niece of both the Bishop of Durham and Lady Crewe, and sister to the famous 'General Tom Forster who conspired in the 1715 Jacobite Rebellion. The Lord Crewe Arms was built in the twelfth century and was part of Blanchland Abbey which was set in the beautiful and picturesque Derwent Valley in the heart of the North Pennines. It is a former Abbots' house from that period, and is now classed as an ancient monument and a Grade II listed four-star Inn.

The ghost of Dorothy Forster dates back from the sixteenth century and it is said she haunts the very room that she waited in for her brother's return from the rebellion. It is said that her sad, lonely ghost has been seen looking out of the window, in torment, waiting for her beloved brother.

IN-DEPTH CASE STUDY: THE LORD NELSON, MONKTON VILLAGE
Good Ghost Rating: 7

Mike was born in South Shields, spent the first years of his life in Hebburn – three, he thinks – before his family moved to Armstrong Terrace in South Shields, where he was inducted, albeit reluctantly, into Mortimer Road Infants School (now demolished). Shortly thereafter his family relocated to Jarrow where he lived, in a succession of well-maintained council houses, until his marriage in 1978. The last of these was a pleasant three-bedroomed semi-detached house in Langley Terrace.

The western aspect of Langley Terrace intersects with York Avenue, a busy dual carriageway. By crossing the road and turning right, one can follow York Avenue northwards until one reaches the entrance to a large circle of houses called the Crescent. The Crescent leads to the Monkton Stadium, a modern sporting and athletic complex. Another turn left puts you inside one of the most pleasant areas of South Tyneside, Monkton Village.

Monkton Village is an oasis of calm in a troubled world. It plays host to the imposing but attractive Monkton Hospital, a number of pleasant housing estates, a smattering of small shops and – last but not least – an old inn by the name of the Lord Nelson.

The Lord Nelson is not actually 'old' in the strictest sense of the word. Some of the old-timers who still drink within its walls can remember it being built when they were only knee-high to a grasshopper's garter, as they say. But in terms of continuity the Lord Nelson is old, for it stands on the site of a much older inn of the same name. When the first Lord Nelson was built, no one really knows.

Despite the fact that they shared a common name, the two taverns were radically different. The new Lord Nelson is extremely picturesque, festooned with a profusion of flowers on the outside, a mock-Tudor finish and a spacious beer garden at the rear. The interior is roomy, well-aired and nicely decorated. So far it has resisted all attempts at modernisation, which brings joy to the soul of old-fashioned types such as Mike who think that wine bars and discos are the Devil's own playgrounds.

Mike and his wife visited the Lord Nelson on the morning of Saturday, 5th August, 2000. The sun was shining brightly, and they spent a pleasant ten minutes talking in the beer garden before the doors opened for business at 11.00am. On entering they were introduced to the deputy manager, whom they had arranged to see by prior appointment. Over in a quiet corner, they asked him to discuss the spectre which allegedly roamed around Monkton Village's only watering hole.

Initially they were disappointed. Yes, the deputy manager had heard vague rumours, but was unable to furnish any details. But he did offer a glimmer of hope.

'Look', he said, 'There's a chap who wandered into the bar a minute ago, and he's drunk in the Nelson since he was young. If anyone would know anything about the ghost it would be him. Let me introduce you'.

Mrs H. grabbed her port and lemon, Mike his lager, and they dutifully followed.

'Pip, this man is a columnist with the *Shields Gazette*, and this is his wife. I want you to tell him what you know about the ghost'.

Pip Stonehouse has lived in Monkton Village all his life. His sister-in-law, Gladys, ran a corner shop just a hop, skip and jump away from the old Methodist chapel down the road. This immediately brought back a flood of happy childhood memories, for, as a child, Mike would often pop into 'Gladi Stonehouse's' for a quarter of sweets. Corner shops like this are a dying breed. So many like it have been crushed underfoot by faceless hypermarkets, much to the detriment of local communities. The interior of the shop was small – too small, some would say – but retained an overpowering ambience of the 1960s, when the world was a safer and more settled place. Gladys Stonehouse was not just a shopkeeper. She was a grief counsellor – offering kindness and sympathy when someone died – an encyclopaedia (she knew where everyone lived or was moving to) and a purveyor of every commodity you would care to name. What she didn't have in stock she would get, and quickly.

After reminiscing with Pip over a pint, Mike returned to the matter of the ghost. What could he tell him? Pip looked like the sort of person who could tell Mike what he wanted to know.

'The ghost? Well, there's not much to say. I've never seen it, I can tell you that much'.

'But you've heard the stories?'

'Not really. Can't say I've heard anything'.

'Vague rumours, then?'

'Not even vague rumours, I'm afraid. I really don't remember hearing anything about a ghost at all'.

Mike then asked Pip about his memories of the Lord Nelson, and on this subject he had much more to say.

The old Lord Nelson bore no resemblance to the new one, he stated. It was smaller, for one thing, and not nearly so picturesque. The picture he painted was of an inn which, in some ways, was rather dilapidated. But was it a nice place to drink?

'Oh, yes', he said, 'Most definitely'.

The old Lord Nelson was managed by an elderly lady, although he could not recall her name. It was, he said, a friendly, welcoming place, very much a pub for the local farmers and residents.

'Everybody loved the Nelson', he said fondly.

In one sense, nothing changed after the old Lord Nelson was demolished and the new one built in its place. It had the same atmosphere, and was frequented by the same clientele.

'See that part of the bar over there? Well, at one time there was a wall there. The room beyond was called the Green Room, and that was where most of the farmers gathered. You paid an extra penny on your pint, mind you, but you got service for that'.

'Table service, you mean?'

'Yes. You paid extra, but you got service'.

'And you're sure you haven't heard anything about the ghost?'

'I've drank here since I was a young un', and I honestly can't remember hearing anything about a ghost'.

Sadly, Mike could tell that Pip was telling the truth. If there had been talk of apparitions in the Lord Nelson, then they'd passed him by when he wasn't looking.

There was a menu on the table, and both Mrs H and Mike decided to stay for lunch. In retrospect Mike later said that it was one of the best instinctive decisions he'd made whilst carrying out his research.

Mike confesses to being something of a connoisseur when it comes to pub grub. He's not easily pleased, and has a built-in abhorrence for poor cuisine. Serve him with a battered cod swimming in grease, for example, and he begins to get violent thoughts and/or a desire for retribution. This may include putting in an official complaint to the brewery or, if he is so disposed, tying the chef to a chair and making him or her swallow the thing whole.

Jackie chose the ploughman's lunch, Mike the scampi and French fries. Both meals were served promptly by a smiling waitress-cum-barmaid who actually looked as if she enjoyed her job – another rare commodity nowadays.

The ploughman's lunch was something to behold. The salad was fresh, crisp and plentiful, containing slices of carefully cut pepper and juicy tomato wedges. It was complimented by three triangles of cheese – mature cheddar, Danish blue and Cheshire – which could easily have fed a family of five for a week. Resting on the side of the platter – which wasn't far short of being the size of bicycle wheel – sat a crusty cob of *QE2* proportions. And then there was the cole slaw; a generous helping of real cole slaw, mind you, and not the bitter pap that one is often served, tasting like elastic bands which have been marinated in battery acid.

And Mike's meal was no less inviting; huge, beautifully battered pieces of real scampi which were nothing short of perfect in size, texture and taste. Only at the Marsden Grotto had Mike ever tasted pub grub like this. For those of you whose idea of cuisine is three anchovies artfully arranged on a plate beside a sliver of watermelon, we would say do not visit the Lord Nelson. Your sensibilities will undoubtedly be offended.

After settling the bill and saying farewell to Pip, Mrs H. and Mike ventured outside to take some photographs of the inn's exterior. Just before he started clicking the shutter, it suddenly dawned on him that he hadn't asked for a receipt. Mrs H. and Mike went back inside to rectify matters, which turned out to be their second good decision of the day.

The barmaid turned out to be the same person who'd served them with their first drink on entering the Lord Nelson, and she had mentioned then that she had heard one or two stories about a ghost. Possibly a woman, she recalled, and maybe she'd been seen upstairs. But she couldn't be sure. She also had difficulty printing the receipt, and solicited the help of a male colleague behind the bar.

'This gentleman is researching ghost stories, and he'd heard about the one which is supposed to be here in the Nelson', she told him.

'Really?' he replied, 'Then you should have a word with chef – she's seen it'.

At this point Mike's astral antennae started twitching like mad, and I knew that his luck was in.

'Can I speak with her?'

'No problem. She'll be out in a minute'.

Kath Reynolds was the person who had transported Mike and his wife into a state of culinary nirvana, and now it seemed that she was also going to put some flesh on the bones of what had, until that point, been something of a non-story. Her tale was simple, but interesting nonetheless.

Kath and her husband had moved to Monkton village in 1989, her employment at the Nelson commencing some time thereafter. One day she was sitting in the bar when she saw a man behind the counter. The years have naturally dulled her memory of the incident somewhat regarding details, but she recalls that he looked 'completely normal, not like a ghost at all'.

Kath recalls that he was dressed in completely conventional and contemporary clothing – an open-necked shirt and slacks, she thinks. As she looked at him, the man just walked from one end of the counter to the other and promptly disappeared.

Paranormal researchers are, obviously, in their element when listening to tales of spectral pirates and ghostly Cavaliers. Their period-style dress and demeanour enchant the imagination, and sometimes we can become a little disappointed when an apparition presents itself in an entirely conventional way. But there is another side to the story. The ghosts of people who have died relatively recently are easier to research and identify, and the simplicity of both the tale and its telling can often be a hallmark of authenticity.

Kath had asked several drinkers in the bar if they had seen the man, but none had, despite the fact that he must have walked right past them. Who was he? The spectre of a past landlord? No one knows, and if Pip Stonehouse is unable to say it is unlikely that anyone else will have an answer.

Mrs H. and Mike left the Lord Nelson and basked in the sunlight once again. As they headed off down the road towards Stonehouse's corner shop – Mike wanted to take a sentimental glance at the place – they agreed that this friendly inn has a unique charisma and personality. Are there spectres within its walls? The authors think so, and await their next appearance eagerly. They just hope someone lets them know when it happens.

In-depth Case Study: The Manor House, Ferryhill
Good Ghost Rating: 10

The Manor House in Ferryhill lies roughly 7 miles south of the city of Durham. In the sixteenth century, when first erected, the building served as a farmhouse. In 1642, a certain John Wilkinson sold it to one John Shawe, and when Shawe died ownership passed to his grandson, Ralph. By the early 1700s, the house and surrounding land had been through a succession of owners. However, by 1885 only the house remained as the land had been sold on to a local colliery. In 1891 the building was fully renovated and subsequently occupied by a man called Henry Palmer. Since Palmer's death it has been rented and/or owned by many other occupants. In 2001 a family bought the premises and turned the Manor House into a thriving hotel, which is still open to this day.

This sixteenth century one-time orphanage, manor house and now hotel is reputedly haunted by a number of ghosts and spirits that once had some connection with the locality. The spectre of a woman is said to amble along the stairwell looking for her child. Those who have seen her claim that she looks as if she is in anguish. It is also said that the bones of several youngsters were found buried in the grounds adjacent to the house, leading some researchers to hint at the possibility of murder.

Rooms 7 and 8 have also been subjected to extremely aggressive poltergeist-like activity and spectral apparitions have on occasion resulted in the present owners becoming quite literally terrified. Other investigations and two attempts at exorcism – which did not succeed – did nothing to curtail the strange phenomena in the residence. In fact, things became decidedly worse afterwards.

One inclement Saturday night several years ago, a team of researchers from G.H.O.S.T. plus a few selected guests, carried out an investigation which Darren actually attended as a member of the team.

The researchers arrived at approximately 8.30pm and were shown rooms 7 and 8. They made themselves comfortable and then carried out their preliminary checks. A temperature drop of 4° was noted and both Darren and a Drew Bartley recorded very high readings on their EMF meters over both of the beds in Room 8. No anomalies were detected in Room 7 and the adjoining corridors. The average temperature sat around 20° in the bedrooms and 25° in the corridors.

The team then set up a trigger object in Room 7 and a 'flour tray' experiment in Room 8. The trigger object in Room 7 was a crucifix. The flour tray experiment consisted of a long, plastic tub of flour placed upon a sturdy surface. A number of objects were then carefully placed into the flour. The objects consisted of several crystals and a red lollipop, as some of the spectres were said to be those of young children.

The team then split into two groups and began the investigation proper. For a while nothing seemed to happen. Then, later during the vigil, the researchers started to hear the odd click or tapping noise. The distinct odour of vomit was also detected by the investigators.

After the 'split vigils' the team members all regrouped back in Room 8. Earlier in that location it had been reported that the motion detectors placed in the doorway had been turned around whilst the investigators present were sitting upon a bed. Strangely, the detectors were not activated when the beam was broken. After a short discussion it was decided that it might be of some value to attempt a séance in that room. Before the séance took place, several light anomalies were recorded on the night vision video camera and an intense feeling of something or someone present in the room was noted by the investigators.

Darren and fellow investigator Drew Bartley did not take place in the séance, but monitored the proceedings whilst the rest of the group sat in the circle and attempted to make contact with who or whatever may have been in the room.

Prior to the séance beginning, Darren had the presence of mind to take a control photograph of the flour tray containing the ten crystals the red lollipop. He also took several other photographs of the room for further analysis and reference.

The séance began when Suzanne Hitchinson, the North East Ghost Research Team psychic, became aware of a 'spirit presence'. She sensed the proximity of two children, a boy and a girl, and said they were related to each other. Suzanne actually asked the children if they would like a lollipop, and told them that they were welcome to take the one the team had left as a trigger object in the flour. After a minute or so, Darren shone his torch onto the flour tray to see if there had been any movement of the objects. He was not disappointed. He had noticed that the flour had indeed been disturbed, as if someone had literally dragged two or three fingers through it, thus leaving it piled up at one side of the tray. The real surprise came when they noticed that the red lollipop had completely vanished from within the tray! Darren was monitoring the séance from the area where the trigger objects were located, and so knew that no one had touched it. Drew Bartley was on the other side of the room, and everyone else was sitting in the séance. So, who took the lollipop? It does not take a great leap of faith to assume that it was probably one of the spirit children.

The disappearance of the lollipop was a first for the team. During many of the trigger object experiments they had set up over the years, some did indeed move from their positions, but only slightly – perhaps an inch at the most. However, in this case the object had completely vanished and was taken away from under their noses never to be seen again.

Later Darren commented, 'I can assure everyone that no one touched the flour tray objects. Everyone turned out their pockets and was checked for the presence of flour on their hands and clothes as a precautionary measure. Everyone turned out to be 'clean', physically and metaphorically, but we always knew that this would be the case'.

Interestingly, patches of flour were later found on the carpet. One, near the door, was identical in size and shape to the missing lollipop.

The investigators also found traces of flour in the bathroom, outside on the landing and down the stairs in the corridor. The researchers could only conclude that it had been taken from the flour tray by the spirit children before they transported it out of the room, into the corridor and down the stairwell. After all, the investigators knew that no one living had left the room whilst they were present. This incident baffled the team members, and they all became convinced that they had experienced genuine ghostly phenomena. Those present were so impressed, in fact, and spent the rest of the night talking it as well as trying to locate the missing lollipop. They never found it.

There is an interesting postscript to the lollipop tale. Before the investigators realised that it was missing from the flour tray, Darren took a number of photographs of the séance as it progressed. He also took one of Drew Bartley. When Darren analysed the picture of Drew the following day he noticed something decidedly odd. Behind Drew, on the floor, could distinctly be seen the red lollipop!

Darren has stated categorically that neither Drew nor anyone else would have been able to remove the lollipop from the flour tray without his knowledge. Darren has concluded that the lollipop must have been removed from the tray by the 'spirit children' – the only persons present who would have been able to remove it without Darren spotting them. Darren believes that they must also have dropped it onto the floor near where Drew was standing and then removed it for a second time later.

The investigation certainly proved interesting, and some of the best results ever ascertained by the team had been forthcoming that evening. Although the malevolent entity that is also said to reside in Room 8 never did manifest itself in the way the investigators had hoped, the spirit children really did themselves proud. If you ever decide to book into Room 8 at the Manor House in Ferryhill, make sure that you don't leave your lollipops lying around....

- **PUB:** THE MARQUIS OF GRANBY
- **LOCATION:** WHICKHAM
- **GOOD GHOST RATING:** 7

On an interior wall of the Marquis of Granby pub there is the story of the resident ghost. The pub is situated on Streetgate in Sunniside, near the Ravensworth Castle estate. The inn stands en-route to probably the earliest wagonway in the north-east – which was created around 1700. The pub was used as a stop-off for rest and recuperation and was once called The Granby Arms. The ghost is said to be that of an old woman that appears in various places in the pub but more often than not she is in one of the bedrooms in the private living area. She has allegedly been encountered by almost every landlord and landlady dating back to the late 1800s. The very first sighting was witnessed by more than one person.

It is also said a murder took place here in 1865, but details are vague and no one knows who the murderer was although there were suspicions. A chap called Joseph Leybourne was brutally killed after an ongoing feud that came to a head one night after a drunken brawl. It is believed that whoever killed the victim did so by striking him on the head with a sharp and heavy slab of stone, which was found covered with his blood and hair, near to where his lifeless body was discovered. It is said this chap – Joseph Leybourne – also haunts the inn and the surrounding area, perhaps looking for the murderer who so unjustly took his life all those years ago.

In-depth Case Study: The Marsden Grotto (Smuggler Jack's) South Shields
Good Ghost Rating: 10

Believed by some to be the most haunted pub in Britain, the Marsden Grotto cave bar is a public house situated at the foot of the limestone cliffs of Marsden Bay, South Shields, Tyne & Wear. There is an imposing lift shaft which takes the inn's patrons from the cliff top down to the beach below. For those who do not know, the Grotto is actually built into the foot of the cliff face itself. For quite some time now Mike has been researching the history of this strange dwelling, and has recently had a book published on the subject (*The House That Jack Built*, Amberley Publishing, 2008). What you are about to read here is a synopsis; a brief history of the Grotto and the characters who have inhabited it over the centuries. The authors will also tell you of its ghosts.

In the mid-1700s, a lead miner called Jack Bates from Allenheads, Northumberland, arrived at South Shields (then in County Durham) with his wife Jessie. He gained work as a quarryman at Marsden, and later retired. In 1782 Jack and Jessie were, at the age of eighty, evicted by an unscrupulous landlord. Having nowhere else to go, they took refuge in a small cave in the cliff face at Marsden Bay which faces directly onto the tempestuous North Sea. Despite his age, Jack blasted a set of steps in the cliff face to afford both he and his wife easier access. For this reason the old miner was – and still is – known as Blaster Jack. Before too long they had turned their cave into a comfortable dwelling which was, to quote one local toff, "delightfully quaint". Jack added windows and a door, and furnished the home with items salvaged from wrecks and with furniture which he'd made himself from driftwood.

Jack and his wife then went one step further, and turned misfortune into favour by enlarging the cave and opening a small café which sold tea and refreshments to the summer tourists. Jack had seen potential for making money, and in the warmer months he and his wife entertained their visitors as well as providing them with tea, scones, 'singin' hinnies' and spice cakes – at a price. You could also purchase gin, ale and porter 'from under the counter' if you were discreet. To enhance their income, Jack and his wife also engaged in poaching, fishing and acting as look-outs for the local smugglers.

For ten years, dignitaries from the surrounding towns and cities – Newcastle, Sunderland, South Shields – came to marvel at "the cave dwellers", and when the couple died in 1792 they were moderately wealthy.

The 'house in the cliff' was left abandoned and uninhabitable until 1826, when a man called Peter Allan renovated the derelict establishment and made it habitable once more. He named it The Tam O' Shanter, but it was not long before it was renamed The Marsden Grotto. During his time there the smugglers of the day would often frequent Marsden Bay, and they actually became friendly with the landlord. It is almost certain that the smugglers used the nearby caves as a hideaway for themselves and their contraband.

At some point a protracted legal battle broke out between Peter Allan and a group of local dignitaries, led by none other than John Clay, the first mayor of South Shields. Clay and his pals were fuelled by a complex mixture of motives, the primary one being that, in ancient times, Roman legionnaires from the nearby Arbeia fort had stashed away a large hoard of treasure in the cliffs at Marsden. Clay wanted to gain control of the Grotto, believing that Peter Allan was already way ahead of them in the search for hidden treasure. In the final event neither side won. Clay would eventually gain control of the Grotto, the courts decided, but only after more than two decades had passed by, as Allan was granted a lease for the interim. Clay was frustrated because his plans would have to be delayed for over twenty years. Allan was broken-hearted that he would eventually have to give up the Grotto, which he had planned to hand on to his children. Days after the court hearing he took to his bed and 'pined awa', eventually dying of a broken heart'.

Since Peter Allan's death the Grotto has changed hands several times, and seen a succession of tenants and managers come through its ancient doors. Few, if any, have stayed there without experiencing paranormal activity of some kind. The reader should note that the ghost tales attached to the Grotto have, over the centuries, become confused. Indeed, it took Mike eighteen months of solid research to untangle them and get to the truth.

The most famous tale associated with the Grotto concerns the Smuggler's Tankard. In fact, there are two separate legends attached to this pewter drinking vessel, both of which the authors will relate here.

One of the regular drinkers at the Tam O'Shanter, as it was then called, was a smuggler who's name is now lost to us. By all accounts he was a young man who possessed a devil-may-care attitude and who enjoyed the dancing and drinking which had become part of the Tam O'Shanter scene. One evening he was standing at the second bar, which Peter had erected in the large cave known as the Ballroom, enjoying a pint of ale. He was drinking from a plain but well-crafted pewter tankard. Having one's own tankard in the bar was a sign of some status. It identified the drinker as a regular who was known to, and accepted by, the management.

A review of the contemporary evidence indicates that the young lad had already had a bit to drink. Perhaps because his senses were somewhat dulled by alcohol, they did not set any alarm bells ringing when a polite and friendly stranger idled up to him and offered to buy him a drink. Why not, he thought?

The two chatted for a while, and the stranger enquired politely as to what his new-found drinking partner did for a living. Was he a farmer, perhaps, or a fisherman? The young man sniggered: not much, but enough to draw the attention of Peter Allan who was himself behind the bar and serving the ale that evening. The youngster went on to tell the gregarious stranger that he was, in fact, a smuggler.

To Peter Allan's dismay, the young contrabander then proceeded to divulge to the stranger the most guarded secrets of local smuggling operations. Peter had no way of knowing whether the man was an Excise man or not. He certainly didn't recognise him, but that counted for nothing. The boy was playing with fire.

Even though by now in an alcoholic stupor, the smuggler suddenly seems to have realised that the stranger who was plying him with beer seemed unusually interested in what he had to say. It was too late, for now he felt the barrel of a pistol pressing firmly into his ribs. The stranger, who obviously had been a Preventive or Excise man, told him he was under arrest.

Horrified at what he had done, the smuggler reacted and lashed out at the Preventive. The blow caught the officer on the head and he fell backwards towards the floor. By this time the smuggler was already taking off through the door which led from the Ballroom onto the wooden patio outside. With one leap he vaulted over the sea wall and landed upon the beach. He had to escape, but the question was which way to run? South was out of the question. The tide was in, and he could go no more that one hundred yards before hitting a large outcrop which would bar his escape along the beach to Whitburn. He would have to head north towards South Shields.

Despite being drunk the youth built up an impressive speed. The wet sand and shale was substantially firmer underfoot, and if he could make it to the myriad of caves which encircled the area known as Velvet Beds he could hide in any one of them. There, the Excise men could search for a year and a day and still not find him.

By the time the young smuggler had made his mind up which way to take off, the officer was already in hot pursuit. As he chased after the smuggler he was watched by a crowd of gawking farmers, fishermen and smugglers. And of course, a distinctly worried Peter Allan.

Breathing deeply, the Preventive raced across the sand but the man was still pulling away from him. At this point that he made a decision which would colour the legend of Marsden Bay forever. He raised his pistol and carefully took aim. The smuggler turned around to see how close his pursuer was. Seeing that the officer's pistol was raised and pointing directly at him he turned to run again, but it was too late. The ball of hot lead hit him directly between the shoulder blades. In all probability he was dead before he hit the ground.

According to legend, the stricken smuggler fell next to a large, stone pillar which has graced Marsden beach for untold centuries. It is a natural formation, over twenty feet in height, and has the appearance of an elongated salt cellar. For as long as anyone can remember, the pillar has been known as Lot's Wife.

Back inside the pub, Peter asked beckoned to his wife Elizabeth and asked her to fetch his toolbox. Once it was placed on top of the bar he removed his hammer and a large nail. Taking up the hammer, Peter drove the nail into the limestone wall of the bar. Then his eyes fell upon the pewter tankard which also stood upon the bar exactly where the smuggler had left it. It was still half-filled with beer. Solemnly, the landlord poured out the remainder of the ale the floor and then hung the tankard upon the nail. Incandescent with rage, Peter then instructed everyone present, 'Let no man drink from this tankard from this day forth, lest he be accursed.'

Over the centuries, several people have broken this rule and drunk from the tankard. Mike's research has indicated that, on each occasion, a disaster of some kind rapidly followed. On one occasion a 'flash flood' filled the bar with seawater. The damage was so extensive that a complete refit of fixtures and fittings was required.

On another occasion – Tuesday, February 8, 1996, to be precise – the southerly aspect of the arched Marsden Rock collapsed entirely.

Ever since the tankard was hung on the wall of the bar by Peter Allan it has been the focus of both suspicion and negative attention. Peter himself set the tone, of course, when he uttered that rather chilling curse.

We know that a great deal of superstition surrounded the tankard from that day onwards. The vessel seems to have been treated reverently by Peter Allan and his successors, indicating that they believed to do otherwise would bring 'bad luck'. Even so, there is little indication that the tankard was actually associated with the alleged ghostly activity at the pub until after Peter's death.

In 1874 the pub was taken over by one Sidney Milnes Hawkes and, in 1898, Vaux & Sons, a local brewers, leased the building. Eventually they took it over completely in 1938. In fact, it is only after the arrival of Sidney Milnes-Hawkes that the tankard seems to have begun to influence life at The Grotto at all.

Early one morning – one account says it was a Saturday, but we can't be sure – Hawkes was polishing the glasses and tankards which stood behind the bar. At some point he removed the Smuggler's Tankard from its nail and started shine it with a cloth, but as he did so he began to hear a peculiar rattling sound. To Sidney, it sounded for all the world as if someone had dropped a pebble on the roof. He ignored it. But then the sound returned, and louder than before. Now it sounded as if handfuls of pebbles were being thrown onto the roof. Naturally curious, put down the Smuggler's Tankard on the bar and went outside to investigate.

When Milnes-Hawkes looked up upon the roof he could see absolutely nothing, and yet as soon as he put his head inside the door it sounded as if a torrential hailstorm was in progress. Milnes-Hawkes knew that what he was witnessing was neither normal nor explicable. Puzzled, the landlord sloped back inside, once more surrounded by the cacophony of thousands of invisible pebbles bouncing off the roof.

If the bizarre sounds outdoors were disturbing Milnes-Hawkes, they were nothing compared with what was to follow. On returning to the bar he was dumbfounded to see that the Smugglers' Tankard had been actually been filled with ale. Stunned, he simply walked away and found some other tasks to take care of.

Later, his duties required that he returned to the bar. To his further astonishment he found that the tankard which had been so mysteriously filled with beer was, now, just as mysteriously drained! That evening, after the inn had closed, Milnes-Hawkes placed yet another tankard of Scotch ale on the bar for 'the ghost'. The following morning it was empty – and thus began the tradition of leaving out the Smuggler's Tankard full of ale every evening.

From that time, every tenant or manager of the Marsden Grotto kept up the tradition of leaving a drink on the bar for the spectral bibber. Some mornings the tankard would still be full of beer; on others it would be drained of every drop. Sometimes 'the ghost' would drink half of the ale and leave the rest in the tankard. Because Sidney Milnes-Hawkes was the manager of The Grotto when the tradition first began, there was been a house-rule that only the manager of the pub could touch the tankard unless he happened to be away on business or vacation. Then the duty would fall to the next senior member of staff, or whoever was left in charge. Other customs dictated the brand of beer that should be left out. Scotch seemed to be the ghost's favourite tipple, although from time to time he would gladly down brown ale or a fine-conditioned cask ale as a special treat. Curiously, under no circumstances would the spectre drink lager – a beverage that, in life, he would not have been familiar with. On one occasion, after being left a tankard of ale that was not to his liking, he made his displeasure known by tipping over two tables in the bar and smashing several pieces of crockery in the kitchen. There is a story in circulation that strong cider was once left in his tankard by way of an experiment, and that he drank a little of it and did not, apparently, kick up a fuss.

The entity connected with the tankard – the authors think it reasonable to henceforth refer to him as 'the Smuggler' – could become quite annoyed if his tankard of ale was not left according to custom and tradition. However, unlike occasions when the tankard was actually drunk from, the consequences never seem to have been disastrous. When forced to go without his ale he merely seems to have thrown a temper tantrum.

Many years ago, so the story goes, one landlord became rather lackadaisical about leaving the Smuggler's ale out at night. On the first two occasions nothing happened – perhaps the Smuggler was away doing whatever ghosts do when they aren't engaged in haunting, or maybe he has a tolerant streak, who knows. However, on the third evening the tenant was woken up by the sound of a tremendous clattering. He ran downstairs and entered the bar, fully expecting to find some intruders present. Instead he was confronted by a scene of absolute chaos. Tables and chairs had been overturned and a number of glasses broken. Ashtrays had been thrown around and, inexplicably, dozens of fresh eggs had been cracked upon the carpet. But there was more. On the bar stood the empty tankard. Invisible hands had seemingly removed it from its normal resting place and left it there, the message to the landlord being blatantly obvious – don't forget to leave out my pint of ale.

The next evening the landlord, erring on the side of caution, filled the tankard with ale and dutifully left upon the counter. Order was restored, the Smuggler's thirst was quenched. As long as the ale was left out, there was never any bother.

How seriously can we take the legend surrounding the tankard? Well, in June 1999 Mike decided to put it to the test.

Mike and a former friend spent a night in the Grotto with the (then) landlord, Nick Garvey. After closing time and the last of the patrons had departed, Nick and his family engaged in some cleaning and tidying up. By midnight, only Nick, Mike and the other chap remained in the bar. Naturally they struck up a conversation and got round to covering some interesting topics – psychic phenomena, the nature of apparitions, dowsing and other rather Fortean subjects. Politics also came into the conversation on several occasions too, as Mike recalls. At about 2am Nick remembered that they had actually forgotten to fill the tankard, which is embarrassing, considering that verifying the stories concerning it was the entire point of the exercise. Hastily, but not without due ceremony, the landlord filled up the tankard and placed it upon the bar in what was then known as the Copenhagen Room. At 3.20am they checked the tankard. The beer, now somewhat flat, was still there. Just before 4am, Mike's colleague heard a faint sound like a crate of bottles crashing to the floor, and they investigated. The noise seemed to be coming from the Back Bar, or Cave Bar, as it was generally called. Nothing seemed out of place. At 5.20am they all went into the Copenhagen Room together, via the bar, and watched as Nick picked up the tankard. To the astonishment of all present it was dry. Mike and his colleague took photographs of the tankard, and noticed that the lip of the pewter receptacle was totally devoid of moisture. The tankard had obviously not just been emptied. Both Mike and his colleague later testified that no one – and we mean no one – approached that tankard before Nick picked it up.

Sadly, the tankard was stolen from the inn whilst it was closed for repair and renovation. Later, three separate spirit mediums claimed that the tankard was located in a caravan. Intriguingly, there are several caravan sites in the area, some of them close to The Grotto itself.

Jibber John is another well-known Grotto character who is sometimes confused with Blaster Jack, Peter Allan and the aforementioned unknown smuggler whose young life was ended so tragically. What we are about to relate is the true story, or at least the legend stripped of its historical impossibilities and errors, which is, admittedly, not quite the same thing.

John was a member of the smuggling gang which operated out of Marsden Bay. At some point, it seems, his comrades began to have doubts about him. Perhaps he just seemed to have a little too much money in his pockets. Maybe he'd been seen in the wrong company, who knows. But suspicion set in. Someone was tipping off the Excise Men, and John became the chief suspect.

The gang was not about to wreak revenge on one of their own without having incontrovertible proof that he was guilty. Even the smugglers had some standards. So they decided to test John out. One of the leading lights in the crew had a covert meeting with John, probably in the Marsden Grotto itself, and told him that a consignment of rum and tobacco was coming in from abroad the following Wednesday. All hands were needed to help in the offloading operation; was he up for the job? John declined. He had other business to attend to, but thanked his fellow smuggler for the offer.

What John didn't know was that John was the only person to be told, up to that point, exactly what cargo was being delivered, when it was arriving and where. If the Excise got wind of the delivery and turned up, then only one man could have been responsible for the treachery; John. To cover themselves, the smugglers posted look-outs along the shore at Jackie's Cove at Whitburn – where the drop-off was being made – to give an early warning should the authorities make a show. Each look-out was accompanied by two large dogs, and had been instructed, at first sight of the Excise, to discharge his gun and order the dogs to bark. Hopefully, one noise or the other would alert the captain of the vessel bearing the contraband that the authorities had arrived.

Sure enough, the Excise turned up on cue. However, as soon as the first musket shot echoed across the bay, the smugglers put a well-rehearsed plan into action. Firstly, the captain of the lugger lying just offshore veered away. As fast as the wind would take him, he made for Souter Point. The smugglers below on the beach disappeared into a series of hidey-holes which had been previously prepared.

The Preventives realised that they had been rumbled. All that remained now was to work out where the lugger was headed. Ironically, they discounted Souter Point as being too dangerous an option – which in real terms it was – but forgot to take into account the bravado of the sea-smugglers, who were more than prepared to take the risk of being grounded on the perilous rocks. Shortly afterwards, whilst the Preventives were scouring Marsden Bay, the smugglers were off-loading their precious cargo at Souter Point.

From this point onwards, the fate of John was sealed. Only he could have tipped off the Excise. For that he would pay an exceedingly high price indeed.

The following day, several smugglers called on John and asked him to help them move some contraband. When he asked where the contraband was stored, he was told Smugglers' Cave at Marsden Bay.

At this juncture we need to detail something of the nature of Smugglers' Cave. There were, and still are, many caves at Marsden Bay. Two of them however, in times past, shared an unusual feature. Smugglers' Cave, to the south, was an extremely large cavern which sat just a short distance in that direction from the Grotto Inn. To the north, near the outcrop known as Velvet Beds, stood another large cave known as the Hairy Man's Cavern. Neither cave exists, both having collapsed long ago. Both caves had a strange, vertical shaft which went from the roof of the cavern to the cliff top some one hundred and twenty feet above. Whether these shafts were man-made or natural fissures has long been debated. Personally I believe that the former option is more likely, but I digress. The point to make is that Smuggler's Cave had such a shaft, and that it would now be put to macabre use by the smugglers who so detested John's treachery.

On entering the cave with his fellow smugglers, John was pistol-whipped into unconsciousness. He was then forced into a barrel – some say a wicker basket – and hauled halfway up the shaft by a rope. He was left there for sixty days, only lowered down occasionally to be given the odd scrap of bread or mouthful of water. He was not even allowed out of the barrel/ basket to perform ablutions, so one can only try to imagine the appalling state the man was in after two months.

Eventually John expired, mercifully, and the smugglers continued about their business. However, before long there were dark rumours circulating that the traitorous contrabander had come back to haunt his persecutors. John had been branded 'John the Jibber', or 'Jibber John', jibber being a colloquialism similar to the modern 'dobber', which means cheat, turncoat or traitor. Unearthly moans could be heard coming from the interior of the cave, even when it was deserted. Passers-by decided not to pass by, and gave the cave a wide berth.

To this day, even though the cave has long since collapsed, reports of strange moaning sounds emanating from that locality still trickle in. Some years ago a rather well-known football player – a striker for Sunderland AFC – was unnerved to hear wails and shrieks which 'sounded like a man being tortured' as he walked nearby on the beach.

Is there any validity to such stories? From an entirely subjective point of view we have to say that there may well be. Several times Mike stayed overnight at the Marsden Grotto whilst researching material for this and other books. One occasion, in June 2000, was the most memorable. Over a dozen researchers and investigators, including Mike, 'staked out' the Grotto in an effort to witness some of the paranormal phenomena which allegedly takes place there. The vigil was well-organised, and produced some interesting results which were later featured in two documentaries.

At one point in the evening Mike began to feel tired and decided to go for a walk along the coast. On leaving The Grotto he turned right and headed for the direction of Smugglers' Cave.

Marsden Bay at night is awesome. Illuminated only by starlight and moonlight, the bay reverberates to the sound of crashing waves, howling winds and screeching gulls. Nature is king at Marsden Bay.

Mike found a rock and sat down, staring out across the ocean. This was a peaceful place, he thought. And then, suddenly, the wind dropped. Not partially, but totally. There was an eerie silence, not even punctured by the screeching seabirds, for they had gone silent too. In fact, other than the waves, he only heard one sound – a sickening thud immediately to his right. He jumped. Something heavy had landed right beside him. And yet, search as he might, he could find no sign of anything having landed on the sand. He also detected what he later described as a 'malign presence' which disturbed him greatly.

So what did he hear? Strictly speaking we have to confess that we simply do not know. The fact that the wind stopped so suddenly (and then resumed again immediately afterwards), coupled with the strange silence of the birds, leads us to conclude that the episode may have been more supernatural than mundane. Marsden cliffs have, unfortunately, been the scene of many suicides over the years. Troubled souls have often ended their inner torment by throwing themselves from the cliff top to the rocks below. Did Mike hear a macabre echo of a past suicide – the sound of a human being's life being snuffed out as their body collided with the beach? Perhaps. Or maybe he heard the sound of Jibber John's body being cut down from the shaft and falling down to the cave's interior. Yet another ghostly – and ghastly – reminder of the fact that not all of Marsden Bay's past has been happy. Mike promptly returned to the Grotto and rejoined his colleagues.

But we have by no means exhausted The Grotto's repertoire of ghostly goings-on. Other spectres have been seen on numerous occasions, and this volume would be woefully incomplete if we refrained from mentioning them.

When Nick Garvey and his family moved into The Grotto, they quickly became aware that something strange was going on within the confines of this strange, old pub. One day before opening, Nick entered the gents' lavatory and immediately noticed something odd. All the disinfectant cubes (Nick called them pineapple cubes, because they were yellow) which had been placed in the urinal trough had been removed and placed on the floor in a neat circle. No one could have done this, Nick assured Mike that he checked the toilets that evening and was the first to go in there the following morning. This bizarre habit of rearranging common objects into geometrical shapes is common with poltergeists, although no one is sure why it happens. The authors think it may be a subconscious effort on the part of the 'focus' in the case to demonstrate that there is an intelligence behind the phenomenon. A screeching noise may be dismissed as faulty piping. A whistling noise may be put down to a draught. A plate toppling from a shelf may be dismissed as the fault of a heavy lorry going past and making the shelf vibrate. But geometric patterns formed by invisible hands from everyday objects cannot be so easily rationalised.

Nick told Mike that the entity in The Grotto – what or whoever you may consider it to be – could be unusually helpful when the mood took him/her/ it. He gave Mike an example of this.

Periodically new beers would arrive at the pub to add a little variety to those already on sale. Just prior to their arrival, Nick would receive a box containing some fancy metal badges or plaques bearing either the logo of the beer or its manufacturer. These badges were then attached to the beer pumps which deliver that particular brand so that the public is aware of them. Sometimes, said Nick, the badges would arrive without the small retaining clips that secured them to the pumps. This meant that either Nick, Sue or one of their staff would have to search through a box full of old clips to see if they could find one to fit. One night, Nick opened a parcel containing some new badges when he noticed, to his irritation, that the retaining clips were missing. He searched through all the old clips but could not find one to fit. Tired, he simply put the old clips away and went to bed. The next morning he came down to open up the pub and saw – as soon as he walked through the door – a retaining clip lying in the middle of the floor. Later he told Mike, "I knew it definitely hadn't been there the night before. If I'd dropped it I would have heard it hit the floor, but in any case it wasn't where I'd been standing. It was as if it had been strategically placed there so I would see it as soon as I entered the bar.

"I knew before I even tried the clip that it would fit the badge. Things happen like this all the time. You can sense that it's trying to help you."

There is also one particular spot at the bar which, by tradition, "belongs to the ghost". If someone stands there and the spectre is around, he'll tap you firmly on the shoulder in an effort to get you to move. Most people do, and quickly. Several times whilst drinking at The Grotto Mike has stood at the bar in the hope that he would experience that paranormal prompt from the ghost, but to date nothing has ever happened. Maybe the spectre and he are like ships that pass in the night – never in the bar at the same time.

The first paranormal encounter Nick Garvey had in the Marsden Grotto took him by surprise. He was in the kitchen adjacent to the restaurant on the first floor when he noticed a black and white cat in the middle of the floor. Concerned at this inadvertent breach of the hygiene regulations, he immediately went to get hold of the creature and put it out. Well, that was the plan. Unfortunately it did not come to fruition, for his hands passed straight through its body as if there was nothing there. At that point, Nick realised he was dealing not with a flesh-and-blood feline, but with something of a stranger nature altogether. Stunned, he watched as the cat walked straight through the refrigerator nearby and, presumably, through the wall beyond it.

Nick is not the only one to have encountered the ghost cat. Drinkers playing the one-arm bandits in the bar have often felt it brush up against their legs, just as a real cat would do. Just before Nick and his family departed from the Grotto, he was approached by an irate customer who wished to remonstrate with him.

'I think it's a bit hypocritical, actually. You've put a notice up there saying 'NO DOGS ALLOWED', and yet you'll let your cat wander all over the place'.

'And which cat are you referring to, exactly?' replied Nick.

'That black and white one standing on the...'

'Yes?'

'It's gone'.

Nick told the gentleman concerned not to worry, as spectral cats were not thought to be a health hazard.

Other, more conventional ghosts have been seen in the Grotto. A former barman told Mike he had seen the face of a bearded man with curly hair staring at him in the restaurant. Mike later found a rare portrait of Peter Allan, and it matched his description perfectly.

The shade of one of Peter Allan's daughters was also seen in the 1920s, standing at the foot of the stone stairwell which leads to what was then referred to as the Circular Room, but which now is called the Cocktail Bar.

Darren Ritson has also been hunting down spectres and spooks at the Grotto, along with his colleagues from The Answers People Seek (TAPS) and fellow researchers The North East Ghost Research Team.

During their vigil at the Grotto the team was subjected to the usual array of strange noises, weird lights, temperature changes and even phantom apparitions. Chains even rattled in one or two places in a thoroughly Dickensian fashion. However, what intrigued Mike about this investigation were the names 'picked up' psychically by some of the researchers, as he was able to check their authenticity against the hundreds of historical documents he's accumulated in his archives about the history of the pub.

Two investigators – Suzanne and Glenn – ascertained the presence of a young boy called Samuel. Samuel was apparently ten years old when he lost his life during a rock-fall from the cliffs nearby.

What we do know is that rock-falls were not uncommon at Marsden Bay. In fact, in 1865 a near disaster occurred when huge boulders broke away and demolished the cottage adjacent to the pub. The Allan family, who ran the Grotto at the time, were lucky to escape with their lives. There are two mentions of deaths being precipitated by such falls, although names are not recorded. The idea that one of them could be young 'Samuel' is a tantalising possibility.

Another researcher picked up on the name 'Jossie', and Darren speculated that this could have been actually been 'Jessie'. The first inhabitants of the cave where the Grotto now stands were Jack 'the blaster' Bates and his wife. Her name? As previously detailed, it was Jessie.

However, there is another intriguing possibility. In 1842, two Grotto 'regulars' from Sunderland had a falling out. One chap was a magistrate by the name of Richard Spurr, the other 'a professional man' called Joseph 'Jossie' Wright. A duel was fought, but neither man was hurt, as the landlady Lizzie Allan had substituted the lead balls in their guns with wads of cotton!

Was this the 'Jossie' picked up by the investigators? It's tempting to think so.

Another researcher put forward the name Archie. This could have been Archibald Allan, brother of landlord Peter, who was born on 4 May 1803. A more likely candidate, however, is Peter's son, also called Archibald, who was born in 1836.

One of the most interesting names to be suggested was that of Catherine. There is no Catherine associated with the Grotto directly, but the author Catherine Cookson visited there many times and alluded to the Grotto (and the mysteries surrounding it) in her novel The Harrogate Secret. Better, she based her work Mrs. Flannagan's Trumpet on it directly.

Another researcher 'got the impression of a long, bustling dress'. In fact, Lizzie Allan was photographed on two occasions in just such dresses, and her ghost has been seen at the Grotto on numerous occasions.

Finally, one investigator saw 'a man in a black suit standing with his hands clasped behind his back, wearing white gloves'.

Mike is convinced that this may have been the ghost of Peter Allan Sr, who was a Scots Presbyterian and always dressed in black. Although a gentleman, Allan was large in stature and an imposing figure. Intriguingly, one investigator said he looked 'something like a pub bouncer'.

Some years ago Mike was involved with the making of a TV documentary about the ghostly presences at The Marsden Grotto. Since then the programme has been aired repeatedly on satellite TV, a testimony to the allure that this fascinating pub-cum-restaurant creates in the minds of those who want to know more about the paranormal.

One of the psychics, Suzanne, sensed a man sitting at a seat at the back of the Cave Bar. He was, she said, 'sweaty and grumpy', and his name was Tommy. 'Tommy' could well be a historically identifiable character.

In 1833, an athlete and sharpshooter from Sunderland started to frequent the Grotto. He was, by all accounts, rather arrogant and bad-tempered.

On one occasion he shot at the Landlord Peter Allan's pet raven, Ralphy, and took off one of its legs. The bird survived, but Peter gave the braggart – a man called Tommy Stokes – a severe beating for his effrontery.

Could this be the grumpy 'Tommy' whom the psychic detected in the oldest part of the pub, the only part of the pub actually open for business in 1833? One wonders.

During the making of The Ghost Detectives, Mike and the others managed to pick up a number of strange orbs on camera. These luminescent spheres may have a scientific explanation, but one orb, videoed by a member of the film crew, seemed to have a human face in the centre.

Darren Ritson and his fellow investigators also detected several of these orbs, substantiating the fact that, whatever causes the phenomenon, it is persistent.

During the making of a second documentary about the Grotto – Anatomy of a Haunting – the investigators' walkie-talkies, camera batteries and other electrical equipment kept failing repeatedly. Freshly-charged batteries would be drained of all power within seconds. Again, exactly the same problems were encountered by Darren and his fellow investigators.

Glenn, another investigator at the same location, felt as if he'd been hit on the back of the neck and developed a headache. This was in the same spot where, in 1831, the Preventive or Customs Officer was attacked by the aforementioned young smuggler.

Sue Birbeck, who was at that time the manager of the Grotto, accepted that there were spirits there but said that they didn't in the least make her feel uncomfortable. Had she seen anything herself, we wondered?

'I have, actually', she said. 'It was in the Cave Bar. Not long after I started here I saw the silhouette of a young boy – maybe five or six years old – just standing there'.

Other staff members have seen things too. A large, wild-haired character has been spotted, and his physical appearance tallies with a description we were once given of the smuggler Jibber John.

Darren and the North East Ghost Research Team also investigated the pub on a later occasion. They arrived on a cold November night to begin their series of vigils, which took place on 19ᵗʰ November and 17ᵗʰ December 2004. The investigations began about at midnight.

On the first occasion the researchers split up into their respective teams and the investigation got underway. The Family Room and the beer cellar were the first areas due for inspection, and the first thing they all noticed was how cold these particular areas were in comparison to the rest of the building. Although closed and locked fire doors were nearby, the researchers recorded a temperature drop of 5° – and it was getting progressively colder. They thought that there may have been a draught coming from the fire doors but tests ruled this out. Later on the temperature returned to normal.

The next location for investigation was the circular cocktail bar and adjacent restaurant upstairs. The first strange occurrence took place as soon ad Darren and a fellow investigator arrived. Both felt an ice-cold blast of air rush past them, and despite their best efforts they were unable to work out where it had came from. 'Orbs' and other light anomalies were recorded on night-vision video cameras, and tests proved that they had not been caused by any conventional means, such as torchlight or camera flashes.

All very interesting, to say the least. One of the strangest things that Darren ever saw at the inn occurred when, during an investigation, he happened to walk into the restaurant area. Inside the restaurant, North East Ghost Research Team psychic Suzanne Hitchinson was sitting down against a wall with her eyes closed. Suddenly, Darren saw a bizarre, white mist emanate from the front of her face and rise up into the air before completely disappearing. Darren called her name, and Suzie seemed to leave her trance-like state with a start. She then told Darren that she had been trying to contact a spirit and had actually been successful. This spirit had 'got way to close' to her, and was actually beginning to take her over. Suzie was quite shaken up by this episode. Later Darren commented, 'Whatever happened to Suzanne I will probably never know for sure, but I know what I saw – and it was incredible'.

The researchers eventually retreated back into a small bar area. They didn't have to wait long before they glimpsed a rather spectacular apparition; that of a misty, white torso and head.

An acquaintance of the researchers, a journalist from the *Shields Gazette* who had been invited to accompany the investigators, also seems to have espied this apparition. She described seeing a woman aged 60-70 years old, thin in stature with grey hair and a gaunt face. She was also said to be wearing 'a frilly garment' of some sorts. This took the journalist by complete surprise, and she could do nothing but watch in stunned silence as the woman floated past the bottom of a nearby narrow stairwell. When Darren asked if anyone could get a name for this lady, one of the team's psychics said he believed her to be called 'Josie'.

Darren's group decided to continue with the investigation by relocating to the large Cave Bar. Intriguingly, another group had already been in the same place earlier on in the evening and had allegedly 'made contact with a male spirit'. This spirit had, by all accounts, been demonstrating its presence by precipitating some interesting phenomena such as temperature drops and light anomalies. A guest psychic accompanying the researchers asked if the entity would be kind enough to give the next group to visit that room a definite sign of his presence. That group was, of course, the one that Darren was leading. Unbeknown to Darren's group, the spirit had said he'd be happy to oblige.

When Darren's group entered the Cave Bar, the fresh batteries that had previously been inserted into their video camera and torches drained of energy almost immediately. Suzanne Hitchinson then 'picked up the essence' of a man near the cave wall adjacent to the security light situated at the south end of the bar. Later, in exactly the same spot, another investigator saw a figure of a man standing upright with his hands clasped behind his back. It was at this point that the security light on the wall went out altogether. By law these lights are required to be on 24 hours per day, and when the team asked if they could turn them off for the investigation they were refused. Darren wondered if any other strange phenomena were being reported elsewhere on the investigation at this point, and when he located the manager Sue Birkbeck, she informed him that all the security lights had went out anyway, and she did not know why. Nobody had interfered with them, and upon inspection they were all found to be connected up and switched on. For the next ten minutes or so the place was in utter pandemonium as other lights that were unplugged suddenly came on, and lights that should have been on mysteriously went out. One set of lights came on even though they were not connected up to the mains. The researchers also noticed that the CCTV monitor was continually flickering on and off. Was this the sign and 'verification of presence' that the guest psychic had asked for prior to Darren's vigil with the others in there? Darren seemed to think so, and said it was unlikely to have been a mere coincidence. After the investigation, all the lighting went back to normal and further tests proved there was nothing wrong with the electrical system.

The Grotto still retains the same mystique it possessed over two centuries ago. Marsden Bay has a fascinating history – and an enchanting public house with no less allure.

IN-DEPTH CASE STUDY: THE MCORVILLE INN, ELWICK, NR. HARTLEPOOL

Good Ghost Rating: 9

Elwick is a quaint village situated near Hartlepool in Teesside, approximately eight miles north of Middlesborough. It is off the beaten track, and when one stumbles across it one automatically gains the impression of being in the heart of the English countryside. Elwick is an enchanting little hamlet with only a handful of watering holes, a number of houses, a post office and a village green. The village is rich in history and there are many ghosts said to reside in some of the wonderful old houses and properties in the area.

Elwick's most famous legend concerns a local woman who, many years ago, was accused of being a witch. Darren spoke to the [now] resident of the witch's house, Jayne Lavelle, and she told him that the witch had lived at what was known as 'B cottage, Elwick'. Locals knew her as Old Mother Midnight of Elwick, or Widow Pavey. She was a herbalist and had attained something of a reputation as a medicine woman. One day, she made up a batch of potion for a sick local resident, but unfortunately – after the administration of her herbal remedy – the patient died. Because of this incident, Old Mother Midnight was subsequently tried and allegedly burnt at the stake outside of Hart Church. She is believed to be buried on the spot where she was killed in unconsecrated ground.

Across the road from the two pubs that are situated in the village lies an old house of considerable size. It is said that here, one night, the owner of the house woke up to see a shape described as 'a glimmering mist' floating over his bed. When he shouted for his two sons to come and see this spectacle, they too managed to catch a glimpse of it before it disappeared into the ether. What it was they never discovered.

The local post office also has a reputation for being haunted. It is said that doors often open and close on their own, things are constantly being moved around and 'flitting shadows' have been seen occasionally. It is our hope that we can visit the premises one day, in to investigate these strange occurrences and try to shed some light on them. However, it is one of the pubs in the village, The McOrville Inn, that Darren and the GHOST team were called in to investigate.

The McOrville Inn was given its present name sometime between the years 1845 and 1894. Previously it had been known as The Fox and Hounds. Its current epithet belonged to a horse named McOrville. McOrville was the offspring of another horse called Orville, who won the 1802 St Ledger. Every summer for twenty years this stud stallion, McOrville, would tour the area on a weekly basis for all to see. He died on 21 February 1842, aged 32 years. Such was McOrville's reputation that the local coroner even issued a death notice for him. Locals believed that the horse, colloquially known as 'Old McOrville', is now buried in the village field with a large stone marking his grave. Local historians believe that some parts of the inn date back to the 1600s. Their determination is based upon the age of beams they discovered in the loft area of the building. If true, this would make the inn very old indeed. Darren spoke to the pub owner and landlord, Darren Holmes, and he told the author a little about the history of the inn and the ghosts that are said to reside herein. He went on to say:

A number of strange things have occurred here over the years. Before we actually bought the place there was another couple in here. They went on to tell me that the bedroom, which I now sleep in, was once occupied by them. They woke up one night to find the room was literally full of smoke or mist and they could not see a thing. They jumped out of bed thinking their property was on fire, and when they ventured out into the hallway there was no sign of smoke! They checked the whole place over, looking for a potential fire, and when they ventured back into their bedroom all the smoke – or mist – was gone. This happened on more than two occasions.

'Another story concerns my brother who has a room at the back of the house, which was once a kitchen. On a number of occasions he has told me that he has woken up and saw a figure of a man standing in the room looking over his bed. Sometimes he sees this figure and at the same time can feel the bed shaking. This frightens him quite a lot.

We know of one person who has actually died in the bar area. The guy [who shall remain anonymous] by all accounts was a well-known figure in these parts. His family had owned the pub for a many years, and the story goes that, while having Sunday lunch here at the McOrville, he dropped down dead with a heart attack. Because the pub was so busy and most people were drunk, people did not actually know he was dead and just left him where he lay, stepping over his lifeless body to get past him. It was not until some time later they made their grim discovery.

'Another past landlord I spoke to once told me of the ghostly happenings that occur down in the cellar. He went on to say that on countless occasions, he would go down to the cellar thinking that he needed to change a pump as the beer flow would cease. When he got down there he'd find that the pumps had been mysteriously turned off. This is exactly the same experience that we have had here since moving into the pub seventeen months ago. I have also seen weird light formations and a strange radiance over in a corner near the side door. I have sensed people in here with me when I know I am on my own.

'Let us not forget the old stables that are housed out back too. They have a certain feel to them, and we currently use one as a coal-house. On occasions when I am out back getting coal I often have this overwhelming sense of presence and I feel that something or someone is coming towards me. I am more interested in than afraid of these phenomena.

'There is also a story concerning a handprint of a small child that can be seen in one of the bricks in the walls of the old stables. The story goes that children were employed in those days to make bricks as well as work down the local mines. One day, when a young lad was working, a whole load of newly-built bricks accidentally fell down upon him and crushed him to death. During his brief fight for life under these new, but not yet hardened, bricks his handprint was impressed into one and it can still be seen to this day. It is believed that the ghost of this boy haunts the area of the stables near to where his handprint is still seen in the wall, although no one is sure exactly where he died.

'The pub has an amazing atmosphere, and the people who frequent it – both past and present – are just lovely! I'm not frightened of the ghosts in this place one bit'.

Darren felt that, in the light of what Darren Holmes had told him, there was 'plenty to go on' and, all things considered, the location could provide an opportunity for an interesting investigation.

On the evening of the investigation, a spiritualist medium called Peter Crawford, who had organised the event, came along with one or two other guest mediums. The man sometimes called Britain's top exorcist, Ralph Keeton, was also there with his partner and fellow team member Nikki Austwicke.

Ralph, famous for his exorcism work, was also part of the Most Haunted team for five series. He is also the founder of the International and National Psychic Team which has featured many times on Sky and national TV.

At approximately 10.00pm the investigators entered the pub, which was still busy with all the Friday night drinkers who were out enjoying themselves on that cold, December night. The team members sat down and made themselves comfortable in front of the roaring fire that stands in the main bar area. They began to chat amongst themselves, and it wasn't long before they were introduced to the else who others who were going to be partaking in the investigation. Everyone hit it off very well and got on like the proverbial house on fire. Ralph, when he ventured in, came across to the team and began chatting to them straight away. As well as getting down to the nitty-gritty of ghosts and the business at hand, he also regaled the investigators with some serious but humorous stories from his Most Haunted days with the likes of Richard Felix, Derek Acorah and the rest of the crew. He is a total joy both to listen and chat to, and he is a man with incredible knowledge of the world of paranormal phenomena.

The researchers figured that if they proceeded with the investigation as normal in their usual professional manner, they would have nothing to worry about. That is what they did, and at the end of the night Ralph said he would like to work with them again. On with the investigation: By the time the bar had emptied and the team members had sorted themselves out it was about 12.30am, and they were ready to begin.

The first port of call was to investigate the cellar under the pub, and everyone except Darren, who joined them later, ventured down the steps to conduct a séance. Their hope was that they may be able to make contact with any of the spirits of the McOrville Inn. The séance proved quite interesting, and considerable amounts of subjective data were picked up by some of the mediums. The first entity they made contact with was the spirit of a woman with grey hair and a parting down the centre of her head. Peter Crawford sensed the presence of this spirit first, and he told the team that the woman was scurrying around as if looking for something. He went on to say that she was a nice old lady who was simply searching for something she had lost. When the spirit was asked to give all the sitters a sign, knocks and bumps were heard. A number of people were subjected to mysterious pains, ailments and feelings of extreme cold. At this point all members of the team captured a number of light anomalies on their night-vision video cameras.

Another team member, Drew Bartley, joined Darren and the pair proceeded to monitor the proceedings with their EMF meters and digital thermometer guns. Sure enough, a number of anomalous readings were indeed recorded. Ralph Keeton proceeded to call out in response to the spirit and, every time he asked a question, the investigators were rewarded with bumps and bangs emanating from within the room somewhere, although everyone present had remained perfectly still. Then the sitters began to sense 'impressions', including the feeling that, in the past, the cellar, may well have been used to as a place to slaughter animals.

Darren then ventured upstairs to talk to Darren Holmes, the landlord, about this and he confirmed that in the past animals were indeed slaughtered in the area, but where exactly he could not say. It would be interesting to find out if it was indeed in the cellar of the old inn.

One medium said that she got the impressions of 'stables' and 'the death of horses', which is interesting indeed as there are old stables at the back of the inn. Also, readers should remember that the horse 'Old McOrville' is buried under the village green. When asked if she knew anything about the old stables out back, the medium told Darren she did not, and was indeed quite surprised by the revelation. It must also be noted that it was after this séance when the pub owner, Darren Holmes, announced that he was taking the group outside to see the old stable area! Darren Ritson had known about the stables simply because he'd interviewed the landlord prior to investigation. so it was an interesting start to the enquiry.

On leaving the cellar, Darren proceeded to take a few photographs. The first two pictures came out normal, but the third image was obscured by what can only be described as a dense, anomalous mist. Later, Darren said he found it rather odd that this should happen just after the séance. Could something have been 'brought forward' by the séance? It's a teasing thought, and if true, it may just have been caught it on camera.

The team retired upstairs for a short break and were treated to sandwiches and cakes courtesy of the landlord. Afterwards, the team spilt into two groups to cover more of the building. One group ensconced themselves next to the disused fireplace at one end of the huge L shaped bar, whist the other ventured to the other end of the pub where a fire was roaring away merrily. Darren's team along with Ralph, Nikki, and several of the mediums, decided to hold a table-tipping experiment while Peter Crawford and his group sat in silence, monitoring their respective area.

Before the vigil began in the bar, Darren and a fellow investigator ventured downstairs into the cellar to set up some 'lock-off' equipment. A set of motion sensors was used along with a trigger object – a crucifix. On venturing back upstairs, they re-joined their group and proceeded with the investigation.

A circle was formed around a table, and Ralph proceeded to ask any spirits that may have been present some questions. In a sturdy, dominating voice he called out;

'If there are any spirits here in the room with us tonight, please try and give us a sign'.

Nothing happened, so Ralph called again.

'If there are any spirits here in the room with us tonight, please try and give us a sign'.

Still nothing, so the medium tried a different approach.

'If we can ask our energies and our guides to combine, to bring forward any energies within this room, any energies in this area. I am going to ask that you step forward so that we can use this table to communicate. I am going to ask the group sitting at the table to combine their energies and focus on the table; please make sure your hands are touching, thumbs to thumbs, and little fingers to little fingers. I am now going to ask the energy to go through to the table and the first thing I am going to ask the energy to do is….'

At this point one of the team members filmed a light anomaly moving across Ralph's torso. He pointed this out to Ralph and he said, 'Yes, it's just stepped forward. I am now going to ask you to creak the table, don't force the table but slightly creak the table so we know that you are here.'

A little time passed by, and then everyone heard the table creak distinctly.

'Right, I am going to ask the energy to step forward and make yourself known to us. Please, make yourself known'.

The sitters then reported that the table was beginning to move, ever so slightly.

'Please creak the table.' Ralph said.

'If anyone is here with us, can you move the table?'

At this point everyone heard a wooden leg belonging to the table scrape across the floor.

'Thank you! Can you do that again please?'

Sure enough the table began to move.

'Okay, can you show us a yes?'

The table moved one way.

'Can you show us a no please?'

The table moved another way.

At this point Darren and Drew were both trying to get under the table in the hope that they could see the table actually lift off the floor. Others had the same idea, and were attempting to take photographs between the legs of the sitters. I was also monitoring closely the hands of all the sitters and took great care to study them all meticulously. I filmed each and everyone's hands close up so I could perhaps get a better look to see if any foul play was being administered but my later inspections proved fruitless. It appeared that everybody's hand were resting so lightly upon the base of the table and cheating, at this stage in my enquiries, was ruled out.

By this time the table was rocking extremely violently and was up on one leg. The table came so close to lifting up off the floor completely, but alas, this did not happen. However, knocks, bumps and the occasional sound like a footfall or two were heard in the bar. It was as though someone was strolling around in the bar area trying to make themselves known to the investigators. Darren even walked the length of the bar simply to prove to himself that no one was in area. He then asked the group stationed at the other end of the bar if anyone had been walking around, and they replied that no one had. So who, or what, had they just heard? And who, or what, was trying to communicate by moving the table?

Ralph, now curious as to what was clumping around the bar area, decided to venture over and have a look. When he got to the middle of the room he suddenly stopped and said 'I am feeling a presence right here'.

'Is it male or female?' Darren asked him.

'I can't quite tell, at the minute, I just know we have somebody here'.

This astounded Darren, simply because when he was interviewing the landlord earlier on, he'd told the author about the person who had died right there at that very spot. Could Ralph have been picking up on this person's spirit? It could well have been the case. For Darren, this was another true-life encounter with spirits that went a long way to supporting the existence of both ghosts and the afterlife. It certainly supports the theory that some people are gifted with an ability to engage in spirit mediumship! Darren knew for a fact that none of the researchers knew about the spot in the pub where the man had died, but Ralph had sensed it. Could this have been the same person they all heard moving around not more than two minutes earlier? It looks likely that it could have been. The table at this point had 'calmed down', and whatever spirit had came through seemed to have dispersed. It was a fascinating experiment to watch, and it is something the author will not forget in a hurry. Whether the table-tipping experiment can be deemed as good, objective evidence is another story, but nevertheless it proved very interesting indeed.

The other group was also having some success with their attempts at spirit communication. Darren ventured over to see what was happening. He was told that the door to the top of the cellar stairs kept opening on its own even though the handle was firmly engaged. He sat down and 'called out to the atmosphere' in the hope this would occur again. Never in a million years did he expect to see the handle move down, and the door slowly open, but he did – twice in the space of ten minutes:

'It was absolutely incredible, and there was no way that a draught or rational explanation could explain that one. This has to be one of the best ghostly phenomena I have ever witnessed on investigations, and believe me; I have seen some incredible phenomena! I just wish I'd had my spare videotape with me. When I retrieved it from my holdall, the door (surprise, surprise) would not open for us anymore! I put my camera away and taped the proceedings with my dictation machine.

'When I asked Peter Crawford about any other impressions or anything else that may have happened, he told me that he'd picked up the benign energy of a lovely lady. He felt her presence for about five minutes until it faded, and then he told me her name was Sarah. She resembled the lady in the Mona Lisa picture. Then, with my naked eye, I then saw two amazing light anomalies float across the top of the door'.

It was time for one last break before the last vigil of the night. The team then ventured outside into the old stable area. The wind was howling through the trees, and the rain was lashing down upon them. The stable doors were crashing in the wind and it was cold beyond belief. Most normal folk would be tucked up in bed, nice and warm at that time in the morning, but not us!

The vigil in these barns proved rather fruitless to say the least, and it was quite hard to determine what noises may have been paranormal due to the gale force winds reverberating around both outside and inside most of these old stables. However, one stable proved rather odd. This is the stable that Ralph had wanted to be inside for a while and, when the team entered, they were not disappointed. The wind was confined to the outside of this particular stable, and after asking 'Alice' – the lady whom Ralph sensed – to show some signs of her presence, the light flex hanging from the ceiling moved back and forth and to and fro, on command! It stopped when asked, and resumed when it was commanded too. It was quite incredible to say the least. Some cynics will say it was the wind, but they weren't there. Darren is a sensible investigator; had it been the wind, he would have said so.

So, the investigation came to an end – and what an investigation it had proved to be; a fabulous venue, reputedly haunted by the ghosts or shades of the past.

* PUB: THE NICKY NACK (NOW THE DALESIDE ARMS)
* LOCATION: CROXDALE
* GOOD GHOST RATING: 4

Harvest time is a gruelling season for farmers, and when the work is done labourers will often celebrate by supping a pint or two of ale. This tradition is an old one, and was kept up religiously in the Durham village of Tudhoe.

Last century – or some say in the century before, we cannot be sure – a group of farmers gathered one evening in Tudhoe Mill farm with a generous amount of alcohol. Their work having been completed, they now had time to relax.

Late into the hours of darkness the liquid refreshment started to run out, and a young farmhand was asked to walk to the nearby village of Croxdale to gather fresh supplies from a local inn that was still open. A large jug of whisky had taken their fancy, and he promised to return promptly with exactly that.

An hour ticked by, then two, and still the lad had not returned. One of the others decided to play a trick on him by way of revenge for his tardiness. He took a white sheet and headed off for a nearby field that lay between Croxdale and Tudhoe.

'I'll dress up as a ghost and frighten the daylights out of him as he comes back across the field', he had told his pals with a mischievous grin.

Another hour or two passed, and suddenly the first young man staggered through the door of the farmhouse looking petrified.

'I was passing through the field, when suddenly a white ghost jumped out and frightened me!' he stammered.

His friends laughed hysterically, knowing full well that the 'ghost' had merely been their other friend playing pranks. But the laughing soon stopped when the frightened youngster carried on speaking.

'The white ghost was bad enough, but when the black one appeared it was even worse'.

Now they were puzzled.

'What black ghost?'

'Well, it was bigger than the white ghost, and it fell on top of it. Then there were terrible screams, and they both disappeared into the night.'

Concerned, they all traipsed down to the field. All that remained was the shredded remnants of the white sheet, covered in blood. Their friend was never seen again.

One curious postscript to this tale is that the first worker to cross the field – the one who was supposed to be the victim of the ghostly prank – claimed that as he ran back to the farm terrified he could hear the Devil calling out to him, 'Knicky-Nack! Knicky-Nack!'

Later, this mystery was explained when it was found that the young man's heel had come loose and was making the 'nicky-nack' noise when it slapped against the road as he ran!

Later, the field was renamed the Nicky Nack Field and still bears that title to this day. The public house in Croxdale was renamed the Nicky Nack, too, although it now carries the slightly less curious epithet of the Daleside Arms.

Some versions of the tale indicate that the farmer who heard the Devil calling him and the one who had the terrible experience at Nicky Nack Field were two separate persons. We don't know, but whatever the facts it's a terrific story anyway.

- **PUB:**   THE NOAH'S ARK
- **LOCATION:**   SOUTH SHIELDS
- **GOOD GHOST RATING:**   6

The Noah's Ark, long-since demolished, once sat in Shadwell Street, South Shields. Like other inns it was also mentioned in the Pigot's Directory of 1834. Although not too far from the aforementioned Hop Pole, it was an altogether different type of establishment. It had a Long Room in which 'ship-launch dinners' were held for local toffs whenever a ship was 'bottled' down at the river.

The Ark was also the home of the first Mission School in the area, and various religious denominations held their meetings there. The Noah's Ark must have been a strange sort of ale house indeed; either that or the clerics of the nineteenth century were not as opposed to the demon drink as we may like to think.

The Ark, formerly known as 'Bella Booth's' is reputed to have been haunted, but we have been unable to find out any details about the spectre other than that it became something of a celebrity around the East Holborn area.

Could it be that the Noah's Ark – home to religious meetings and business dinners alike – was also a contraband stash-house? Geographically it was in the right place, and its reputation as a respectable establishment may well have caused the Excise men to overlook it. Perhaps the Ark's ghost was also a myth; perpetrated – like the Red Lady of the Hop Pole – to scare away those who may see or hear too much and blab to the Peelers.

Then again, maybe the Ark really was a respectable drinking house. Perhaps the ghost which frequented the Long Room really did exist. The question is, who was it? We may ever know for sure, but we do have a likely suspect.

One of the most popular local ghost tales concerned a character with the ominous – sounding name of Jack the Hammer – not to be confused with Jack the Blaster, of Marsden Grotto fame, whom we dealt with in a previous chapter.

Several locations have been suggested as to the location of Jack's home, the Holborn area of South Shields being the most likely.

At one time Jack seems to have been marginally wealthy, some reports suggesting that he owned a hardware store near Templetown. At some point Jack fell on hard times, and it appears that if he did run a business it was forced to close. Jack – still finding it necessary to earn a living – took to peddling the stock he had accumulated from door to door. When finances allowed, he would frequent the local inns and alehouses of Holborn, no doubt chatting with old acquaintances and putting the world to rights over a tankard or two. Again, confusion exists as to which pub was Jack's 'local', but the Noah's Ark in Shadwell Street has been mentioned to us more than once.

Jack seems to have been a rather mercurial character. Whilst enjoying the company of friends and patrons of his business, he also seems to have craved moments of solitude. Whilst most of the patrons would be gathered in the larger public bar, old Jack could often be found sitting in the Snug next door quietly sipping his ale. What thoughts ran through his head we cannot say. Perhaps he recalled past visits to foreign climes, for in his younger days Jack had been a sailor.

Due to his experience at sea, Jack proved quite adept at predicting the weather. With uncanny accuracy he could foresee forthcoming changes in the climate, and was definitely the person to ask if you were unsure whether to take your topcoat with you. Much as locals appreciated Jack's talents, they were sometimes unnerved by his rather dramatic way of demonstrating them. During opening hours he could often be found looking out of the Snug window, and, if he saw clouds gathering, he would hit the dividing wall between the Snug and the bar violently with the flat of his hand and shout, 'There's a storm comin'! Mark my words, there's a storm comin'!' This rather eccentric habit allegedly earned him his nickname of Jack the Hammer.

Eventually Jack passed away, but before long poltergeist-like phenomena started to manifest themselves both in the Noah's and one or two other inns which Jack had frequented. Without warning, pounding noises would echo through the building – noises which sounded exactly like those made by Jack's leathery fist when he was alive.

To those who remembered the old sea-dog-turned-peddler in the flesh, there was no doubt that Jack had returned. The sound was too distinctive to be mistaken. Before long Jack's customers began to report banging noises on their doors and walls, and yet on investigation there would be no one there.

One of the things that convinced the locals that it really was Jack 'back from the grave' was the fact that whenever the mysterious banging noises occurred they would inevitably be followed by a violent storm. The louder the hammering the worse the tempest would be. It seems that in death, as well as in life, Jack the Hammer was still determined to warn his drinking compatriots that 'There's a storm comin'! Mark my words, there's a storm comin'.'

- **PUB:**   THE ODEON CINEMA BAR
- **LOCATION:**   SOUTH SHIELDS
- **GOOD GHOST RATING:** 6

One night some years ago, Mike happened to be sinking a pint in the Alum House, just off South Shields' Market Square, when he bumped into an old friend of his who, for the purposes of this story, prefers to remain anonymous. We'll simply refer to him as 'J'.

J told Mike that, some years previously, he had been employed as a bar manager in the bingo hall which had formerly been the old Odeon cinema in King Street, South Shields.

Cinemas and theatres have a well-deserved reputation for being sites of intense paranormal activity. An old theatre in New Mexico, for example, is said to be haunted by the ghost of no less a personage than Wyatt Earp. The building is now a museum, but visitors and staff alike have frequently reported hearing the ghostly sounds of honky-tonk music drifting from the vicinity of the stage in the main auditorium.

On several occasions, when the staff have opened up on a morning, cigar ash, half-finished glasses of whiskey and poker chips have been found on the table at which Earp was reputed to sit.

Not to be outdone, the old Odeon was also subject to some strange paranormal happenings, and J was able to supply Mike with a number of interesting details. Another WraithScape fan added some other facts, and when the two stories are put together they make an interesting tale.

More than one person who worked at the premises reported feeling a "presence" in the stalls, both during the Odeon's days as a cinema and as a bingo hall. On one occasion a member of staff opened up the building and saw a lady in a grey dress "glide up the aisle" before disappearing. Regardless, as he had locked up the premises the night before, after checking the building thoroughly, he knew that no one had been locked in there.

J's story was even more interesting. One day, a fellow employee had approached him in a state of great agitation. He was, says J, barely able to speak. He pointed towards the main hall and J, intrigued, accompanied him in an effort to find out what was wrong.

In the hall was a large organ, a relic of the old silent movie days. Many, many years previously this imposing instrument had been disconnected from the electricity supply, and some of the internal wiring had also been removed. By all standards of logic the organ should have been unworkable.

Despite the fact that the organ was not connected to the electricity supply, to all intents and purposes it appeared to have been switched on, and its decorative lights filled the old cinema with an eerie glow.

J naturally thought that he was the victim of a cleverly orchestrated practical joke. Two things convinced him otherwise.

Firstly, his colleague was obviously quite traumatised. Secondly, he inspected the organ and could see with his own eyes that no electricity was being fed into the machine whatsoever. At this point they both made a rapid exit!

Since speaking to J, Mike has interviewed several ex-employees of the bingo hall. They all said that certain areas of the building had an 'eerie' feel to them. One said that objects would 'move around without anyone touching them'. Another said that she also had heard the organ playing when it was definitely disconnected.

The old Odeon was definitely quite haunted it seems; but by whom? Theatres and other public buildings are often haunted by the apparitions of long-time employees or patrons who had strong connections of the place.

It is not necessary to believe that all ghosts are conscious entities. Sometimes they may be images from the past which are somehow transported through time. This doesn't explain how the disconnected organ burst into life, however, and we'd love to know who the lady in the long, grey dress was.

- **Pub:**   Offshore 44
- **Location:**   Newcastle upon Tyne
- **Good Ghost Rating:** 8

As mentioned earlier in the volume, the authors visited a number of public houses in Newcastle's Sandhill area on the Quayside that are all run by the same manager, Joyce Wemyss. Offshore 44 is a splendid drinking den with a very high ceiling, a solid stone floor and has like all good, old-fashioned pubs, wooden beams on the ceilings. The interior is marvellously festooned with nautical features such as ships' steering wheels, beer barrels, ropes, nets, buoys, and even large models of galleons and schooners.

When you step inside, you are automatically taken back to the days of smugglers, sailors and press gangs and a sudden rush of yesteryear washes over you as the pub's instant atmosphere takes hold of you with a firm and sturdy grip. However, don't be fooled by the theme of the pub, as that is all it is – a seafaring theme. Actually, before the building was used as a pub it was once a shop.

The back wall in the building is said to form the outer walls of old Newcastle castle, and it is believed that this area was where the lifeless corpses of criminals were displayed after been hung on the gallows. The authors admit that looking at this wall, and comparing the area to old maps of Newcastle, this could well indeed be the case.

During their research and compilation of this book the authors made many visits to alleged haunted pubs and inns. They sampled a good variety of ales along the way, listened to tales of yesteryear and relished the wonderful ghost accounts that many kinds of people, from all walks of life, relayed to them. This pub was no different. They were informed by one of the bar staff that when they were in the bar alone, tending to their duties, they were always looking over their shoulder and listening out for strange and unexplained noises. The barman believes that when he was alone…well, he actually wasn't alone, if you catch our drift. A sudden 'sense of presence' would envelope him from time to time, alerting him to the eerie feeling that someone, or 'something from the other side' may not have been too far away. When asked by the authors whether he liked working there side-by-side with a ghost, he simply replied, 'No, not on my own…but I just get on with it'.

Another fascinating account came from our colleague Steve Taylor. He went on to tell us, 'I witnessed what looked like a man in a blue, velvet jacket with ruffles around the neck but worn very loose. It was rather unnerving to see, and it made me feel rather unwell. Another odd thing I noticed was that he was displaced from the visible setting, as if he was sitting behind the seating'.

The authors were also informed about the 'resident psychics' who have often visited the premises – one of them being related to the manager. They too have sensed otherworldly individuals, with one tale concerning a man who had somehow had his arm ripped from its socket on the premises and subsequently bled to death. However, details of this alleged incident are rather difficult to obtain. With other stories of blood letting, witchcraft, murders, public exhibitions of the recently executed, and black magic, it is no wonder that this pub lays claims to having a spectre or two.

- Pub: THE OLD GEORGE
- Location: NEWCASTLE UPON TYNE
- Good Ghost Rating: 10

The Old George Inn is a fine drinking den that is nicely tucked away down an ancient, cobbled back lane called 'Old George Yard' and is situated to the east of Newcastle's Cloth Market. The pub is believed to be one of the oldest pubs in Newcastle upon Tyne (after The Cooperage) and has been described as a veritable oasis of serenity in a troubled world. Looking at the pub from the cobblestoned lane outside, one gets the impression of a traditional-style olde world pub serving fine, olde worlde ales and beers – and you would be right, for this is exactly what the Old George is. It actually dates back to the early 1600s, and was once used as a coaching inn. It is also believed that there are royal connections associated with the pub too. King Charles I reputedly drank there back in the mid 1600s. There is a room at the inn named after him, and a chair he allegedly once sat in to 'sup his ale' is still there. The authors have been told that the chair is actually a replica of the original, however.

Stepping inside the Old George inn (as the authors have done quite often – in the name of research of course – is metaphorically taking a step back in time. The past comes to life and one is transported into a quaint world of yesteryear as you are greeted by a warm and welcoming feeling of days gone by. A large, open fire sits near the main entrance, the walls are panelled and the Old George retains its ancient, low ceilings with thick oak wooden beams. These give the inn an air of grandeur and magnificence that is still obvious to the visitor – even after 400 years or so.

Like all ancient hostelries, it too has its resident ghost – as a matter of fact, the Old George is known as one of the north-east's most famous 'haunted pubs. Perhaps it is famous because the ghost that is said to reside there is none other than King Charles I himself. Along with phantom footfalls across the wooden floors in the empty rooms, the spectre of King Charles I has reputedly been seen standing at the bar – complete with his head!

It is interesting to add that at the time of one of his visits to the Old George pub, in 1649, he was seized, taken to Whitehall in London and beheaded. One may presume, then, that this could have been his last visit to a favourite drinking hole just before his untimely demise. Maybe that is why he chooses to haunt the very bar he may well have drunk his last tankard of ale in.

- PUB: THE OLD SHIP
- LOCATION: HARTON VILLAGE
- GOOD GHOST RATING: 7

The Old Ship is one of the oldest public houses in South Shields, dating back to the year 1802. It sits on Sunderland Road, in the area known as Harton, and in its time has seen the advent of two world wars and the horse and cart replaced by the horseless carriage. Entry is made via an inconspicuous side door which leads directly into the bar.

There is something curious about the Old Ship. The diversity of its patrons is quite striking, and as Mike sat quietly once upon a time, supping his pint he noticed how a strange admixture of businessmen, manual workers, teenagers and pensioners all intermingled. Perhaps it is a testimony to the friendly atmosphere the inn generates.

Now let's get down to business. There is no doubt in the minds of the authors that the pub is haunted, for Mike once spoke to the then manager, Brenda, and she told him that she had seen the apparition herself, along with other members of staff. Curiously, it seems that the haunting is connected with a large boulder which sits outside on the south-east corner of the inn. The origins of the boulder are a mystery. One theory is that the stone, which is the size of two large sacks of potatoes, is a meteorite. This is impossible, of course, for as Mike pointed out to one of the locals, if a meteorite that size had landed in Harton there would have been nothing left of Harton itself and precious little else of South Shields.

A second theory is that the stone was found when the foundations were being dug, and that because of its size it was easier to roll it to one side and leave it there rather than have it taken away.

A third, and far more intriguing, tale is that the boulder is a ballast stone. When ships used to off-load on the river Tyne, the space formerly occupied by the cargo was filled with large ballast stones to give the ship stability on its return voyage. Empty ships arriving at the port would have ballast stones removed to be replaced with cargo. The spare ballast – which could be quite substantial – would then be deposited on one of the numerous ballast hills that were in the area. It is said that a cart full of ballast was making its way past the inn when the boulder in question rolled off and came to a halt by the Ship, where it has remained ever since. The difficulty with this theory is that it is hard to fathom why ballast would be taken as far as Harton village when there were ballast hills far closer to the river. Nevertheless, it is not impossible.

A fourth theory is that the stone was deliberately placed there as a 'mounting stone', so that riders could stand on it and mount their steeds more easily. Indeed, to this day it is still sometimes referred to by some as 'the Mounting Stone'.

During the nineteenth century it is said that a man stood upon the rock in order to climb his horse. Unfortunately the horse reared, and the poor chap fell backwards hitting his skull upon the very same rock. He died soon after, and it is said that his ghost can sometimes be seen standing beside the mounting stone, staring vacantly into space.

Eyewitness testimonies to this apparition are few and far between, but this is most certainly not the case concerning the ghost which is said to frequent the interior of the inn. Brenda told Mike of her own experience. She first saw the apparition in the corridor which leads from the bar to the exit. It was, she said, a 'dark, man-shaped shadow' which walked past and was gone in little more than a second or two. The same entity has been seen by other staff in the lounge, and also, apparently, by a rather startled drinker or two.

It is tempting to think that the shadowy entity within the pub is connected with the apparition of the horseman who appears beside the Mounting Stone, but the authors think we need to exercise some caution here. Ghosts are frustratingly intangible and almost impossible to verify scientifically. However, they are usually consistent in the way they present themselves. Because the ghost of the horseman always appears in a normal anthropomorphic form, we are forced to conclude that this entity has nothing to do with the shade which manifests inside the pub itself; a shadowy, insubstantial apparition of indeterminable origin. (An exception to this rule may be the Grey Lady who frequents the Ladies' toilet in the Alum House. She occasionally appears as a dark shadow, and in such a small geographical location it is reasonable to assume that the two are connected. The two spectres which haunt the Ship Inn, however, appear in different places.)

There are other explanations for the appearance of this entity. In an altogether darker age it is said that victims of the plague were buried in pits adjacent to where the Ship now stands. Others say that a graveyard existed there in the sixteenth century. As burial pits and graveyards are notorious for generating hauntings, there may well be some truth in these stories. Perhaps the rather shadowy entity which confronts the staff from time to time was himself a victim of the Black Death, who knows.

Brenda remarked that the haunting phenomena always seemed to increase when there were changes taking place in the pub, such as decorating or refitting. This tallies perfectly with the experiences of other landlords, such as Nick Garvey, a past landlord at the Marsden Grotto, who reported exactly the same thing.

Those who wish to research pub hauntings could do worse than start off with this friendly little inn. Whilst doing his research, Mike was taken under the wing of Joe, Walter, Harry and several other regulars, each of whom lost no time in feeding him with their own variations on the legends surrounding both the stone and the ghost. Walter, a Welshman who has lived up in Geordieland for thirty-plus years, informed Mike that he remembers the Mounting Stone before it was painted. 'It was jet black', he recalls, 'and not like any of the local stone around here. It must have been ballast'. Joe, listening sage-like, drew slowly on his cigar and pondered.

'Could have been...could have been...' he said.

Mike left the Ship, reluctantly, and promised to return in a day or two to talk to some more of the master storytellers who frequented the place. He hoped that one of them, perhaps, could reveal the secret of the Mounting Stone and the spectral rider who stands beside it.

- PUB: PATIE'S INN
- LOCATION: DARLINGTON
- GOOD GHOST RATING: 8

There is a lonely road that leads from Great Stainton to Great Burdon, near Darlington. Known then – and sometimes now – as Catkill Lane. The road gained its strange epithet because it was said to be a place where cats would convene at Hallowe'en and, bizarrely, on April Fools' Day. On one occasion, centuries ago, the bodies of dozens of local cats were found dead there under mysterious circumstances.

The footpath still runs from Petty's Nook to Salters Lane at nearby Ketton. Petty's Nook is actually a bastardisation of Patie's Nook, and this provides the authors with a suitable opportunity to introduce the ghost story attached to this eerie stretch of road.

'Mr Patie' was by all accounts an innkeeper who ran a run-down drinking establishment on Catkill Lane. Putting it bluntly, the pub-cum-hotel had a terrible reputation. Researcher Alan Tedder has called Catkill Lane 'the haunt of footpad and thief', and the inn itself he describes as 'a wicked halt for strumpet and criminal'.

One evening, two local farmers (some say butchers) decided to spend the night at Patie's Inn before travelling home the next morning. However, being fully cognisant with the pub's scandalous reputation, they deemed it wise to take a look in one of the windows to make sure that the place wasn't filled with undesirables. Later, they must have wished they hadn't bothered.

On peeking through the window, the two travellers saw Patie himself and a farmer called Pringle holding down upon the floor a third person, another farmer by the name of Race. They watched in horror as Pringle took up a knife and, slowly but steadily, ran it across the throat of the prostrate and terrified Race. Within a second the man's neck had been opened from ear to ear. Pringle grabbed a basin and held it to the wound, catching the spurting blood as it pumped out of the wound. Patie, for his part, held the writhing man down until he was exsanguinated.

Absolutely terrified, the two would-be patrons decided not to visit Patie's Inn at all, and fled into the night. According to legend, the body of Race was either cut up and fed to some pigs or, alternatively, cooked in an oven. Whether Patie and Pringle actually feasted upon him afterwards or merely snacked on a water biscuit or two is not recorded.

Not long after the gruesome murder, the ghost of the victim, Race, was said to have been seen in the premises on numerous occasions. The inn was eventually demolished, but that didn't stop the haunting. The spectre of the hapless Race simply took to haunting the adjacent road from Great Burdon to Great Stainton where, some say, he can still be seen to this day.

- PUB: THE PHOENIX
- LOCATION: SUNDERLAND
- GOOD GHOST RATING: 6

The tale of the Phoenix pub haunting was relayed to the authors by a colleague, and this particular story bares relation to an ancestor of his who actually once ran the pub.

This chap's old relation, known only as Mr Downey, seemingly ran the Phoenix in Lombard Street, between the years 1843 and 1863. For two decades, then, he dished out ale, porter and spirits with gusto. Like the traditional good publican, he also allegedly took to haunting the bar after his death.

Of course, time and tide has washed away much of the detail, but witnesses described him as 'a little old man wearing a grey suit'.

At the time, few disputed that it was indeed old Downey who was haunting the bar. Sadly, the area has been transformed since those days and the older properties have been replaced by new and modern edifices; so, what became of Mr Downey's ghost?

With the demise of the Phoenix – which sadly did not rise from the ashes despite its name – Downey had to find somewhere else to haunt. With common sense and impeccable taste, he plumped for another bar which was quite literally around the corner; the White Lion in High Street East. Once again, the 'little old man wearing a grey suit' put in an appearance, although to our knowledge he never offered to buy a round.

One wonders if this really was old Mr Downey or perhaps another spectre altogether; the old regulars certainly seemed to go with the former notion.

In-depth Case Study: The Red Hackle, Jarrow
Good Ghost Rating: 9

The Red Hackle opened for business on September 25, 1966 at 11am, to the sound of a Scots piper who had been hired for the event. For over thirty years the inn has served as a watering hole for locals, and boasts both darts teams and pool teams of no mean reputation.

From the exterior the premises are reasonably unassuming, the building being typical of its genre. Nevertheless it is well kept and neatly painted. The interior of the pub catches the new visitor by surprise, and for a multiplicity of reasons. Firstly, although the décor is not ambitious it has a character which belies its relatively short lifespan. The sturdy dark-oak fittings and solid counter give a distinctly Victorian atmosphere to the bar. The bar itself is also unusual because of its sheer size. It is refreshingly spacious, although on Friday, Saturday and Sunday evenings – by far the most popular – it can still get quite packed.

Like most ale houses of this type, the Red Hackle provides a variety of entertainment for its patrons, including a popular karaoke evening. It has a reputation for serving excellent beer, which the authors can vouch for having visited the place as part of their research for this book.

When Mike first visited the pub, researching his *Ales & Spirits* book, the manager, Alan, confessed to having drank in the inn for a number of years before taking over the running of it. Mike found his help invaluable, as he arranged for several customers and staff members to be there when he arrived so that he could interview them. As Mike arrived first, he took the opportunity to ask Alan what he knew about the paranormal happenings allegedly associated with the pub.

'Remember when you first rang me this morning, and I thought you were playing a joke? Remember how at first I thought it was a 'wind-up'? That was because just a few nights ago I actually experienced something myself. I thought someone I'd told about it was playing tricks'.

Mike asked Alan what did happen, and he told him. It seems that he had said goodnight to the rest of the staff and locked up the premises, which left him entirely alone. Without any feelings of foreboding, he carried out a succession of small tasks which would leave the pub ready for business the next day. It was approximately 2am by the time he had finished, and he was just about to retire to the flat upstairs. As he walked along the short corridor adjacent to the lounge and the bar, he suddenly heard a voice. It was, he said, a deep voice – almost husky – but definitely female. It uttered only one word; 'Alan'.

'It was really close...just behind my ear. It was loud and clear. I jumped round expecting to see someone, but the place was deserted. I admit I was shocked. It's easy to joke about this sort of thing, but I know what I heard'.

Anyone who talks to Alan about his experience will easily be convinced that he's telling the truth, and believe us, we don't fool easily. But if any sceptics are still doubtful, they should know that he is not the only one to have had such an experience.

After twenty minutes or so Mike was joined by local man and Hackle regular Sammy H. Sammy, a joiner by profession, has drunk in the Hackle since it opened. He had seen a succession of managers come and go, and could recite with perfect accuracy the names of some of the characters who had frequented the pub over the years. Had he experienced anything untoward in the Red Hackle? No, but he had heard the stories. Before he even took a sip from his glass, Sammy left the Hackle and went to see another old-timer called Charlie.

'I'll be back in a minute – I'll go and get some information from Charlie. He knows a lot about this place'.

And so he did. Within minutes Sammy was back with some welcome facts and figures about the Hackle. Characters like Sammy and Charlie are invaluable when it comes to research, as are others, like regular Nicky C, who was actually a hod-carrier on the site when the pub was being erected.

Within half an hour Anita, an ex-employee of the Hackle, arrived. She had worked at the pub as a barmaid, and was adamant that there was a 'presence' in the building. She should know, for one evening she had an encounter with it herself.

Although she couldn't remember the exact date, Anita was pretty certain that the incident occurred in November, 1999. Again it was late at night, and the last of the inn's customers had turned up their collars and set out into the cold, winter air to wind their way home. Anita was alone in the bar and, as was the custom every evening, she went to remove the plug which attached the juke box to the mains. She had done this many times before, and on each occasion the plug had slid from the socket effortlessly.

But this time it was different. As Anita tried to remove the plug it stubbornly refused to budge. The harder she tried, the more determined the plug seemed to be to stay exactly where it was. Eventually she managed to remove the plug a small distance, but to her astonishment found that this was not to someone's liking. Exactly who that 'someone' was will undoubtedly be a matter of debate for some time to come, but the fact is that Anita distinctly felt an invisible hand press against her own and, quite literally, force the plug back into the socket.

The authors are sure that some of the wags who frequent the Red Hackle will undoubtedly try and engage Anita in some good-natured banter, but to be honest it isn't really a laughing matter. Experiences such as this can have a profound effect on people.

'Just talking about it makes the hairs on my neck stand on end', she said.

But if Anita's experience was frightening, it was nonetheless eclipsed by an incident which involved a local taxi-driver and Hackle regular. Alan had asked Dave to pop in to the pub to meet me, and his story was, to say the least, quite startling.

Dave told Mike that five years previously he had been drinking in the Red Hackle one evening. Come closing time, the (then) manager and two other friends sat talking with Dave, no doubt engaging in animated dialogue about sport, politics or some other topic. Time flew by quickly, and before anyone realised it the clock struck 1am. Just as they were preparing to leave, Dave noticed something out of the corner of his eye. Something, stealthily, was moving in the corner of the bar.

Professional paranormal investigators know that apparitions often disappear if you try and focus on them, and that they most often appear initially in the field of peripheral vision. Naturally, however, Dave did what anyone else would have done under the circumstances and immediately turned his head to see what it was. With hindsight, he may have wished he'd turned the other way. Standing in the corner – apparently invisible to Dave's companions – was a dark, shadowy figure. It was, says Dave a male figure, but he was unable to state whether it was old or young, or what sort of clothes it was wearing.

Seeing a phantasm like this would unnerve the stoutest of souls, but what happened next was chilling. The apparition slowly raised its arm and pointed directly at the stunned taxi driver before promptly disappearing. Shocked, Dave turned to his colleagues and said, 'Did you see that?' But they hadn't.

In folklore, apparitions which interact with humans in this way are not always seen as sinister. Although the apparition itself may cause alarm, even downright terror, some researchers believe that they are actually trying to do the witness a favour by 'warning' them of something which has yet to occur. Was the phantasm trying to warn Dave of some impending disaster or negative experience? Judge for yourself, but the fact is that, the following morning, Dave's car suffered a blown tire whilst he was driving through Moffat Avenue, which is adjacent to the Red Hackle. Out of control, the vehicle only came to a halt after it careered into a lamppost and demolished it. We can but wonder.

Other staff and patrons have heard and seen strange things, too. One night, when two of the bar staff were sitting talking, the gaming machine across the bar suddenly 'dropped its jackpot'. No one was near the machine at the time.

Other staff members have heard rapping sounds coming from the lounge, and have identified the noises as identical to those that customers make when they tap their knuckles on the counter to gain the attention of bar staff. It's as if spectral drinkers are knocking on the bar in an effort to place an order.

If the Red Hackle is haunted – and it is difficult to imagine otherwise – the question is, who or what is doing the haunting? Alan distinctly heard a female voice speak to him. Dave saw the apparition of a distinctly male figure. Perhaps there are a brace of ghosts in the Red Hackle, then.

Often it is tempting to assume that pub apparitions are the spirits of well-loved characters who frequented the place and do not wish to leave. This is a quaint idea, but one we should treat with caution.

The first manager of the Red Hackle, we are informed, was a gregarious chap by the name of Geordie Mason. Sammy described him as a large, powerfully-built man with a shock of white, curly hair. 'He was a gentle giant', says Sammy, 'a real character'. Mike asked one of the locals whether Geordie was still alive. 'Nah…died years ago', he said.

Nothing, as far as we can tell, connects the strange goings-on in the Red Hackle with Geordie the Gentle Giant, and so the nature of the haunting must, for the time being at least, remain a mystery.

For connoisseurs of good beer and ghost stories, a visit to the Red Hackle is a must.

PUB:	THE ROBIN HOOD
LOCATION:	JARROW
GOOD GHOST RATING:	8

The Robin Hood is situated at Primrose Hill, Jarrow, and has a long and interesting history. When Mike was in his early twenties he used to live only a stone's throw from 'The Robin' and used to pop in every Sunday night for a pint with some chums. He also recalls 'wetting the head' of his first son there after witnessing the traumatic events that took place in the delivery suite at the hospital, and, as all first-time fathers know, it can be a nerve-racking experience.

As far as Mike recalls there was never any talk of ghosts back then, but there certainly is now. In November 2008 he visited the pub to interview the proprietor Jess McConnell, who had an interesting tale to tell. Just a few days previously the bar staff had locked up for the night and were standing by the door when they heard an almighty crash. A large, ornate brewery clock had seemingly 'fallen' from the wall and was lying several feet away. The staff were puzzled.

Several nights later the same thing happened again, this time in the presence of two workmen, Alan and John, who were helping with extensive renovation work that was being carried out on the premises. Once again they fixed the clock and replaced it on the wall.

When Mike spoke to the workmen they told him that on both occasions the wooden back of the clock was still left hanging on the wall whilst the rest of the apparatus had seemingly sauntered through the ether to its final resting place.

The clue to the sudden onset of this paranormal activity might well be due to the fact that renovations were being carried out at The Robin Hood. It is a well-known fact that ghosts do not seem to like changes being made to their haunting environment, and will often make their displeasure felt by throwing things around as if engaging in a psychic temper-tantrum.

The Robin Hood has real spirits as well as real ales, then ...

• PUB: THE SAXON INN
• LOCATION: ESCOMB
• GOOD GHOST RATING: 5

Escomb is a village that lies close to Bishop Auckland and takes great pride in its rich Saxon heritage. We should not be surprised, then, to find there a public house by the name of the Saxon Inn, although records show that it had previously been called the Royal Oak.

According to legend the Saxon Inn is haunted by the shade of an ancient Saxon farmer whose attachment to the land pre-dated by a long way the existence of this pleasant watering hole. No one knows who he is, of course, but he often appears in a cowl. Other witnesses simply see a 'hazy figure' flit across the bar, or a slight movement out of the corner of their eye. But they know something is there. Not knowing his name, some locals have simply taken to referring to the ghost as 'the Saxon', which seems quite fitting.

When Sunderland ghost hunter Alan Tedder visited the inn, he was told by one of the locals that the ghost loves to play pranks on unsuspecting patrons. One of his favourite tricks is to throw full bottles of whisky down the cellar steps, and yet, mysteriously, none ever seem to break. They may bounce, but will never shatter, for which those who enjoy a drop of the hard stuff must be forever grateful.

One of the curious aspects of this haunting is the affection the Saxon demonstrates towards landlords who are about to leave the inn. One departing manager found a number of used glasses behind the bar washed, dried and put away when he was the only one on the premises. This occurred two days before he left.

An even stranger incident occurred when an extremely popular landlord decided that it was time to retire and hang his bar cloth over the taps for one last time. He chose to throw a farewell party for all the patrons who had befriended him during his tenure, but it seems that the emotion of the moment got to him and he imbibed slightly more alcohol than he probably intended. Without warning he suddenly found himself vertically challenged, and, rather than disgrace himself by falling over, stretched out on two adjacent chairs in the bar.

To their astonishment, a number of patrons observed the spectre leaning over him with its hands resting upon the landlord's chest, almost as if by pressing him down he would impede his departure.

Another witness – described by a friend as 'a no-nonsense bloke' – recalled one amusing incident while he was drinking in the bar. Suddenly his glass of beer began sliding along the counter, which sent him into a panic for two good reasons. Firstly, glasses are not supposed to move of their own accord. Secondly, blokes always panic when someone, invisible or otherwise, tries to pinch their beer.

Quite miffed, the patron bellowed, "Hoi! Bring that back!"

And lo and forsooth, the glass immediately slid across the bar back to him.

It is not only the Saxon Inn that is haunted, but also its immediate environs. The riverbanks at Escomb are a haunt not only of fishermen but also of ghosts. One local chap, citing an example, described the time he saw a figure walking along the bank towards him. Thinking it was a friend he hailed him with a wave, but the figure vanished before his very eyes.

Like many other pubs in this guide, the Saxon Inn has an unrivalled reputation for food – you should try the rack of lamb or the stake and ale pie. The landlord will make sure you don't go away without a belly full of the finest scran and a ghostly tale or two to get you thinking.

IN-DEPTH CASE STUDY: THE SCHOONER HOTEL, ALNMOUTH
Good Ghost Rating: 9

The Schooner Hotel is situated on the coastline of Northumbria, close to Alnwick. Previously a coaching inn built in the seventeenth century, this 32-roomed hotel is reputedly the most haunted hotel in the UK. No one knows exactly when this listed building was constructed.

The village of Alnmouth where the Schooner Hotel is located, has an interesting past. The Luftwaffe once bombed it during World War II. On

November 8, 1941, two bombs hit the village; one landed in Argyle Street and the other in a street not too far away. The resulting explosions precipitated the deaths of many civilians and three houses were completely destroyed.

On September 6, 1940, a Spitfire from 610 Squadron based at Acklington crashed on the beach at Alnmouth. Flying Officer C.H. Bacon was killed instantly. Going further back along the historical timeline to the thirteenth century, we find Alnmouth being hit by the Plague.

The Methodist preacher John Wesley also had some negative thoughts about Alnmouth, describing it as 'a place of all kinds of wickedness'. The hotel also has a macabre past, with tales of mass murders, suicides, smuggling activities and all kinds of mysteries dating back throughout its 400-year history. The Schooner has also had its fair share of famous faces staying there, such as Charles Dickens, Basil Rathbone, Douglas Bader, and even King George III. Even John Wesley, despite his rather dim view of the place, reputedly lodged there for a time.

The Schooner Hotel has become one of the most well-known haunted hotels in the country. It is famed for its ghostly inhabitants and paranormal activity. Investigators from all over the UK visit the hotel in their droves in the hope of uncovering some of the Schooner's macabre history and sordid secrets – allegedly including lost loves, rapes and other salacious events.

It is no wonder, then, that the Schooner Hotel claims to have so many resident spectres.

An oft-related tale of a young lady who took her own life and sacrificed the life of her unborn child, intrigues patrons of the hotel and other visitors to the village.

It had been a month or so since Eleanor had heard from her husband Jack. He'd been working overseas and she was desperate for some contact with her spouse. Daily she would wait by the harbour, for hours on end, in the hope Jack would soon return home to be with her. Eleanor, you see, was carrying Jack's unborn child.

As the days wore on, Eleanor's concern increased and she became physically ill. The owners of the Schooner Hotel looked kindly upon her, as she had no family in the locality. Patiently they looked after the heavily pregnant woman and consented to care for her until – hopefully – her husband returned home from his seagoing activities.

Early one morning, Eleanor was woken up and informed that her husband had been lost at sea some time ago and would now never return to her side. Devastated at the fact she would not see her husband again, combined with the knowledge that she would have to raise their child on her own, she fled to her room and killed herself along with her unborn child. The method

Eleanor chose to dispatch herself into the afterlife was particularly horrific; she knifed herself in the stomach, killing both herself and the child in one blow. As she lay bleeding to death, her blood spilled across the bed and ran in rivulets down onto the floor. Hearing her blood-curdling wails, her friends raced to her room – but it was too late. By the time they burst through the door both Eleanor and the child she was carrying were dead.

Eleanor's body was cremated and her ashes were scattered on the nearby beach. What actually happened to Jack no one knows, but his body was never returned to Alnmouth.

Eleanor's spectre reputedly wanders around the hotel, still awaiting the return of her dear husband. On some occasions, her spine-chilling screams have been heard echoing around the premises – making the blood of those who hear them run cold.

September is said to be a busy time for spirit activity at the Schooner. Local legend has it that, in the year 1742, the Schooner Hotel began to brew its own, special ale and a cask of it was presented to the local cleric, known as Parson John. As he fumbled to open the cask in eager anticipation, the tap is said to have fired off and hit him on the head, killing him instantly. The tap was returned to the Schooner Inn and, supposedly, was never used again.

Locals believe that should they ever use the 'cursed tap', or return it to the cask, the parson's blood will surely flow from it. During the month of September the ghost of the parson supposedly walks the corridors of the Schooner Hotel holding the offending tap above his head for all to see.

One of the most famous ghost stories concerning the Schooner Hotel is that of a family massacre that allegedly took place several hundred years ago. Rooms 28, 29 and 30, all situated at the top of the hotel, are said to comprise some of the oldest parts of the premises. They are also said to be the most paranormally active areas in the hotel, although when the massacre took place it is believed that they were all one, large room in which the family resided.

One dark winter's night, supposedly, 'William' came home after a night spent in several local taverns and, for some unknown reason, brutally killed his wife and children. Contrary to what people may assume, it is actually the ghost of William that is said to haunt this upper section of the hotel rather than his butchered family.

However, the sounds of a woman crying and the screams and wails of tormented children have occasionally been reported over the years by staff and guests alike in other parts of the hotel. Could these sounds be attributed to William's murder victims? William is not only reported to haunt rooms 28, 29 and 30, but is also said to make his presence felt throughout the rest of the hotel. His evil presence has sometimes been felt in Room 7, resulting in paying guests fleeing from the premises in absolute terror. Room 4 of the hotel is also believed to be one of William's haunts, if you'll excuse the pun and the room is consistently cold even during the summer. In fact, Room 4 is colloquially known as 'the Cold Room'. Even the mention of William's name to locals and hotel staff may send shivers down their spines.

Christmas Day, 1806, saw the worst storms in Alnmouth history. As the winds howled and the rains lashed down, a small family was crowded around the fire in what is now the Schooner Hotel's 'Chase Bar'. They were anxiously waiting for their father to return home from a fishing trip out in the North Sea. One of the daughters was lying asleep in her mother's lap when, suddenly, a number of fishermen burst into the room holding the lifeless body of their father. The mother quickly stood up to see her husband, forgetting that her child was sleeping on her lap. The youth subsequently fell into the fireplace, hitting her head upon the hearth. After frantic efforts she was pulled out of the fire – burnt, charred and choking on her own blood. She later died of her terrible injuries. She was only six years old.

On countless occasions the ghost of a small girl has been seen and heard in this area. One lady said that, whilst sitting in the restaurant adjacent to the Chase Bar, she heard the distinct sound of a young girl crying. Knowing the bar was empty at the time, she ventured around to see whom the girl was with. At that juncture the eerie noises abruptly ceased and there was no sign of her. Another witness claimed that whilst she was sitting in the bar having a drink a young girl ran in, looked at her and then simply vanished in front of her.

The Schooner Hotel is also said to be haunted by a number of other spectres and visitors from 'the other side'. These include a lady who walks the corridors of the hotel, tapping and knocking on the walls and doors. Another woman who was brutally beaten and strangled to death is said to haunt the first floor of the hotel. A man in an RAF uniform is said to appear, glide down the corridors of rooms 15-19 and then promptly disappear at the end of the hall. However, the most sinister apparition was seen adjacent to Room 20.

Two employees of the hotel were doing their rounds one morning when, out of Room 20, came 'a black figure'. It flew out of the room and collided with the fire exit door opposite creating a loud bang as it did so. To their utter horror, it then, came padding down the corridor towards them. They dropped everything and ran away terrified. Allegedly, these eyewitnesses were extremely shaken due to their experience.

In 2007, Mike visited the Schooner Hotel with his wife Jackie and was able to elicit a good deal of information about the ghosts of the premises from the staff. Taken with the ambience of the inn, he had no difficulty in believing that at least some of the legends may be true and that the hotel may really be haunted. Darren and his team have investigated the Schooner Hotel on a number of occasions and have had many strange things happen to them during the course of the investigations. Locked doors had been found unlocked and wide open on their return from their night vigils when the team were the only people on the premises. Trigger objects had been moved from their respective positions whilst in locked off and controlled environments, and on one terrifying occasion Darren was actually chased along a corridor by a threatening, yet invisible presence. It was accompanied with the sound of heavy footfalls and resulted in Darren running headlong into a wall gashing his wrist, bumping his head, stubbing his toes...but worse still, smashing his clipboard he was using for note taking.

Of course ghost hunters are not supposed to run from what they are seeking but Darren admits 'we are dealing with the unknown here and I suppose my survival instinct told me to get the hell out, so I did, at some speed, I can tell you'.

- Pub: THE SCOTIA
- Location: SOUTH SHIELDS
- Good Ghost Rating: 8

At the juncture of Mile End Road and King Street lies the Scotia Hotel – one of the borough's most interesting public houses. Once a rather unsophisticated beer bar, the inn's increasing popularity with drinkers dictated that an extension was added. Even this proved insufficient, and eventually the original structure was demolished and much more sophisticated one built in its place.

The Scotia is, essentially, a Victorian 'long bar' which runs from the aforementioned King Street through to the other entrance on Mile End Road. Upper stories once open to the public have been blocked off for many years and, we believe, are no longer accessible.

Originally pronounced scot-ee-ya, emphasising the 't', this was later changed to the more up-market sounding skoe-sher, which it retains to this very day.

The Scotia is allegedly haunted by a spectre known as Tommy the Cellarman, who seemingly passed away in the mid-70s. Some say he died on the premises. Tommy walked with a limp and always used a walking stick. Staff have repeatedly heard the sound of his distinctive gait as he walks up and down the cellar steps.

The authors have visited the Scotia on numerous occasions, but have never seen the shade of old Tommy. However, they were told by one of the bar staff, that a former landlady once took a picture of some staff members at Christmastime and, when it was developed, Tommy was standing there as large as life. Attempts by the authors to track down this photograph have been unsuccessful.

- **PUB:**　　　　　　　　　THE SEABURN HOTEL
- **LOCATION:**　　　　　　　SEABURN
- **GOOD GHOST RATING:**　4

The renowned artist L.S. Lowry actually hailed from Manchester, but until his death in February 1976 his favourite pub was said to be The Seaburn Hotel.

Lowry, known for earthy paintings such as The Accident and The Empty House, excelled at painting industrial scenes from the north of England in his distinctive 'matchstick men' style. We are the less for his passing. Whether the rugged painter haunts the Seaburn Hotel we cannot say, but other ghosts are said to.

One female phantom is described as being 'middle aged, and with long grey hair', the latter feature being the only one to our knowledge that would explain why she has been labelled 'The Grey Lady'.

One of the peculiarities of this haunting is that the spectre seems to make a real effort to get on with the patrons, chatting to them and even addressing them by their names! She also looks solid enough, which makes one wonder how many times she may have appeared to punters at the bar when they didn't even realise that she was dead.

Like Lucinda who haunted the late, lamented Half Moon Hotel in Gateshead, the Grey Lady has a mischievous sense of humour. She has been known to creep up behind the staff and touch them gently on the back of the neck. However, she never lingers around for too long, and always vanishes rather quickly into the ether. The staff members at the Seaburn Hotel are at pains to stress that that the ghost is a model citizen who sees to it that everything is kept in its proper place. God bless her, we say.

- **PUB:**　　　　　　　　　THE SHIP INN
- **LOCATION:**　　　　　　　FELLING
- **GOOD GHOST RATING:**　4

The Ship Inn on High Heworth Lane, Felling, is reputed to be haunted but no one seems to know exactly who by. However, like many other pub ghosts, this one also seems to take great pleasure in turning the pumps on and off, much to the dismay of the bar staff.

On one occasion we were told, the old innkeeper, on popping down to the cellar to find the cause of the problem, discovered that the gas bottles had been manually turned off and yet the cellar had been empty all morning.

This particular spectre seems to have the interests of the bar at heart. This may not be surprising if, as some suggest, it is the spirit of a former manager, who, having died on the premises, was laid out in the very cellar he is now said to haunt ...

- **PUB:** SOUTH SHIELDS POLICE CLUB
- **LOCATION:** SOUTH SHIELDS
- **GOOD GHOST RATING:** 4

On the floor above the old Crime Prevention Department at South Shields Police Station, in Keppel Street, was the Police Club; a popular retreat for officers and civilian employees alike who wanted to down a cold pint of ale before wandering off home. The bar was popular, but so too were the toilets, for obvious reasons.

The Gents' Toilet was said to be 'haunted' – although certainly not by a ghost.

A number of officers reported that if they stood at a particular urinal they would feel as if a large drop of water had splashed upon their head. Instinctively they would raise a hand to their skull but would inevitably find their hair (or bald pate) bone dry. Further examination of the ceiling – in a search for pools of condensation that would explain the phenomenon – were always fruitless. One CID sergeant became so unnerved by this occurrence – which happened to him repeatedly – that he refused to use the toilets again.

Mike, during his tenure as a Special Constable, often used to visit the Police Club and experienced the 'phantom drip' phenomenon himself.

Bizarre though this tale is, it is actually true and other such reports, almost identical in nature, have been made in places as far-flung as the USA and Scandinavia.

The authors are puzzled, and if readers have any explanations ... well, answers on a postcard please!

- PUB: THE SPORTSMAN
- LOCATION: EAGLESCLIFFE
- GOOD GHOST RATING: 5

Eaglescliffe is a small town that nestles within the borough of Stockton-on-Tees and lies just north of the Tees river.

North of Eaglescliffe in the beautiful Tees Valley, which makes the area a favourite haunt of tourists who want to get away from it all. A leisurely walk around the woods, taking in the flora and fauna of one of the North's most revered beauty spots; what could be better?

Well, you could always visit one of the local hostelries for a decent pub lunch and an ice-cold pint, for starters, and, back in the mid-1990s, you could have done worse than pop in to the Sportsman's Hotel.
Providing you didn't mind sharing the bar with a spectre or two, that is. 'The Sportsman's', you see, was at that time rapidly gaining a reputation for being well and truly haunted.

The unusual thing about the spirits – and we're not referring to the alcoholic variety – found at this delightful little pub was that they seemed to operate to a very strict schedule. Indeed, they only seemed to appear on Wednesdays, which is market day in nearby Stockton.

One common feature of haunted pubs is that the resident spooks seem to have a penchant for messing around in the cellar. The spectres at the Sportsman's Hotel (now renamed simply 'The Sportsman') was no different, and gas bottles and keg taps were continually turned on and off by unseen hands. In addition, glasses were found left on the bar when no one was present, a cleaner once saw a disembodied pair of feet in the cellar and, to top it all, a Victorian-looking lady in a grey and black dress once appeared in the flat upstairs.

So, what – or who – could be responsible for the eerie events at The Sportsman? Our research didn't turn up any local characters associated with the pub in times past, although readers may know differently. However, one of the bars used to be a waiting room at the adjacent railway station before being subsumed into the pub.

Could the ghost hail from an era before the Sportsman's Hotel took over the room, and perhaps have some connection with the railway station? Vague rumours of a woman being hit by a train at the turn of the twentieth century kept cropping up, but nothing you could actually hang your hat on, so to speak. The then manager Norman Hart has moved on, but the Sportsman still thrives. However, as the pub doesn't have a phone, we weren't able to find out whether Wednesdays were still filled with all sorts of paranormal pandemonium.

Our saviour turned out to be Anna from The Waiting Room – there's a coincidence – a highly-regarded vegetarian restaurant just across the road. Acting as our unofficial researcher she happily ferried messages to the Hotel for the authors and found out what she could.

We're happy to add Anna to our roll of honour for her efforts, and unashamedly give The Waiting Room a plug for her kindness.

Next time you happen to be passing Eaglescliffe, why not pop in to the Sportsman and see for yourself whether the Grey Lady is willing to make an appearance? If she does, please let the authors know what happens...

Sources: The personal archives of Alan Tedder.

- PUB: THE SPRING GARDENS
- LOCATION: SOUTH SHIELDS
- GOOD GHOST RATING: 6

Elizabeth 'Betty' Heron was something of a character, apparently being related to the wealthy nineteenth-century South Shields shipping magnate Sir Cuthbert Heron. Sir Cuthbert did have a daughter called Elizabeth, although it is highly unlikely that they are the same person. Sir Cuthbert's daughter was a lady of grace and social standing. Our Betty Heron was slightly less refined, shall we say.

Betty lived in a cottage near to where the north-west entrance to the South Marine Park now looks out onto Ocean Road. The locals were slightly suspicious of her, although she had gained something of a reputation as 'a wise woman'. Betty also kept goats. We don't know what breed they were, but by all accounts they had a psychopathic quality which made them want to kill everyone who came near them. Betty herself often got on the wrong side of her pets, and on more than one occasion had to be carted off to the infirmary in a serious condition after they turned on her. Nevertheless she always seemed to recover.

Betty earned her living in several ways. She took in washing – a popular 'guvvy job' back then – rented out small boats to pleasure trippers and also sold 'ginger beer and sweet cakes' to passers-by.

Always one to buck tradition if she felt like it, Betty did a large wash for a neighbour one Good Friday and hung the clothes around the picket fence which surrounded her cottage. This bothered her more pious neighbours who said that no good would come of it. Working on a Good Friday in those days was tantamount to dancing with the Devil himself. Betty ignored their comments and got on with her chores.

Several hours later Betty ventured outside to check the washing and see if it was dry. To her horror she noticed that huge splashes of blood were covering the clothes and sheets, and there seemed to be no natural explanation as to how they got there.

Betty's neighbours knew of course. This was a sign from the Almighty that she shouldn't have worked on a Good Friday. The authors have another theory.

The famous South Shields naturalist William Yellowly once remarked, 'I have frequently seen the ravens in early morning sailing in graceful circles at a great altitude above their nests; and once I saw a pair of these sable marauders each carry away a gosling as large as a partridge, which they bore away to their young in the cliffs. I was informed by my uncles that they not only lost chickens and goslings, but frequently had young lambs killed by these voracious birds. During the lambing season the ravens would sit near the ewes, croaking the while; and if the opportunity arose they would at once seize and carry off the newborn lamb. And sickly and dying sheep would have their eyes picked out by the same birds'.

Bear in mind that the seagulls which we now see in their hordes did not dominate the coast then; the ravens did. The authors think there was probably a dog-fight of sorts above Betty's cottage between two birds and the blood that was spilt during the carnage ended up over the freshly washed clothes. (Mind you, its possible that one of Betty's killer goats gobbled up a passer-by and the washing got splashed with blood in the ensuing frenzy. Only joking).

Still, The authors think they may inform their 'significant others' not to wash next Good Friday. Best not take chances, we always say, and we'll tell you why. The north of England has a rich mine of folklore the equal of any other in the world. The authors were stunned to find old records from Cleveland which stated that anyone who washes clothes on a Good Friday would find them 'spotted with blood'.

Betty's cottage eventually became a hostelry known as the Spring Gardens, although the name was eventually appropriated by another drinking den nearby. A number of spectres were said to haunt the pub, although the tales have become confused – always the case when dealing with two establishments which bear the same name.

In-depth Case Study: The Stately House [Pseudonym], Near Haltwhistle – *Good Ghost Rating: 9*

The beautiful old public house we take you to now lies in a serene area of the Northumbrian and Cumbrian countryside. Due to the nature of the haunting activities the authors felt compelled to include it. However, due to the disturbing nature of the paranormal phenomena and the owners' concerns regarding them, all concerned felt it necessary to keep its location secret and the names of the principal experients will therefore remain anonymous.

In the past few years or so, a male ghost has been seen inside the property – emerging from a wall and slowly walking along the bar area until he gets to a certain point in the room. Then he simply disappears. He has been seen countless times by the pub owners and has also been 'sensed' and seen by visitors to the establishment.

The owners of this pub are obviously very distressed and frightened by these episodes and recently called in G.H.O.S.T. in the hope that they could give them some answers as to who the ghost was and why he was haunting their bar. We arrived at the location at about 11.00pm, but did not get started until the early hours of the following morning. We split our team into two, while one group went into Room 1 upstairs and the other stayed downstairs in the bar. It was Darren's group that ventured upstairs first and went into Room 1. The first thing they noticed was how cold the room was. By all accounts the room is always that cold and no matter what the owners do to try and heat it up, it remains that way! Anyway, they sat there for a short while, just listening and observing.

Darren asked his colleague, Lee Stephenson, if he was drawn to anywhere in the room as he tends to get 'feelings' about certain places, and he told Darren he was, for some reason, 'drawn' to the door that led into the room. This was odd to say the least, as that's where Darren found his eyes being drawn, too. Why? He doesn't know. He admitted to being 'trigger-happy' with his digital camera whilst in that room, and that in itself proved fruitful to say the least as he took a great photograph of what we believe to be a 'ghostly mist'. When the investigators purposely tried to reproduce this effect with their breath they could not. After a while, as nothing much else was happening, they headed back downstairs for the first séance of the evening with the other team members. The owners of this fine establishment also participated in this experiment.

At 2.46hrs, the séance started. After asking any presence to make itself known to those gathered, the researchers all started to hear noises and sense movement coming from around the circle area. Light anomalies were caught on camera and a temperature drop was recorded in the middle of the circle. After a while things seemed to calm down a bit, and then Darren was asked to lead the séance to see if a male voice would make the ghosts respond any better. Everyone sat back down, all joined fingers on the table and Darren asked all present to focus on their breathing and uncross their legs whilst keeping their feet flat on the floor. He then asked any spirits in the room if they would make themselves known. He repeated the request, but this time addressed the ghost by his name, as through research carried out by Drew Bartley prior to the investigation they believed they now had the name of the frequently seen apparition. For reasons already stated, this name too must be kept anonymous.

'Mr X', Darren asked. 'If you are here with us and can hear my voice, and understand what I am saying, please give us a sign'.

He then asked if there were any more ghosts other than Mr X listening in, could they too make their presence known.

'Give us a knock or a rap ... tap on something or touch someone ... please let us know you are with us tonight'.

It was at this point, to Darren's front right and behind two of the sitters, he saw (or he thought he saw) a black shape with a human form. It was standing right in the spot where the resident ghost is said to come through the wall. Darren looked away, admittedly frightened, and when he turned back around to catch a second glimpse of the entity, it was gone.

This actually happened twice during the séance. Knocks and bumps were also heard throughout the proceedings and all present thought they heard the shuffling of ghostly feet. The other amazing thing was that, as the séance was drawing to a close, the table tilted right off its feet and no one admitted to having done it. Darren asked them repeatedly if anyone had 'faked' the incident, but everyone was adamant that they had neither pushed nor tilted the table – or moved it back again. Then Darren's arms, and especially his thighs, went bitterly cold and he said that he 'did not feel right'. Suddenly the table vibrated as though it was in the centre of an earth tremor – and then it stopped. It vibrated once more before the close of the séance and Darren later commented that it had 'felt weird'. Another sitter present also said his arms and thighs went bitterly cold, and he too felt the table vibrate twice. Not a bad start!

The investigators had a break for a while and, when they asked for the lights to be turned on, a bulb exploded with a bang and an electric fan started to turn; even though the researchers were told the fan had not been switched on! Upon checking the trigger object – the usual crucifix – which had been placed on a chair earlier on, they found it had been moved about 5mm. It is interesting to note that three individuals who attended the séance, when asked what they had thought of the proceedings, told Darren that they were 'sitting in sceptic's corner'. After some discussion, one young lady in particular said 'the whole ghost thing and the séance was literally rubbish' or, to quote her without paraphrase, 'It's all fucking bollocks'. Neither she nor her colleagues were convinced.

After a break the team moved from the area of the first séance and sat at the other side of the bar for séance number two, the idea being that the area in which the ghost was said to walk could be monitored properly while the séance was actually in progress. Darren ran the séance while two other team members, Drew and Fiona, monitored the area. Darren initiated the séance and almost immediately the proprietor's wife suffered immense hot and cold flushes. At the same time she felt she wanted to cry one minute but then felt OK the next. This continued throughout the proceedings. Darren asked her if she was alright time and time again throughout the séance, but each time she told him to continue.

Darren later recalled, 'I think for her it was something she had never experienced before and it had a profound effect. This is where the séance took a turn. While I was asking Mr X to show himself, knocks bumps, footsteps and shuffling were all heard in the area being monitored by our team members. Lots of light anomalies were caught on digital camera and the more I asked for Mr X the more phenomena were being reported'.

A massive temperature drop was then recorded with the laser thermometer gun. In the space 90 seconds the temperature dropped a staggering $14°$. Meanwhile, in the circle, the owner's wife was shivering with cold and was almost weeping. Two of the sitters were now claiming to be able to see the ghost!

'It was pitch black, and I think everyone was excited yet quite scared at the same time. I needed to be over in the bar area; so, without breaking the circle – a no-no in psychical research – I asked one of the sitters to continue with the séance while I ventured across. Another team member, Fiona, had been taking some stills with my camera, catching some good light anomalies and, stranger still, a bizarre red mist. She took a series of photographs and only one came out showing the red mist. I had to ask her if she could have had a finger poised over the flash of the camera, possibly causing a red tint across the frame. I thought that the light could have bounced off her finger, creating this sort of effect, but she was adamant that she took the photos the same way as she had the rest'.

So why did only one investigator come up with this anomaly? Is it not also too much of a coincidence that this photo was taken at the precise time of all the others reported both seeing and sensing paranormal activity?

We must now refer the reader back to the sighting of the ghost by two sitters during the séance. The young lady who earlier on had offered her precise scientific analysis that 'Its all fucking bollocks' was one of these sitters who claimed to have seen the apparition during the séance! As it turned out, after the séance ended she was very badly shaken up, threw up violently in the toilets and then quickly vacated the premises. A total sceptic had been converted, which in turn made her 'sceptical friends' think again as they left immediately after the séance too.

So, after a very slow start to the night, it turned out to be quite an interesting evening indeed. Lots of unusual activity was recorded and documented. Although only two areas in the whole building were investigated (Room 1 and the bar), the results attained were quite astonishing to say the least. With regards to the apparition, Darren explained to the pub owners what he thought.

'Every time this ghost is seen it appears from out of the same section of wall and takes his walk along the bar area. He then disappears at exactly the same point every time, which leads me to the conclusion that this ghost is nothing more than a residual 'stone tape' or 'place-memory' apparition. I explained it posed no threat to them or their family whatsoever. They were happy with my diagnosis'.

Darren later elaborated, 'I think closure and understanding of the haunting of this establishment for the people who live there is a must. I now believe that they are on their way to understanding this particular haunting after our investigation and after I explained a few things to them. The residents now seem a lot happier with the idea of what they have; or at least they now know the ghost or apparition is a harmless playback or psychic recording of nothing more than a nice old gentleman who once lived there'.

IN-DEPTH CASE STUDY: THE STEAMBOAT, SOUTH SHIELDS
Good Ghost Rating: 8

The Mill Dam is a fascinating place. Its proximity to the river generates a rich aura of days gone by, when old sea-dogs stood chatting with a clay pipe in one hand and a hip flask full of rum in the other.

The Mill Dam is, we think, one of the 'forgotten' parts of South Shields with an extremely interesting past.

Over the years, the area has been associated with several fascinating ghost stories. Spectral seamen, ghostly fishermen and even a 'grey lady' who was alleged to float down Coronation Street at dawn and frighten the life out of anyone who happened to be on their way to work.

Alan Tedder – whom we really must appoint as our Researcher and Archivist In Chief, as he sends us so many good ghost stories – told us a particularly interesting tale about the Steamboat inn.

It seems that many years ago – when the Steamboat was merely a 'beer house' and didn't have a license to sell spirits – a regular drinker in the pub had something of a reputation for being a hard drinker and a loud talker. A retired seaman, he would brag to all and sundry of his exploits upon the briny, and could become quite tetchy if he suspected that those listening weren't taking him seriously. One evening, after consuming a surfeit of ale, he staggered to the top of the cellar steps, swayed, muttered something unintelligible and promptly fell headlong down the stairwell to his death.

For a week all was quiet, and then someone reported seeing the old sailor walking past the door which led into the street. They dashed out to catch him, but to no avail. He had vanished into the fog.

But then other customers began seeing him to. Even during the 1950s the old salt made frequent appearances. One winter's evening, a female customer saw an old man sitting in the corner dressed in old-fashioned clothing. Jokingly she asked him which fancy-dress party he was going to, and could she tag along. He didn't reply. Miffed, the lady in question asked one of the bar staff why the old man wouldn't talk to her. The barman tactfully explained that she had been trying to strike up a conversation with a denizen of the spirit world. Her reaction is not recorded.

Some years ago, Mike and his wife visited the Steamboat to check out some of the tales regarding the inn, and received an exceedingly warm welcome from Joe Mooney, the landlord, and the bar manager Dave Joseph. For the next hour and a half they were treated to a fascinating résumé of both the pub's history and its ghostly goings-on.

During the mid-1800s the inn had actually been four separate premises; a ships' chandlers, a post office (the old letter box is still outside), a beer bar and the house of Tyne Pilot Captain George Milton. In 1854 'Captain George' and his sister were found dead in mysterious circumstances, and it was rumoured that they had been the victims of foul play, although nothing was ever proved. It is actually the ghost of the captain, we think, which appeared 'in fancy dress' to the aforementioned patron back in the 1950s, and according to Joe and Dave still put in the odd appearance from time to time. Apparently he gets particularly irate if awkward customers try to stay in the bar after licensing hours.

Joe also showed Mike and his wife two old receipts that had been found in the loft, dated 1831 and 1836 respectively. One was for twelve tallow candles priced at £1 and 18 shillings. Even by today's standards we think that's pretty pricey, but never mind. A frame on the wall also contains a seaman's discharge papers from *c.*1830.

One pub regular is David Walker – also known as Erasmus Bottle (don't ask why) – and he's actually written a hilarious history of the Steamboat, copies of which may still be on sale at the bar.

IN-DEPTH CASE STUDY: THE TOBY CARVERY, CLEADON VILLAGE
Good Ghost Rating: 8

The Toby Carvery – formerly known as the Britannia Inn – is supposedly one of the oldest public houses in the Borough of South Tyneside, and stands at the junction of Sunderland Road and Boldon Lane, Cleadon Village. It is a large, stolid building which looks as if it would withstand anything short of a thermonuclear conflagration. Its stout, stone walls exude tremendous character.

The authors say that it is allegedly one of the oldest inns, and with good reason. The Toby Carvery was originally built as a coaching inn, although there is some slight doubt about exactly when. There is a stone fireplace in the pub which some scholars have described as 'original', giving the impression that it was part of the original structure of the inn and incorporated in the building when it was first constructed. Alas, this is not true. There is a date inscribed on the fireplace; 1675. However, there is evidence to suggest that an inn stood on the site at an even earlier time, at least as far back as 1644.

Despite the great history associated with the inn, the reader should know that the Toby Carvery as you see it today only dates back to the year 1894, although it looks much older. In that year the old Britannia was demolished and rebuilt. It does, however, incorporate some features of the earlier inn, including the aforementioned fireplace.

According to legend the Toby Carvery was originally called the Laughing Cavalier – or, as some say, simply The Cavalier – but to date the authors have not been able to uncover any solid evidence to support this notion.

The mysteries surrounding the Toby Carvery are many. To begin with, there is a tunnel that leads from the inn to an extremely old house across the road, Cleadon Tower. Mike has seen both entrances to this tunnel, so there is no doubt that it exists. Both are now bricked up, however, and the tunnel is therefore inaccessible. The entrance to the tunnel from the Britannia lies in the cellar, and was until recently quite obvious.

Other tunnels are said to exist, too. One leads to a nearby cottage, apparently, whilst yet others are said to stretch as far as South Boldon, West Boldon (the Black Horse public house), Hylton Castle, Marsden Bay and even – incredibly – under the river Tyne as far as Tynemouth. Such feats of engineering boggle the imagination, but they are not impossible. Why were these tunnels built? To answer this question we need to analyse the complex political and religious situation that existed at the time.

During the Civil War, a local cottage was seemingly used as a field hospital for the Parliamentarian troops. Just across the road sat Cleadon Tower, home of the affluent and influential Chambers family. The Chambers were devout Roman Catholics and were persecuted in the most outrageous manner for no other reason than their religious affiliations. Historically the Catholic populace had precious little to thank the Royalists for, but the thought of having Oliver Cromwell in charge of the country absolutely terrified them. Despite being portrayed as a national hero and champion of the people, Cromwell had, to put it mildly, a dark side. He was a religious bigot of the first order who would stop at nothing in an effort to see off those who had the temerity to disagree with him. In fact, our research has led us to believe that the tunnel which stretches from Cleadon Tower to the Toby Carvery and beyond was actually an escape route for Catholics on the run.

To the Catholics, the Royalists were essentially the lesser of two evils. Indeed, some Catholics actually fought on the Royalist side. King James was an overt lover of ritual and had shown distinct signs of wanting to make peace with Rome. Thinking Catholics sensed that if he was allowed to keep the throne a reunion between Rome and the English secessionists was a distinct possibility.

During the Battle of Boldon, which took place in 1644, a soldier was badly wounded and, according to legend, staggered to Cleadon Tower and died of his wounds in the grounds. Stories passed on from generation to generation insist that the soldier was a Roundhead, but our research has led us to believe that he was actually a Catholic fighting on the side of the Royalists. Had he been a Parliamentarian there is no doubt in that he would have made his way not to Cleadon Tower, but to the Cromwellian field hospital at the nearby cottage, which was just yards away. Why, if you were a Parliamentarian, would you make your way to a Catholic household instead of a hospital? The authors believe that the man was hoping to escape from the Parliamentarians by using the tunnel underneath Cleadon Tower as an escape route. Alas, he died before such a plan could be effected.

But what about the Toby Carvery? Is the pub truly haunted? Indeed it is, and possibly by the same spectre who still wanders around the vicinity of Cleadon Tower, although we cannot be sure. We've have heard a story from several sources about a Cavalier who allegedly sits in the corner of the bar, drinking. He appears but momentarily before fading into the ether.

The Toby Carvery is a popular pub in Cleadon Village. It is also a perfectly decent restaurant, being part of the Toby Carvery chain. Until the 1940s, the pub had a rival for business – the Ship Inn, which stood just across the road. Royal Mail coaches had stopped at the Ship Inn twice a day until the advent of mechanised transport. When this practice stopped the Ship lost its main source of revenue, went into decline, and eventually closed. The new 'rival' to the Toby Carvery is the Cottage Tavern, which is even closer.

But back to business. When Mike visited the Toby Carvery to research the story he was greeted by John, who kindly showed him around and told him another interesting ghost tale attached to the place. In one of the anterooms, now used for storage, a member of staff allegedly happened to glance out of the window onto the street outside, and was staggered to see a phantom coach and horses glide by. A customer in the Toby Carvery told Mike a similar story, alleging that his cousin had seen a coach and horses pull up next to the pub one Christmas Eve, before promptly pulling away again and riding off into the distance.

There are other tales attached to the Toby Carvery, including the yarn about a one-legged sailor who supposedly died on the premises in the 1800s. The source of this tale is a bit unreliable, but there is no doubt that one or two real ghosts do indeed walk the floors of this old inn.

- **PUB:**   THE TRIMMERS' ARMS
- **LOCATION:**   SOUTH SHIELDS
- **GOOD GHOST RATING:**   8

Strictly speaking, the Trimmers' Arms – the now demolished premises, and not the current one – should not be included in this volume, for it was not a haunted inn. Nevertheless we have decided to buck convention and tell the reader about it anyway, and for two reasons. Firstly, the tale behind the Trimmers' Arms is exceedingly strange, at least what we know of it, that is. Secondly, it was probably the only public house in the country which is guaranteed not to be haunted, as we shall see.

At the beginning of August, 2000, Mike was giving a talk to the PROBUS fellowship in Harton Village, South Shields, and the subject of his discourse was the research he'd carried out whilst writing his book *Ales & Spirits*. At the end of the talk Mike allowed some time for questions, and one chap who had sat at the back listening very intently raised his hand and said, 'I have a question. We've all heard of 'the pub with no beer', but do you know anything about the pub that never opened?'

Mike had to confess he didn't. The pub that never opened? What sort of pub was that? The gentleman himself was very sketchy regarding the details, but said that there was, allegedly, a public house in South Shields that had been built many years ago, but which never actually opened for business. He said that the inn was apparently called the Trimmers' Arms. Mike put the word about, as they say, and, surely enough, small snippets of information started to drift back. By following the clues he ended up, one sunny afternoon two weeks later, at the end of Commercial Road, South Shields, right next to what little remains of the West End Vaults – another old pub that has now, sadly, bitten the dust.

Standing adjacent to the plot once occupied by the West End Vaults was a general dealers called Trimmers. It was for a short while a café, but by then had restricted itself to a good line in sandwiches, and presumably made its business at lunchtime, when the employees of many local businesses started to feel hunger pangs just before noon.

Mike popped in and had a word with the proprietor. Could there be, as a friend had suggested, a connection between Trimmers and the almost mythical Trimmers' Arms? Indeed there was, the proprietor said, and proceeded to tell him all about it – or at least what he knew.

Trimmers (the shop) actually occupied the same premises as the old Trimmers' Arms. What was now the shop counter would have been the bar counter, and the ornamental shelves behind had once been filled with spirits and bottled beers instead of provisions. Not that any were ever sold, mind you, for, as stated previously, the inn never actually opened its doors for business. Pigot's Directory for 1834 doesn't mention a Trimmers' Arms, and the first mention made of it in local records comes some time later.

We know that the original Trimmers' Arms did not survive long, for above the door of the shop called Trimmers there were some vestiges of the inn left; mere traces from the past, but enough to give us some scant detail. Firstly, there was a stone lintel which bore the inscription, 'The Trimmers Arms; Rebuilt 1891'. If the first Trimmers' Arms was not very old, and it was rebuilt in 1891, then it must have survived in its original form for merely a few decades. Why was it rebuilt? We have not been able to discover the reason, but it may well be that the original was destroyed by fire. If any readers of this volume can shed any light on the matter, then we would like them to get in touch with the authors so that future editions can be amended.

The doorway which would have led into the lounge had been bricked up, although the original stone step and lintel could still be seen. The remains of a further door, also blocked up, could be seen a little further down.

So why did the rebuilt Trimmers' Arms not open for business? This too is a mystery. A colleague from the *Shields Gazette* told Mike that she remembered a reader relating the story behind the Trimmers' Arms to her some time ago, but there were still too many pieces of the jigsaw missing. The most likely reason is that it was not granted a license to sell alcoholic beverages. Could the owner of the inn next door have objected on the grounds that it would have taken away his trade? Even this seems unlikely, for hardly a street in the borough was without a drinking den of some sorts, and they all seemed popular enough to rule out any form of rivalry. In short, there was enough business to go round.

There is, however, a mystery surrounding the old Trimmers' Arms after all, for the proprietor of the Trimmers store told Mike that there was a hidden room on the premises which seemed to have no visible access. Intrigued, he actually pulled up the floorboards upstairs in an effort to gain entry. He found himself staring down into a dark room which seemed to contain a considerable amount of rubble. Deciding against lowering himself down, he replaced the floorboards, thus keeping intact a mystery which was never solved, for the entire building was demolished some time later. Who was responsible for this secret room being built? What purpose did it serve? Was this room connected in some way with the failure of the inn to open for business? We can but ponder.

Happily, there is a new Trimmers' Arms on the same site – the pub's third incarnation – and this one most certainly does sell ales, and fine ones at that. It's a brand new pub, and the authors haven't heard any ghost stories attached to it. Still, give it time…

- Pub: THE TUDOR ROSE
- Location: DUNSTON, GATESHEAD
- Good Ghost Rating: 7

A work colleague of Darren's who is a regular at this pub brought the Tudor Rose to the authors' attention. Knowing that the authors were experienced ghost researchers he decided to enlighten them about the pub's resident ghost. The story appears on the back of the 'pub grub' menu that is placed on every table within the bar and restaurant and is there for the punter to read and enjoy while mulling over the fine beers and cask ales this old wonderful pub sells. The pub is said to be one of the oldest drinking dens in Dunston and was formerly called The Anchor Inn.

Many years ago the area where the pub stands – which is not far form Dunston Staiths – was used by the local shipping industry, and military naval vessels would also often visit the area. Sailors came ashore and drank in the local inns, where prostitution was rife and drunken brawls were commonplace. It is from this era that the resident ghost seems to have stemmed after allegedly being killed in one of these skirmishes.

He is a friendly ghost by all accounts, which is rather odd considering the circumstances of his demise. He has been seen in the bar on so many occasions he is now looked upon as 'just another regular'. The locals have even christened him as 'Old George'. When the authors paid a visit to the pub, they were looked after and treated well by the bar staff and enjoyed a robust meal served with a pint of bitter. Unfortunately, Old George failed to make an appearance that day, but you never know; he may show up in the future. We'll undoubtedly return in an effort to catch a glimpse of this enigmatic pub spectre.

- PUB: THE TURK'S HEAD
- LOCATION: SOUTH SHIELDS
- GOOD GHOST RATING: 2

The Turk's Head was situated on the Lawe Top in South Shields, and most would concur that it looked just like any other typical watering hole. However, this pub had one or two secrets, some of which may still be waiting to be revealed.

Ghosts, if any were here at this wonderful old pub, didn't seem to make their presence known to people that often. This begs the question; was the pub haunted at all? In times past there was talk of a spectre or two residing there – but details proved to be tantalisingly scant. When Mike first visited the pub whilst researching his book *Ales & Spirits*, the punters that frequented the old tavern couldn't recall any specific stories of ghosts or phantoms making an appearance in recent history; but they all recalled that there had at one time been 'talk' about them.

Of course, just because specific details had been washed away by the tide of time that's not to say that the shades of the departed didn't reside there. Rumour had it that under the pub itself there lay an old, disused tunnel that was once used by smugglers and vagabonds for taking away contraband and other ill-gotten gains – hiding them from the local excise men. Perhaps the ghosts, if any, inhabited the dark, unused catacombs under the pub, thus explaining the lack of activity up in the main bar. After all, smugglers' tunnels, caves, and other secret hideouts are classic abodes for denizens of the other world. Or so it is said.

It is also known that, not far away from where the pub stood, there is a blocked-up entrance to the old tunnel network. As far as the authors know this entrance has not been explored. Perhaps one day we will be given the opportunity to explore these avenues and determine once and for all if ghosts resided not in the pub, but actually deep below it. Perhaps the Turk's Head – or at least its legend – holds some mysteries after all.

- **Pub:** THE TYNEMOUTH LODGE HOTEL
- **Location:** TYNEMOUTH
- **Good Ghost Rating:** 9

The Tynemouth Lodge Hotel stands in the middle of Tynemouth Road between North Shields and the village of Tynemouth, and is situated at the junction at the top of Tanners bank. By all accounts it has been trading as a public house since 1799.

A house of correction that once housed petty criminals such as prostitutes and thieves stood right next door to this old inn, and it is said that the circuit judges at the time would stay at the Lodge Hotel while carrying out their trials in the area. Hundreds of these houses of correction were built across the UK, and it seems that this particular one is one of only a few that is left intact. The warm and friendly welcome we received on our visit there a few years ago, one dark and cold winter's night, was very much appreciated – as was the delightful stories we were told about the inn's resident ghosts. It appears that in the upper levels of the building, in the private living area, the ghost of a woman in Georgian attire, and wearing a bonnet – has been seen on occasions chasing two ghost children out of one of the rooms. These children were reported to have had happy, smiling faces as though being chased in excitement and in good fun; so we can safely say nothing macabre is associated with these apparitions. There is no sense of evil presence, no feelings of being ill-at-ease – and no chill factor.

If the haunting is true – which the authors have no doubt it is – these ghosts or recordings of bygone days will of course be seen again sometime, but when is another question. What the authors can predict is when they will pay the pub another visit, if only to sample the good quality ales and beers, and receive more of the fine hospitality that all its customers receive when stepping into this wonderful old pub.

- **Pub:** THE VILLAGE INN
- **Location:** EASINGTON
- **Good Ghost Rating:** 4

The Village Inn at Easington is haunted by the ghost of a lady known as Emily who was killed in an accident outside the property as she walked her dog. Whenever she makes an appearance a strong smell of lavender arises, and dogs show a marked reluctance to enter the cellar which is the principal area of the haunting.

• PUB: THE WATERFRONT
• LOCATION: SOUTH SHIELDS
• GOOD GHOST RATING: 8

The Waterfront is a pleasant pub that can be found in the Mill Dam area of South Shields. The Mill Dam is probably the nearest thing that South Shields now has to an 'Old Quarter', and if one walks through it of a night it is very easy to imagine that the past is only a whisker away.

The Waterfront was, until recently, known as the Railway Inn. According to legend, the pub was once managed by an elderly lady who had quite a forceful disposition. This doesn't surprise us, for even in these relatively sedate times it takes strength of character to be the manager of a riverside tavern. Back then it was even harder, as nineteenth-century sailors and fishermen were not the sort to spend the afternoon sipping a white wine and soda before going home to prune the roses. Nevertheless, she kept an orderly house and ensured that the Railway Inn was a pleasant watering hole for those in need of refreshment.

At some point the landlady reached the point of retirement, and gentle hints were passed that she should perhaps be thinking of hanging her drying towel over the pumps for one last time. But the old dear would have none of it. The Railway Inn was her home, and she fully intended to stay there till the day she died.

Despite her failing health the landlady of the Railway Inn struggled on until things became impossible. However, out of respect for her wishes she was allowed to stay on the premises until she died.

It seems that there was a short period during which there was no paranormal activity whatsoever. But then the old lady decided that she wasn't going to leave her old home at all. Before long drinkers at the tavern began to catch fleeting glimpses of her at the bar area.

Whatever you perceive ghosts to be, it is certainly true that they exhibit many of the characteristics of their flesh-and-blood alter-egos. In life the old lady of the Railway Inn was not averse to tugging the hair of any of the bar staff she was displeased with. Researcher Alan Tedder spoke with a barmaid from the pub several years ago. She told him that, on more than one occasion, she had felt her hair being sharply tugged by an invisible hand. Perhaps she wasn't doing things to the old lady's liking!

Actually, the phenomenon of hair-pulling is common in hauntings which display poltergeist-like activity. 'Shoulder-tapping' is also regularly reported, and we have noticed that this feature seems particularly prevalent in pub hauntings. (The spectre that haunts the Marsden Grotto, for instance – one of several, actually – has been known to tap unsuspecting drinkers on the shoulder if they stand in his place at the bar).

On one occasion a joiner was doing some maintenance work in the bar when an icy blast of wind shot across the room and froze him to the bone. He angrily shouted, 'For goodness sake, shut that door!' and then turned around to find that the door WAS shut and that there was no one else in the vicinity!

Never one to turn away from a challenge – particularly in a public house – Mike paid a visit to the pub one lunch time. The bar staff were friendly, and readily confirmed some of the spooky stories that had been handed down over the years.

Old soldiers don't die, it is said; they simply fade away. Landladies do die, it seems, but then stubbornly refuse to fade away at all...

- **PUB:**   THE WHITE LION
- **LOCATION:**   SUNDERLAND
- **GOOD GHOST RATING:**   4

The Phoenix in Lombard Street, Sunderland, was haunted by a Mr James Downey from 1843 to 1863. After it was demolished it seems that the shade of 'Big Jimmy' took to appearing in the nearby White Lion in High Street East. Little is known about the ghost, other than that it appears to be 'a man in a grey suit'.

IN-DEPTH CASE STUDY: THE WITCH'S CAT [PSEUDONYM], COUNTY DURHAM
Good Ghost Rating: 10

Due to the distressing nature of some of the events discussed in this in-depth haunting study, and at the request of the principal experients, both the names of the experients and the public house concerned have been either removed or replaced with pseudonyms. The Witch's Cat is not the true name of the pub, and the establishment's previous names, found within the text are also fictitious.

The authors understand that in a gazetteer of haunted pubs it will be frustrating for the reader not to be able to identify the building concerned and perhaps visit it. However, the protection of the family concerned must remain paramount, and we do not wish the events to precipitate a negative psychological effect upon the current tenants. Although the location and the names of the experients must therefore be withheld, we trust that this will not diminish the value of the account unduly. The authors wish to assure readers that every incident and event related hereafter is completely true and accurate in every detail.

The old farmhouse formerly known as the Rusting Bell is now known as the Witch's Cat, and was, prior to that, briefly known as the Bouncing Ball.

The pub has long been said to be haunted by an old man – usually espied in the lounge. One former landlord who approached the spectre was astonished to see him vanish in an instant. The ghost has made his presence known at the inn by tinkering with light switches and bar fittings. Those who have set eyes upon him describe the ghost as wearing a white shirt, black waistcoat, and flat cap. But who is he? Could he be, as some claim, a farmer who may have dwelt there in times past? Possibly, but witnesses who well recall the building when it served as a farmhouse told researcher Alan Tedder that they never once heard of a ghost haunting the property.

Ironically, Alan Tedder's own grandmother was once told that there had been a dreadful murder close to the Witch's Cat. Seemingly, an 'unbalanced son had murdered his mother'.

All in all, then, the Witch's Cat seemed to be an ideal setting for a ghost-hunt, and it just so happened that the authors and their colleagues on the North East Ghost Research Team were asked to engage in just such an exercise by a former landlord.

One inclement February night, the authors and their team arrived to begin a series of investigations into the alleged haunting at the pub. The family who lived on the premises at that time had expressed a wish to remain anonymous due to the nature of the events that occurred there. It appears the pub's trade had been slightly sluggish, and in an effort to boost trade, the [then] tenants decided to organise a 'psychic night'. This involved a number of psychics, mediums and Tarot card readers gathering one evening to prognosticate regarding the futures of the pub's patrons. All in all, the event seems to have been a success, but in regards to the haunting at the pub this is also when the trouble began.

Although the family had indeed witnessed the odd strange occurrence within the pub and the surrounding grounds prior the 'psychic night', they seemed quite at ease and happy with their 'resident ghost'. However, when the psychics visited the pub one clairvoyant informed the owner that the spirit that resided there was in actual fact quite disruptive and hell-bent on literally killing the landlord. The psychic seemingly picked up on the fact that the landlord had been plagued with illness and infections during the preceding months and his health was slowly deteriorating. This was indeed true, although nothing had been said to the psychic about this previously. The psychic then went on to say that if the family did not leave the pub immediately, the spirit allegedly haunting the premises would 'continue its grudge and its campaign to rid the earth of this man'.

Pretty harrowing stuff, to say the least. Now the reader will understand why the authors were asked to keep the experients' identities anonymous. This, combined with the fact that the landlord and landlady did not want to trade on the building's past and alleged haunting in any way, indicated a very high level of sincerity and an honest, legitimate belief in the reality of the ghosts that were said to reside within. To the authors, this case had 'authenticity' written all over it!

On the night of the first investigation, the researchers arrived at the pub at about 11.00pm. Mike and Darren subsequently had a chat with the landlord and landlady. Their primary objective was to find out for themselves exactly what had been going on and listen to the first-hand accounts and experiences regarding what had been witnessed at that particular establishment. They were quite amazed at what they were told.

Darren began the interview by asking the publicans what experiences they had had, since moving into the inn.

'A number of things have happened which we find rather odd'. The landlord told Darren.

'The first night we moved into the pub we were all awoken from our sleep to the sound of about 5-6 tremendously loud bangs coming from downstairs in the lounge. They sounded quite 'metallic', like 'metal on metal'. I even put my hand on the bedroom wall and you could feel the vibrations, they were that intense. We looked downstairs in the lounge area and no explanation could be found. We also checked outside, and all was quiet'.

'Interesting', Darren said.

Before the authors got a chance to enquire further, the landlady vouched forth and said, 'I was in bed one night and woke up to find the bed literally shaking while I was on it. It has only happened once, and it is not the first odd experience that has happened to me while being here'.

She went on to tell the authors that, one day, she was getting on with her pub duties when suddenly she felt compelled to move out of the way to let someone get past her while she was in one of the corridors. This unidentified person came from the rear and touched her shoulder as she moved to let this person past. Only no one passed her and she found herself in the corridor alone! She had been physically touched and had sensed the presence of someone. Whom? She could not say.

We were also informed of doors in the corridor downstairs that often slammed shut through the night, keeping the occupants awake at times. No rational explanations for these sounds have ever been found. Other phenomena were reported to the authors during the interview, which had been experienced first-hand by this family and their staff. These included bulbs exploding in the bar, the bar staff being touched by invisible hands, glasses being thrown off the shelves and the family dogs becoming agitated at about 3.00am most mornings for no apparent reason. One chilling account concerns the daughter of the landlord and landlady who was also present at the interview. She went on to explain:

'One day I left the pub to go home as I don't actually live here with my parents, and when I crossed the car park I had the urge to look around me. When I did I could clearly see the figure of a man dressed in a black cloak standing outside the pub on the conservatory stairs. He also had on black shoes and a black hood or hat over his head. There was something otherworldly about him and I just sensed this was not right. I turned away for one second to see where I was going and when I looked back to see this man…he was gone! There is nowhere he could have gone in the time it took me to turn around. This experience has had a profound effect on me. I was sceptical at that point but now I am not sure as this sighting is rather hard to explain. I know what I saw!'

The occurrences outlined above are first-hand accounts obtained from the family. They subsequently found out, not long after moving in, that the locals also believed the pub to be haunted. Locals visiting the pub have often asked the owners if they had 'seen the ghost yet?' The locals believe the ghost is that of a man who once lived in the pub many years ago when, as stated previously, it was actually an old farmhouse that had been built around the year 1900.

The authors were also informed on the night of the investigation that, before the present occupants moved in, the ghost of a man had been seen sitting at the end of the counter in the bar area. Another apparition had also been observed sitting down in the lounge area, behind the tables, 'minding his own business'. Along with the apparition seen on the conservatory stairs, could these three spectres be one and the same? Or are they different ghosts altogether? And are these ghosts responsible for the other activity that has been witnessed there? These are some of the questions the authors hoped they could answer, after first establishing for themselves if something odd was indeed going on.

After the pre-investigation interview Darren and Mike conducted a careful and comprehensive 'baseline test' and left no stone unturned. They had a large number of locations to cover so they got to work quickly. Downstairs in the main bar area and lounge the temperature read between 20-22°, which was quite normal. The conservatory area was a lot colder and read 15-16°, but was indicative of nothing paranormal. EMF sweeps showed no readings unless one stood near the bar where a rather diminutive reading showed. This was due to the presence of the beer pumps and, of course, the electronic till. There were extractor fans on the walls in both the lounge and the bar area which made a clicking and whirring noise every now and again, and the door into the kitchen naturally swings upon its hinges to a certain degree and creaks while doing so. The authors traced a slight draught from along the corridor to a door that leads outside. This accounted for the swinging door! There were no creaky floorboards, or other draughts coming in from the windows or doors, except for the aforementioned draught they had just located. The cellar temperature read 12-15° but when the huge fans are in operation this is quite normal. EMF sweeps were pointless due to all the wires and machinery in there.

Upstairs in the private living quarters the team was allowed access into the main bedroom and living room, as these were the areas where strange phenomena had seemingly taken place in the past. The baseline survey in that location showed both rooms to be at a steady temperature of 23-24° with no EMF anomalies detected. The corridors between these two rooms had very squeaky floorboards and, once again, no draughts coming from the windows. That completed the baseline survey, and the team then had readings to compare should anything otherworldly happen.

The team then split into two groups to investigate the private living areas. These locations were chosen first as the landlady could not stay with us throughout the night and needed some sleep for the next day's work. The authors figured that they could investigate those areas first and concentrate on the actual bar later on. The first location was the main bedroom where Darren headed the first team. Mike and his group staked out the adjacent living room. Darren's vigil proved rather fruitless to say the least, with nothing at all being recorded. However the pub landlord, who was with Mike, saw red flashing lights in the corner of the living room. Mike proceeded to take some photographs of the area and later, whilst examining the photograph, was surprised to find an unusual black, speckled mist obscuring the corner of the room. Analysis on Mike's laptop computer during the break could not determine what it was and further photographs taken in the same area showed no anomalies. The landlord then told the authors that it was in that very corner of the room where other phenomena had occurred in the past!

Later the teams swapped locations for a while, and Darren's team stationed themselves in the living room. Apart from one or two creaks and cracking noises, followed by two loud thumps as though something was in the corridor, nothing else happened. Both Darren's team, and Mike's stationed in the master bedroom with the door closed, heard these thumps emanating from within the corridor. The authors found these occurrences interesting.

During their first break Darren and Mike downloaded the photograph Mike took in the living area so they could scrutinise it. Darren also took a photo of Mike and the pub landlord as they viewed the first picture on the laptop. Later, Darren commented, 'I only took the picture to document what was happening at that particular time, and was taken aback to see that this time we had caught a faint, fine white mist on camera. The mist was in an area where no one was smoking and near the spot where the apparition of a man had been seen sitting behind a table in the lounge'.

The next experiment, carried out after the break in the cellar, involved leaving a 'locked-off' video camera trained on a trigger object; a wooden crucifix. The crucifix was placed on a sheet of white paper and a line was drawn around it before the team vacated the room. If the trigger object moved, the movement would be caught on film. The investigators also left EVP recorders and dictation machines running too, in the hope they would be able to record other sound anomalies. It was in this location where the visiting psychic had said the disruptive spirit that pesters the landlord resided. Hopes were high, and the researchers were not disappointed with the results. Although the trigger object did not move, the investigators managed to pick up some very strange sound recordings coming from within the unoccupied room. If one listens carefully to the recordings, made one can hear the sound of male voice talking. This occurs at regular intervals throughout the recording and at times it is very distinctive. Bangs and crashes are also heard coming from within the cellar, although nothing in there was actually disturbed. A more sinister EVP came in the form of a guttural breath or sigh that sounded so clear it felt like whatever or whoever it was had breathed right into the EVP machine!

During the 'lock-off' period when the cellar was deserted, all present at the investigation were situated in the bar area waiting, watching, listening and hoping that some paranormal activity would take place. This proved rather fruitless to say the least. However, Mike Hallowell, while in the conservatory area, was almost certain he had photographed a face at the window, complete with upper torso, looking in from outside. Darren later commented, 'If I have to be honest, I think the picture is indeed a good one, but one can't help thinking that this is maybe a classic case of pareidolia. Mike is not sure. We looked outside nonetheless to see if anybody was hanging around, and found no one there. So at least that rules out one natural explanation'.

At one point during the investigation, Mike sat quietly in the ladies' toilets as he'd been informed that, on previous occasions, witnesses had seen 'shadowy footsteps' walking past the bottom of the cubicle doors. Mike made some audio recordings at this point, and later, on analysis, found that on one of them a woman can be distinctly heard sobbing for several seconds.

By 5.00am, and after another short stint of EVP lock-off experiments, the team decided to call it a night – or rather, an early morning. It had not been a bad investigation and some decent results were obtained.

Darren summarised, 'The mist photographs, the EVP recordings, and the loud thumps heard during the investigation upstairs... I think we can safely say something odd was going on at that particular location; but exactly what I cannot say at this present time'.

Was there a vicious ghost there that wanted to kill the landlord? The authors don't think so. Are the apparitions that have been seen in the past one and the same person? That is something the authors will try to determine if they get another opportunity to investigate the premises. After all, it takes longer than a few hours to begin to understand what may be going on in a complicated case such as this.

After that night's investigation was concluded, a provisional arrangement was made to carry out some further research on the premises. However, three days before the second investigation was due to be carried out, the authors were informed that the family had decided to flee the premises. To this juncture, they have not been able to return, but hope to do so in the near future.

- PUB: THE WOODEN DOLL
- LOCATION: NORTH SHIELDS
- GOOD GHOST RATING: 8

The Wooden Doll public house is a relatively old drinking den that is situated in one of the best spots in the north-east. It sits high on the top of a steep embankment on Hudson Street overlooking the North Shields fish quay. The beer garden and outside seating area is located at the front of the pub and over a fine pint on a sunlit day, you can experience one of the best views the north-east has to offer. On the north side of the Tyne one can see Tynemouth Priory and Castle, and Lord Collingwood's statue. Across the river in South Shields lie the dramatic cliff tops, the Leas, Marsden Bay and, in the distance, Souter lighthouse. One can also see the two magnificent piers that stretch out over half a mile into the North Sea giving a panoramic view of the mouth of the River Tyne.

The pub itself small, a quaint old building that oozes charm and character. When one steps inside the ambience of yesteryear is immediately apparent. The authors don't know how old this particular pub is, but we surmise it dates back a good few years as it certainly has that 'old feel' to it. The interior is decked out beautifully with wooden flooring and old beams adorn the ceiling, giving a wonderful old-fashioned feel. Many a time the authors have drank the ale and ate the fine pub grub whilst mulling over the possibility of encountering the potential resident spectres.

Darren paid a visit to the 'gents' on one occasion during an afternoon in the pub – his first visit there actually – and whilst enquiring the whereabouts of the toilets he was told they were 'through the double doors and down the stairwell at the bottom of the building'. Upon venturing down the old wooden stairwell he got the certain feeling that there was indeed a presence with him. He felt as though his every step was being watched as he descended, to the point where he actually turned around to see who was there! Of course there was nobody on the stairs other than himself. A sudden chill was followed by an anxious shudder, indicating that his gut feeling may indeed have been correct. It's not the sort of feeling Darren gets that often, but he knew (or at least had a suspicion) that the stairs were indeed haunted. This was confirmed to Darren when he enquired about any 'resident ghosts' at the pub upon his return from 'the little boys' room'.

'Have you seen her?' the barman asked when he enquired.

'No', Darren responded, 'but I think I sensed something down there'.

Darren was then informed about an all-night paranormal investigation that had taken place there previously, in which the team medium (quite respected we are told) had sensed the presence of a woman on the stairwell.

So is the Wooden Doll pub haunted? The authors haven't heard of any other new accounts of paranormal activity, but that's not to say nothing has occurred. It is indeed a wonderful drinking establishment and it wouldn't surprise Darren and Mike if indeed more accounts of ghostly activity come forth from time to time. It would be nice, however, to put a name to the ghostly lady on the stairs – if indeed, she does walk the stairwell of the Wooden Doll.

- **PUB:**   YE OLDE CROSS (THE DIRTY BOTTLES)
- **LOCATION:**   ALNWICK
- **GOOD GHOST RATING:** 10

Ye Olde Cross Inn is situated on Narrowgate in Alnwick, and is tucked away just around the corner from the magnificent Alnwick Castle. The pub, famous for its display of dusty old bottles in the front window, has no ghosts as such at the premises but it does have a macabre and sinister curse which is attached to these aforementioned, ill-fated bottles.

It is said that over two-hundred years ago the [then] owner of the premises was organising his window display when he was suddenly struck down with an unforeseen and fatal heart attack. The window was subsequently closed and locked up, and the display was left as it was.

Local superstition and legend would have one believe that if anyone disturbs or moves the bottle display in the window, they shall suffer the same fate as the old owner did and die on that very spot. It is for this reason that the window has allegedly stood untouched for all these years. It appears that no-one dares risking cleaning up the window display for fear of the 'curse of the dirty bottles'.

The authors have supped fine ale on numerous occasions at this wonderful old inn while carrying out research in Northumbria, and if given the chance to move or disturb the display, I dare say we would also decline...just in case!